Mike's

JET

BOOK

DEDICATIONS

This first reprint of my first book is dedicated to a few people who have kept me focused on the future, sométimes when my life seemed to be going in strange directions.

Firstly to my son, Edward, who I hope will one day understand my decision to start a new life in Holland, to my father who has given me so much moral support over the last couple of years, and also to Bennie and Anita for their confidence in me and the opportunity to explore new challenges.

But most importantly, this book is dedicated to Marijn, and all the other members of the 'Pink & Sticky Jet Team', for their unselfish help and friendship during the last year and a half, and for accepting a 'buitenlander' into their midst so easily!

Mike Cherry
(15 Sept. 2000)

ACKNOWLEDGMENTS

Firstly I wish to thank all the individuals and companies who provided sample products, photographs and information, and those who allowed reproduction of their diagrams and data. I also express my gratitude to the advertisers, who demonstrated confidence in my ability to write and publish this book, and whose funds made it possible to include the full colour pages for the enjoyment of the readers.

Secondly to all those jet modellers throughout the world who have given me encouragement, passed on information, and taught me most of what I know. Without you this book would not have been possible. In particular the following persons who have advised and assisted me during my years in this hobby, and whose opinions I have (mostly) learned to understand and respect: Philip Avonds, Winfried Ohlgart, Steve Elias, Jim Fox, Kurt Schreckling, Marc 'G-Force' Leavesley, Bob Violett, Bob Ryan, Hans Bühr, Dick Spreadbury, Jerry Caudle, Peter Cmyral, Alec Cornish-Trestrail, Bennie van de Goor, Tony Roessen, Wolfgang Klühr, Peter and Paul Thorpe. I offer my sincere appreciation to these gentlemen for persevering with me .... until I got it somewhere near correct !

Lastly, I am especially indebted to my dear friend Ralf Ploenes for his help, technical support & proof reading, and Bob Petrie for his design excellence & unselfish assistance throughout the, somewhat manic, publishing phase!

Mike's JET BOOK

ISBN 1 900371 50 2

Published by:
Traplet Publications Ltd.

Technical Support and Proofing by:
Ralf Ploenes. Bad Homburg. Germany.

Design, layout and technical drawings by:
Mike Cherry. Helmond. the Netherlands

Cover design & digital photograph remastering by:
Bob Petrie & Irvine Ltd. Brunswick Ind. Park, New Southgate. London N11 1JL. GB

Printed and bound by:
Stephens & George Ltd. Goat Mill Road, Dowlais, Merthyr Tydfil, Mid Glamorgan. CF48 3TD. GB.

Front Cover
The author's F-15C Eagle rotates from the strip at the 1995 Jet World Masters, Neu-Ulm, Germany.
(photograph by Richard Seammen)

Back Cover
(top) Franz Walti's immaculate own-design, 1:6.5 scale, twin JPX turbine powered Dassault Rafale B01 taxies back to the ramp after a flight at dusk in Switzerland.

(centre) Just a few of the superb models flown at the 1st Jet World Masters in Germany, including a JMP T-33, a Klühr Mig.31 & Sukhoi 27, and an Avonds Starfighter.

(bottom) A beautiful replica of the famous Belgian F16 Fighting Falcon, built from a BVM kit and finished in this striking Tiger scheme by Oliver Kirch.

CONTENTS

Foreword

R/C jet modelling started about 25 years ago with the advent of the first ducted-fan models, but at that time successful flights could only be accomplished by a handful of patient and very accomplished modellers (some of them full-size jet pilots). Indeed, jet modelling was a new and highly technical matter, requiring the most demanding skills. As a result, the margin between failure and success was very narrow.

In the next few years a lot of learning money and time was spent by those eager to reach their goal of realistically flying a model jet. I went even further; my ambition was to achieve the ultimate accolade in scale modelling, first place at the FAI World Scale Championships, which I was lucky to win twice with my F-15 Eagle in 1988 and 1990.

All of the expertise of that handful of early day modellers has eventually been put together in commercially available jet kits, fan units, engines, tuned pipe silencers, retract systems and even real miniature gas-turbines. This means that, nowadays, any modeller with moderate experience can buy a jet model and equipment off the shelf and be assured of success, that is if he follows the instructions.... this is no place for re-inventors of the wheel!

Of course one needs to learn to walk before you can run, and this is not different with jets. Model jets are high performance airplanes, requiring a solid basic knowledge of both building techniques and piloting skills. A newcomer to the radio controlled model scene will have to display patience, and needs to be prepared to go through all the learning stages.

Gas turbines are the definitive scale power source for jets, as close as we can get to the real thing. However a few words of caution here. Miniature gas turbines need to be treated with the same kind of discipline that is required from full-size jet pilots. You must pass the step of ducted-fan jets before tackling the characteristics of the gas turbine motor, because they are completely new and require some different skills. It would simply be too much to handle both steps at the same time.

This book contains a wealth of information. It shows what has been achieved in this very technical hobby and what is available commercially, although unfortunately not everything obtainable is of the same quality. Only a few manufacturers have built a reputation for making sound designs and good quality products. To select one of these, the best advice I can give is to go to a dedicated meeting of jet models in order to watch the models fly, and to talk to the modellers who are already successful in the hobby. There you will be able to judge with your own eyes what works - and what doesn't.

I have known the author of this book, Mike Cherry, for several years and have watched him progress rapidly in the jet scene. I have always been impressed by his ability to absorb so much specialised knowledge in so little time, and the 'R/C Jet International' magazine which he started in 1992 has been one of the most significant catalysts for the big increase in our hobby in the last few years.

This book gives you the unique opportunity to share much of his remarkable state-of-the-art knowledge in one package. I wish you good reading fun !

Philip Avonds.

Preface

ABOUT THIS BOOK

This book was written for modellers who want to enter, or progress in, the mainstream jet scene with the best chance of success. Consequently it concentrates on current trends, the most popular equipment, kit-built models, and the proven product combinations and methods of today. My sincere hope is that it will guide newcomers around most of the pitfalls, and pave the way for many more people to join in the fascinating, exciting and often challenging, hobby of Radio Control Jets.

From my experience most modellers are uninterested in the theory behind their jets - they just want a reliable model that they can fly as often as possible. Therefore this book doesn't discuss aerodynamic formulas, the technical intricacies of motors, or the design of fan units and models, and it is unnecessary to understand these with the levels of technology incorporated in current products. For more in-depth information on these subjects I recommend that you read David James book "Ducted Fans for Model Jets" as, even though it was written back in 1988, the general principles explained in it are mostly true today, although the products and techniques have advanced considerably.

Of course, experimentation and the natural ingenuity of modellers is the source of many excellent new techniques and useful products, so don't be dissuaded from trying different or new ideas in the future. But first build at least one 'standard' jet kit using a contemporary propulsion system and learn about its construction, operation and flying characteristics - you'll learn more from this experience than anything you can read in this, or any other, book. Nevertheless, the small number of experienced modellers who design and build their own jets provide one of the most exciting aspects of this hobby, and the most successful of these usually become available as kits or semi-kits.

The information on the majority of the products and methods included is from my personal experience, or that of successful jet modellers whose opinions I respect, and I apologise for any deserving items that have been omitted. I have concentrated on the items from reputable and established companies, those from some of the smaller or newer companies either having not yet been proved sufficiently for recommendation, or not being universally obtainable. There are also quite a few kits and other goods still available that are out of date, or of sub-standard quality and performance. Some of these, particularly the semi-kits and older designs, can be modified or updated to work quite well - but this is only achievable after some experience in the hobby, and therefore these are rarely mentioned in this book. Furthermore I have not dealt with the plan-packs and plans for scratch-built jet models, few of these being available now anyway, as most modellers want to build their jet and get in the air as quickly as possible, hence the huge predominance of kit-built models at all events.

I have assumed that readers of this book have, at least, a moderate experience of R/C aircraft modelling, but in any case they need to be a reasonably proficient builder and pilot before attempting to construct or fly any kind of jet model, whether it be electric, ducted fan or gas turbine powered. Actually you will be surprised at how easy it is to fly a well designed, constructed and set-up jet, more than half of the battle is in gaining the experience and knowledge to get to the stage of that first exciting flight.

In a hobby like this, which is at the forefront of current technology, the advances and changes occur at a rapid pace, and some of the products mentioned in this book will, no doubt, be superseded within two or three years. For this reason, and the fact that I couldn't squeeze everything into these 160 pages, is very likely that a second book will be published not too long after this one. Tentatively called "Mike's Jet Book - Volume 2", it will include updates on all the latest propulsion systems and products released since 1997, and much more detailed chapters on construction and finishing techniques than it has been possible to include here.

After much deliberation I decided to compile the whole book using metric units, which most of the world now uses. However, where possible I have included approximate conversions, and there is a complete conversion factor table in Appendix II. For those of you whose native language is not English I've tried to keep the text as simple as possible, and I hope that you'll be able to understand all of it.

I look forward to meeting many new pilots at the flying fields around the world. Enjoy !

Mike Cherry.

The author with his F-15C Eagle during static judging at the 1995 Jet World Masters in Neu-Ulm, Germany, in which he achieved 8th overall. (Philip Avonds kit, Ramtec fan, OS91 motor, BVM pipe, Graupner mc20 radio, Spring-Air retracts)

1 - Introduction

The immense advances in jet modelling during the last five or six years are incredible. Gone forever is the era of noisy, underpowered and temperamental models that required hundreds of metres of hard surfaced runways for successful take-off. With today's efficient ducted-fan systems and miniature gas turbines we have realistic jet-like performance, combined with superb reliability and substantially lower noise levels. The majority of current jets are relatively simple to construct and fly, and many of them are easily capable of operating from the 100 metre length grass strip at your local model airfield.

Sport jets commonly achieving over 200 mph in level flight, 2 metre long exact scale twin-engined models that can duplicate all the manoeuvres of the full scale aircraft, vertical take-off and landing Harrier jump jets, gas turbine powered seaplanes - all these have already been achieved.

A huge choice of properly designed power systems, fully moulded kits and all the necessary ancillary items are now obtainable off-the-shelf, which only require assembling to comprehensive instructions to guarantee success at the first attempt for any reasonably competent R/C modeller. For those considering joining this fascinating and challenging hobby I can assure you that, using the products recommended in this book, your jet can be as dependable as a conventional propeller powered model. Just charge the batteries, check the airframe and fly!

However there are still a number of the more obscure, and usually low cost, kits and propulsion systems that are hanging on from the past, and many of these have caught newcomers unaware - to their personal cost. Some have pitiful performance and a few just don't work at all. Unfortunately, these have cost the jet scene many possible future participants. In this respect my advice is clear: Don't just believe all the hype in the advertisements to select your jet model and power system ... go and see for yourself what really works before dipping your hand into your pocket!

The Future?

At the time of writing this, in 1997, the most rapidly developing facets of jet modelling are gas-turbines, with electric jets following closely behind - most ducted fans already being so reliable and efficient that there is little further progress that can be made. However, I don't believe that turbine models will outnumber ducted-fan jets, at least not in next 4 or 5 years, as currently the cost is too prohibitive for most modellers.

The size and performance of the models will continue to increase, as will the level of scale authenticity, and this should also entice further commercial investment. This is already beginning to develop, for example the use of radio controlled Mig.29 jet models in the recent James Bond 'Goldeneye' movie, and the interest demonstrated by such large corporations as KLM/Fokker. I guess that there will also be many more cases of model jets being used in the movie industry and television advertising in the near future, as the cost of these is far less than full size aircraft.

More sophisticated electronic 'autopilot' modules are being developed for model use, although I haven't seen any that work really well in the high speed jets so far. Nevertheless, they could offer a safer and less risky entry for newcomers. But, as these autopilots become more capable and common, I am sure that they will be prohibited in all contests. However, part of the fun of jet modelling is in overcoming the flying challenges, and as a well known Italian jet pilot's motto states *"No Risk = No Fun!"*

2 - Electric Jets

INTRODUCTION

Although electric ducted-fans require a complete book of their own, I have included this brief chapter as the interest in them is increasing rapidly, and not only in countries with particularly stringent noise laws. Apart from the lack of noise, which is beneficial in many locations, electro-jets present a new challenge for modellers and the performance of some of the latest models is staggering. For example the immaculate own design electric powered F-80 Shooting Star of German expert, Ralf Dvoràk, took 8th place overall at the 1997 German Jet Masters contest - competing against many of the best scale ducted-fan and turbine models in Europe! Many of the current electric sport and scale jets have really sparkling performance, being fully aerobatic and achieving level flight speeds of well over 160 kph/100 mph with flight durations of 4 - 6 minutes.

Just as in the world of internal combustion motor powered ducted-fans, the typical size of electric jets is also increasing, benefiting with lower wing loadings and hence better flight performance. There are now several commercially produced electric fans units that have proved quite efficient when combined with the latest electric motors, the most popular of these having diameters of between 90 and 100 mm. The initial costs of an electric jet system and airframe are a little less than a ducted-fan powered jet, and the running costs almost negligible, but to achieve a performance in any way comparable you need very specialised and expensive motors and nicads.

Electro-impellers is still a very experimental section of jet modelling and most models are own-design and scratch built, although a few suitable kits are just beginning to appear on the market. The photographs nearby show a very small selection of what is now possible in this field. Below is a very brief insight into the main factors of electro-jets, supplied by Hans Bühr, with additional material from Ralf Dvoràk and J.P Schlösser, all of who are regarded as foremost European experts in this field.
Mike Cherry

Perhaps you have some beautiful modern fighters already, equipped with ducted-fans and a Rossi, OS or K&B engine, and now you've heard or read about electric jets and would like to give it a try. So you replace your fuel tanks with some nicads, and put in an electric motor where the internal combustion engine was ... but when you come home from your first attempt at the flying field you let everyone know that electric jets are just a waste of time and money. This situation is just like many i.c ducted-fan models of 20 years ago !

This method is definitely the way things will go wrong. So what is the correct approach to this very young scene of 'electro-impellers', to this almost silent, but fascinating, branch of jet modelling ?

The big difference is that the total energy you carry in your electric model is just a few percent of what a fuel tank contains, and to make it worse the batteries are very heavy. From this you can conclude that the following factors are most important:

• The airframe must be extremely lightweight.

• The model must have clean aerodynamics, both internal and externally.

• The electric components, that is the number of cells, the kind of voltage regulator (speed controller), size and type of motor, and the impeller unit must be properly matched to give the best possible efficiency.

Weight-saving

Remember that electric motors run very smoothly, causing no vibration at all, and therefore you don't need anywhere near the same airframe strength as for a normal i.c ducted-fan jet. Aerodynamic loads are also smaller, as tight turns reduce the airspeed of these sensitive models considerably and are to be avoided.

Don't use heavy materials like plywood and hardwoods, instead use carbonfibre tissue over very lightweight balsa. It is surprisingly strong, and you will also find that your i.c. ducted-fan jets become lighter after you've built a couple of electro-jets. Use just enough glue to hold all the parts together, don't use it to fill gaps. Before installing every part of the airframe, think if there is a way you can lighten it, perhaps by drilling lots of holes in bulkheads. Put only the absolute minimum of lightweight filler and paint on your model, and don't forget you can make the first flight before finishing and painting.

Aerodynamics

The remarkable thrust that an electric fan delivers can be spoiled by drag very easily. This can be caused by several factors:

• Unsuitable wing design and too thick profiles.

• Too high a wing loading; the induced drag from the vortex at the wingtips is often underestimated. Choose an airplane with reasonable wing surface area (eg: Mig.15, Gloster Meteor, Vampire, Pampa, Thunderbolt A10 or Shooting Star).

• Inefficiencies of the ducting system. This can be caused by a too small inlet area or sharp inlet lips, rough surfaces or other vortex creators inside the ducting, or too small an outlet diameter at the jet nozzle. Similar practices apply as used for i.c. ducted fan models (see next Chapter).

Hans and Verena Bühr with their BAe 146 'Whisperjet'. Powered by four home-made 100 mm dia. impellers turned at 15.000 rpm by Graupner RX450BB motors and 28 Sanyo cells, this 2300 mm wingspan model weighs only 5.2 kg and flies extremely well. Wing construction is traditional, and the fuselage is hot wire cut 15mm thick polystyrene over a lightweight framework of balsa tubes. The model features retracts, working landing lights and fowler flaps. Flight time is around 6 minutes.

Now let us look at the different components of the electric propulsion system, which have improved a lot in the last two decades, and very considerably in the last 2 or 3 years. So don't forget that the following text will also be history in just a few years.

The Rechargeable Batteries
Probably 90% of all successful electro-jets fly with Sanyo or Panasonic nicads. The most commonly used cell nowadays is the Sanyo N-SCRC1700, and they weigh 56 grams, or 2 oz each. 1700 mAh is the indication of the energy it can hold. For example, when fully charged, it can give 1.7 Amps for 1 hour, 17 Amps for 6 minutes, or 34 Amps for 3 minutes. There are of course also smaller batteries with less capacity and weight. The voltage discharge starts at about 1.32 volts and drops slowly to 1.0 volt, and then rapidly towards 0 volts.

The number of cells needed to fly varies from 7 - 32. Above 32 cells the voltage becomes dangerously high, and below 7 cells the total energy is not sufficient to fly a model and the speed controller is at its lower voltage limit. The size and weight of the model, as well as required flying time and style dictates a certain amount of energy (ie: the number of cells), which also has to match the motor rating. The voltage needed for your motor is

The two most popular electric fan units in Europe are the Schwerdtfeger 89 mm (left) and the new Aeronaut 90 mm diameter units (right). Also shown is a 12 cell stick of Sanyo SCRC1700 nicads and Aveox motor with speed controller.

reached by soldering the cells directly together into one package.

The Electric Motor
The flow of energy from the battery pack to the motor is measured in watts, which is simply Volts x Amps. All motors available on the market have maximum amount of energy that they are able to change into rpm and torque. They do this with an efficiency of between 50 -90%, depending on the quality of the motor. The losses of 50 - 10% turn into heat, which we definitely do not want, but have to live with. Cooling of the motor is therefore of prime importance.

There are hundreds of different motors, from small and cheap ones that can handle just 100 watts, to very expensive high-tech motors which can transform well over 1000 watts into thrust with a minimum of heat output. But all have something in common, they have a maximum efficiency at a particular rpm. Running them at too low rpm just turns them into an oven and can destroy them very quickly. So the right choice of motor is important as well as careful reading of the instructions. Certainly the future belongs to brushless motors, which are much more efficient (they remain cooler), lighter weight, have almost no wear, and produce less electrical noise to affect the receiver.

The Speed Controller (Voltage Regulator)
The latest devices have now reached a very high standard and the losses (ie: heat output) are negligible. They also have volt and ampere limitations. I strongly recommend a regulator whose ampere limit is well above the expected maximum current that your motor will be running at. These units often have a built-in brake to stop a propeller rotating when the motor is switched off, but is not needed for electro-impellers.

The Impeller

In 1993 I published an article in the German "Elektro Modell" magazine on how to build your own impeller for electro jets. No good commercial impeller units were available then, but a lot has changed since. My favourites, and the most common and successful in Europe, are the Schwerdtfeger and the Aeronaut units, both of 90 mm diameter. Several other new impellers have become available (eg: Electro-Jet and Kress units) recently, also with good efficiency ratings, but I did not have the experience of them so far.

Two of the high-tech kits from JePe Fiberatelier (Netherlands) The F16 is exact scale, 109 cm long and 75 cm span and weighs only 1.7 kg (3.7 lbs) with 12 cells brushless motor and Aeronaut fan Flight times of 7 mins and level flight speeds of 200 kph make it one of the best performers seen so far. The A10 Thunderbolt is a little larger, still quite scale, uses two Schwerdtfeger fan units, 16 - 20 cells, and is very easy to fly. Both kits are highly prefabricated and moulded from composite materials to an excellent standard.

American pilot, David Ribbe, better known for his i.c.ducted-fan jets, also dabbles in electric flight. This neat little scratch-built Mig.15 is fully aerobatic on an Astroflite motor and 30 cells, turning a home-made impeller unit. The model is mainly of traditional balsa construction, with some reinforcing from composite materials, and features retractable undercarriage.

The astonishing own design electric Su35 of Ralf Dvoràk rests on Wolfgang Klühr's 2.5 metre long, twin ducted-fan version. Constructed mostly of balsa, with carbonfibre and epoxyglass reinforcing, it is 1.66 m long with a span of 1.15 m, and weighs only 4.6 kg (wing loading 100 g.m2). Propulsion is by a pair of 90 mm own design fans turned by Graupner Ultra 930-7 motors and 30 Sanyo 1900 mAh cells giving 2.3 kg thrust and superb performance.

If you have the choice to put an impeller of large or small diameter in an airplane, then always choose the larger diameter as it will have better efficiency. A simple note in the manufacturers impeller description that it provides 2 lbs of thrust is useless! The missing data are the input in watts, the diameter of the impeller and outlet nozzle, and to what velocity the airflow is finally accelerated inside the duct. Remember also that the shape of the inlet and duct length influences the thrust, and it is helpful to have this information before making your choice of impeller unit.

Hints for Success

1) The weight of battery pack, regulator, motor and impeller unit should be roughly 50% of the total flying weight of the complete airplane. In other words, the finished and painted model complete with landing gear, servos, receiver and it's battery must be built to equal the weight of the propulsion system, or less if possible.

2) As a rough guide you should not exceed the following wing-loadings for reasonable performance: 60 grams/dm2 for a model with a wing area of 20 dm2 (2.2 sq.ft), which results in a flying weight of 1.2 kg (2.64 lbs). The wing loading may be increased to 100 g/dm2 (33 oz/sq.ft) for airplanes with a wing area of 60 dm2 (6.5 sq.ft).

3) The ratio of the static thrust measured in the completed model, in relation to the overall model weight will give you a good idea of its flying characteristics. To achieve really good performance, for instance in a fighter type, you should aim for the static thrust to be two thirds of the total model weight.

> 1:3 thrust/weight = good flyer.
> 1:2 thrust/weight = good aerobatic performance.
> 2:3 thrust/weight = excellent performance, jet-like!

4) Approximately 150 - 220 watts is needed per kg flying weight, depending on performance required and aerobatic quality of model.

Ralf Dvoràk (right) and Heino Dittmar with their P-80's, shortly to be available as a fully moulded kit from Fiber Classics. A plan is also available for a balsa version. 99 cms long, with span of 110 cms and weight of 1.15 kg (wing loading 70 g/m2), complete with retracts. The innovative thing about this model is that it is powered by two impellers, fitted in front of each other, giving a sparkling performance from a small inlet area. This may well be the way forward.

The 65 mm diameter twin spool fan units in the P-80 Shooting Stars are fitted facing each other, with the impellers rotating in opposite directions. With properly matched motors there is no need for stators. Using Speed 400 6v/480 race motors and 10 Sanyo 1700 mAh cells the thrust is 700 grams, with a 52 m/sec exhaust velocity. It is expected that these fan units will soon be manufactured commercially.

Hans Bühr's latest massive electric jet is this 3.54 metre wingspan Antonov An-225. Power is by 6 own-design 90mm diameter 5-bladed impellers, turned by Lehner 2718/20N motors and 2 packs of 24 Sanyo 1.7 Ah cells, which gives 5 minutes duration. Total thrust is 5kg, which is ample for this 12 kg model. It features retractable landing for all the 32 wheels, flaps, landing lights and anti-collision beacons.

First Models

I strongly recommend that you buy your first electric jet from a reputable supplier who has personal experience in electro-impeller and knows about what he is selling to you. For example the Thunderbolt from J.P Schlösser in Holland, or the Pampa from Vöster in Germany are just two suitable models to start with, and will teach you a great deal. Ask for the best quality components as the cheap ones often turn out to be more expensive in the end. This route is the only guarantee for the beginner that the components will match together, which is even more important than with i.c ducted-fan jet models. Don't believe in all advertising in model magazines, it's better to ask a friend experienced in this field for his advice, as they aren't after your money!

Electro-Jet Advantages

In general, the advantages of electric jets are as follows:

- The equipment needed is not cheap, but will normally last for years without any repair.

- Silent and realistic jet sound.

- Impeller duct is free from cylinder, tuned-pipe, fuel tubes and other vortex creators.

- No oily deposits, making repairs very easy.

- No vibration, and therefore little risk of electronic equipment (servos and receivers) failure.

- Possibility of hand launched take-off with smaller models, which eliminates the need for a long runway and saves model weight.

- All you need on the flying field is a battery charger working from your car battery, and possibly a second battery pack for the model.

- Never any difficulties for starting the motors, and it is possible to switch off, and on again, during flight if required. The almost 100% reliability makes the electro-jet the ideal power system for multi-engine aircraft, especially those with engines some distance apart. There are an increasing number of multi-engined electro models, and even some of the major manufacturers are now producing kits for them.

.... and finally, the answer to all those still asking why on earth should they fly electric jets?

Is your flying field half an hours drive from home, but there's a nice grass field just around the corner? Even noise sensitive neighbours will be surprised by your silent flying, and will most probably enjoy it. Or, do you come home from work in a business suit and a tie, and there is only 1 hour to sunset? Your electric jet is waiting with charged batteries, thanks to the automatic charger, so take-off can be right after having kissed the wife and children!

A lot of well known impeller-freaks who normally fly i.c jets or turbines also have a little electric jet nearby. You ask why? Because the electric jet virus strikes even those who used to say: "It's a waste of time and money". Be careful - it might strike even you !
Hans Bühr

3 - D/F Units & Ducting

Two of the indisputable trends in ducted-fan models since the early 1990's are the rapid decline of 'Pusher' fan units, for the reasons described below, and the reduction in the popularity of the smaller (.45 capacity) engined models. The latter is unfortunate, but there is now little differential between the cost of a complete .45 size propulsion system and that of a .90 size combination. The advent of reliable and powerful larger fan units and models, with their generally better flight characteristics, has also concentrated the commercial development in this area, and therefore the greatest popularity.

DUCTED-FAN UNITS

A ducted-fan unit is basically an air pump. In simple terms it consists of a circular outer tube, called the shroud, which encloses a multi-bladed impeller that is rotated by the motor fitted in its integral engine mount. The motor spins the impeller at high rpm to accelerate the air received at the front of the shroud and force it out of the back of the fan unit, providing the thrust to propel the model forward. Current ducted-fan units are similar in most respects, all including the following major components:

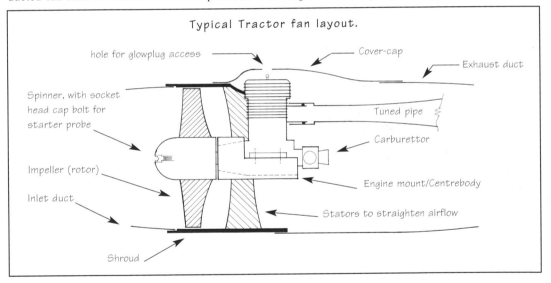

Typical Tractor fan layout.

- hole for glowplug access
- Cover-cap
- Exhaust duct
- Spinner, with socket head cap bolt for starter probe
- Tuned pipe
- Carburettor
- Impeller (rotor)
- Inlet duct
- Engine mount/Centrebody
- Stators to straighten airflow
- Shroud

Shroud

A cylindrical shield which the impeller spins inside, ensuring that all the ingested air passes through it and is accelerated. Most shrouds are manufactured from injection moulded nylon, with either glassfibre or a small percentage of carbonfibre added to enhance the stiffness of the material. All types have the mounting brackets or points moulded as part of, or bolted to, the shroud so it must be strong enough to support the weight of the motor and the operational loads imposed on it.

Stators

Inside the rear of the shroud are a number of aerodynamically shaped stator blades which are fixed at an opposing angle to the impeller blades. These straighten the 'swirling' effect that the impeller causes on the air that it accelerates, further improving the efficiency of the system. The number of stators varies according to different fan designs, but most contemporary fan units have about the same number of stators as impeller blades. Generally stator blades are made of the same injection moulded material as the shroud, and in tractor units they serve a dual purpose as support brackets for the engine mount.

Engine Mount

The engine mount, also called the 'centrebody', provides a rigid base to bolt the engine to, and ensures that the crankshaft is centralised within the shroud. For pusher fan units it usually consists of a 3 or 4 legged 'spider' shaped bracket which is bolted to the front of the shroud. In tractor fans the engine mount is a cylindrically shaped part that is bolted in between the stators, and this normally gives better rigidity which allows closer impeller blade tip clearances. Engine mounts for pusher fans are usually injection moulded from glass-reinforced nylon due to the complex shape, and for tractor fans are either aluminium, or injection moulded nylon with aluminium inserts.

Impeller

All contemporary impellers are injection moulded, either of glass-fibre or carbon-fibre reinforced nylon, and usually have an odd number of blades, generally between 5 and 11. Most are made up from individual blade segments that are securely clamped together by a metal central hub, but a few are moulded in one piece. Although the one-piece moulded impellers are lighter and less expensive to manufacture, they are usually not as rigid and often require some balancing before use. Although more costly, impellers with separate blade segments are usually stronger and stiffer, allow replacement of individual blades if damaged, and are normally pre-balanced at manufacture. Most current fans have separate blade segments.

For maximum efficiency, and therefore thrust, there should be the smallest possible gap between the impeller blade tips and the shroud to reduce aerodynamic losses. To maintain the minimum tip clearance the motors crankshaft must be accurately centred in the shroud, requiring a rigid engine mount, and the impeller must be well balanced. Anti-vibration mounting of the fan unit also minimises the chance of the blade tips touching the shroud in hard landings and other shocks while the motor is running. The minimum tip clearance that is usually maintainable is about 1 mm, anything less than this will result in the tips scraping the shroud due to the combination of natural motor vibration and blade stretching due to centrifugal forces.

Most fan units need some assembly, but this normally quite simple. A typical fan unit comprises the shroud, pre-assembled & balanced impeller, stators, centrebody, crankshaft adapter spool, and all bolts etc., needed. All the recommended units in this chapter come with comprehensive instructions. The fan unit shown is the acclaimed Ramtec.

Assembly

Many fan units come in several parts and need some final assembly. The up-to-date units all have adequate instructions and are not difficult to complete, but care must be taken to ensure that the instructions are followed exactly. Pay particular attention to the manufacturers recommendations with regard to the use of thread-locking compound (eg: Loctite™) during assembly, using the correct grade and amount specified. Do not use more thread locking compound than instructed, or it may prove difficult to disassemble the unit or remove the impeller in future.

The balance of the impeller is extremely important, as at high rpm any errors are greatly magnified and will produce serious vibration which is detrimental to all parts of a model. Most of the contemporary fan units (eg: Dynamax, Viojett, Ramtec) come with pre-balanced impellers, making assembly rapid. However if your impeller needs balancing it can be done statically using one the commercial units that are designed for this purpose, the Robart 'High-Point' unit (RB#425) and Dubro 'Tru-Spin' being particularly fine. Balance is adjusted by removing weight from the heavy side, and this is normally achieved by drilling shallow dimples in the spinner backplate. Under no circumstances should you adjust the balance by sanding or re-profiling the impeller blades.

There are also companies who will balance impellers for you professionally, and this is usually done dynamically with the impeller spinning in special machinery, as in the balancing of car wheels. Accurate dynamic balancing produces the best results, giving negligble vibration, lower noise levels and often a slightly higher rpm. In Europe one company that provides this service is Modeltechniek Koullen, in Holland, and their work is recommended.

Generally the engine mounts are pre-drilled and threaded for your engine choice, but in a few instances it is necessary for the modeller to do this. It is imperative that the mounting holes are drilled very accurately, and I recommend that a vertical drill-press is used. Any misalignment of the engine in the mount will cause corresponding problems with the centralisation of the impeller in the shroud, hence increasing the tip clearances, and may also damage the engine due to stresses set up in the crankcase. Likewise it is important that the shroud is truly circular, so with the types that have separate stators you must be careful to tighten all retaining bolts by equal amounts.

Pushers and Tractors

There are two main configurations of ducted-fan unit; 'pusher' and 'tractor' types, and they have very different characteristics. Pushers have the motor in front of the impeller, the incoming air passing around it, the engine mount and the tuned-pipe, and then being pushed through the fan unit and into the exhaust duct. Tractor types have the motor behind the impeller, sucking the inlet air through the shroud and then passing it around the motor before it exits through the exhaust duct.

In comparison with tractor impellers for similar engine capacity, pusher impellers tend to be of slightly larger diameter resulting in the need for larger inlet areas, although often producing a little more static thrust. There is usually less pitch on the impeller blades and they generally turn at a lower rpm, normally about 18,000 - 20,000 for the most common Gleichauf and Byrojet units. This combination gives much lower exhaust air velocities, in the region of 170 - 210 kph (105 - 130 mph), and therefore slower flying models. Due to the larger inlet areas required, pusher fans often have auxiliary (or 'cheat') inlets under the fuselage or wing to ingest enough air to prevent the impeller blades stalling. These not only detract from the appearance of the model, but also cause a great deal of induced drag at flying speeds, as well as a few other unwanted effects. One of these is the suction effect which can actually prevent the model leaving the ground during take-off, as demonstrated by a few models in the distant past. The pilots soon found a way around this though; after achieving maximum ground speed they would close the throttle just long enough to rotate the model, and then go back to full power!

There are other disadvantages to pusher ducted-fan units. The tuned-pipe and engine are positioned in front of the fan unit, where they do not benefit from the passage of high velocity air to aid cooling, and the motors often run at higher temperatures. This location also causes significant turbulence to the ingested air, which decreases overall performance considerably, but has the benefit that motor access is normally very simple. The carburettor faces into the inlet air, where it is more likely to ingest dust and foreign particles. The use of air filters does alleviate this, but can also restrict the amount of air entering the carburettor, and hence performance. Pushers are generally much noisier than tractor types, as there are very few properly muffled tuned pipes made for these units.

Pusher fans are old technology. They were designed in the days when it was thought imperative to have as much 'static' thrust as possible and that an unrestricted exhaust duct was the most significant factor, but it is now established that 'dynamic' thrust (produced when the model is moving forwards) is the most important criteria to give good flight performance. For these reasons the dominant tendency in the 1990's has been away from pusher powered models, and therefore available products are dwindling quickly, however they can be suitable for beginners who don't want high speed jets, and offer a superficially less expensive entry into jet modelling. Nevertheless you should beware of the drawbacks mentioned above, particularly the noise problem which may make you an unwelcome pilot at many jet events and model flying fields.

Tractor fan units have many advantages over pushers. The motor, glow plug and tuned-pipe are better cooled by high velocity air, even at low throttle settings, which prolongs the life of the propulsion system and improves reliability. The location of the motor and tuned-pipe behind the impeller allows the inlet air to enter the shroud with no induced turbulence, which has proved beneficial for maximising overall performance. Tractor fans are normally a little smaller in diameter and therefore require less inlet area, and the contemporary units are far more efficient. They produce much greater dynamic thrust than pusher types, typical .90 sized units turning in the region of 21,500 - 23,000 rpm and producing exhaust air velocities of around 250 - 300 kph (160 - 190 mph) which give higher flight speeds.

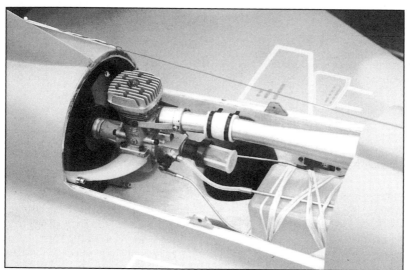

A typical pusher fan installation in a Mirage model. OS91 motor with heatsink head installed in a Byrojet fan, with an air filter fitted to the carburettor and pipe connected to exhaust header with teflon sleeve and high-temperature cable ties. Note single fuel tank arrangement and large open main wheel openings that are used as 'Cheat' inlets to allow sufficient inlet air to the fan unit.

Operation, installation and starting procedures are simpler than for pushers, it is far easier to apply anti-vibration and noise reduction techniques, and the carburettors suffer less from ingested debris. There are many pre-set length tuned pipes available for the current tractor fan units, most of which give optimum performance combined with low noise output. All of the contemporary fan units are very similar in diameter (approx. 125 mm), mounting dimensions and methods, and this often allows a choice of different fan units to be installed in most airframes.

For these reasons almost all recent fan development has concentrated on tractor units which, in turn, has meant that the vast majority of new jet kits are also designed around this configuration.

Power Matching

To get the best performance and reliability all of the propulsion system components must be well matched. In the past a lot of experimentation was necessary to find motors, fan units and pipes that complemented each other. However the experience gathered in recent years, together with the process of natural selection, has simplified this matter considerably, and there are now a number of proven combinations.

There are several factors which should be taken into consideration when determining an efficient propulsion system combination. At full throttle the fan unit used should allow the motor to run at, or very close to, the rpm at which it produces it's maximum brake horsepower. The tuned-pipe, glow plug and fuel used must also allow this, and the fuel system must give an adequate supply at all times.

The load that the impeller places on the motor, which limits it's maximum rpm, is governed by several factors; the diameter of the impeller, the number and pitch of the blades, and the solidity factor of the complete fan unit. Impeller diameter is fixed, typically about 125 mm (5") for most fans, only the Byrojet and Gleichauf Maxi pusher units being much larger at 150 mm. The latest units have generally tended to reduce the number of impeller blades and stators, and increase the pitch to harness the high power of the current motors, whilst reducing the solidity to allow the greatest air flow. Solidity factor is the ratio between the projected area of the impeller blades (when viewed from the front of the fan) in comparison to the total area of the fan shroud.

In the past it was thought that the rpm of the fan (and therefore motor) increased considerably during flight, but recent tests with on-board tachometers that record the highest rpm reached, have finally and indisputably disproved this theory. Therefore for the maximum thrust you should synchronise the static maximum rpm of the motor to that of it's highest power output. For example - the OS91VRDF motor produces it's maximum power (about 4.8 bhp) at around 21,700 rpm, so for the best efficiency it is preferable to chose an impeller that allows it to run at this speed. Of course turning the same impeller at a higher rpm will give additional thrust, assuming sufficient air flow so that the impeller blades don't stall, but possibly at the expense of reduced motor reliability and life.

Luckily for modellers the recent huge expansion of the jet scene has resulted in increased development and resources invested by many of the manufacturers. To some extent this has made the choice of appropriate motors for particular ducted-fan units much simpler, as nowadays all the commonly used fans are generally only available pre-configured for the relatively small number of suitable and proven motors.

Installation

Installation of a ducted-fan unit is really no more complex than for a conventional motor driving a propeller - the main differences being that it's totally enclosed in the airframe, and subject to much higher rpm, stresses and high-frequency vibration.

There are two common mounting methods used to fix the fan unit in to the airframe; the 'Beam' or 'rail' mount, and the 'Bulkhead' mount. The beam mount is used by all current tractor fan units and consists of a flange on either side of the fan unit, usually close to, or on, the horizontal centreline. Each flange has a pair of holes, which are used to bolt the unit to a pair of horizontal beams between two bulkheads. Be especially careful that these bearers are parallel to each other, in side view, so that no twisting force is induced on the fan shroud. It is simple to incorporate anti-vibration (isolation) mounts, as discussed in Chapter 11, and several fan unit manufacturers and accessory companies make suitable examples for use with this mounting method.

The bulkhead mount is most commonly used with pusher fans (eg: Byrojet & Gleichauf), where the front lip of the shroud has moulded-in fixing points which allow it to be bolted into an appropriately sized aperture in a vertical bulkhead or former. It is still possible to install anti-vibration mounting system, although not quite as easy, and there are less commercially available items.

It is common practice to use bolts and captive nuts for holding the fan unit in position, as it's often difficult to get at the other side of the bearer or bulkhead, and the old method of using self-tapping screws is not advisable with the high power of today's units. If using an anti-vibration mounting system, which is beneficial to the airframe and all of it's components, be especially careful not to tighten the mounting bolts too much - or you will eliminate the isolating advantages.

Starting Methods

There are three common methods of starting the ducted-fan motor. The majority of tractor units use a 'Starter Probe'. This is basically a rod with a hexagonal ball-drive on one end that engages in a matching socket head cap bolt in the spinner, and a cone on the other end that fits the standard rubber insert on an electric starter. The probe is inserted either through the inlet duct, or more commonly through the cockpit opening or special access hatch, and engaged in the spinner bolt, the external sleeve is gripped with one hand to support the probe, and the starter is applied to the other end.

Pusher units also use a starter probe, normally consisting of a larger diameter tube of about 750 mm (30") length with a hexagonal socket drive at one end that locates on the nut that retains the impeller to the crankshaft, and a cone on the other end to engage with the electric starter. Some pusher probes, also called starter extensions, have a free-wheeling clutch mechanism which disengages automatically when the motor starts. Of course, for pusher fans the probe needs to be inserted through the exhaust duct.

The final method is generally used for the smaller (up to .45 capacity) fan units such as the Turbax 1, and for all sizes of Thorjet units. This method uses a 'V' belt which is engaged in the pulley groove on the electric starter, and a similar pulley slot or toothed area on the impeller spinner. The circular belt is slipped over both items, then the electric starter is lifted to pull the belt taught, and activated - so turning the impeller and motor.

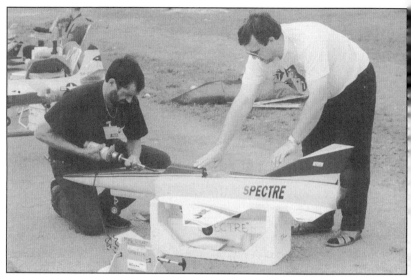

Author & assistant starting a Trim Aircraft 'Spectre' using a JMP starter probe & electric starter. Make sure model is firmly supported and no loose wires or other items can be sucked into inlets. A simple foam stand is a great help. As soon as motor fires, release pressure of starter cone on end of probe, and then pull it swiftly out of the bolt in spinner with motor at idle.

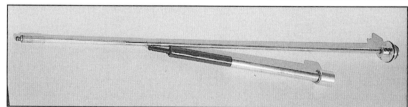

All tractor fans that are designed for starter probe operation use the same 1/4" AF socket head cap bolt in the spinner, and therefore most probes are universal. The ball-end allows the probes to be inserted at angles of up to about 20° without losing drive.

Typical tractor starter probes, with 1/4" hex drive ball ends, are available from most jet companies. Shown here are the extended BVM type (top) & the PMP 'professional' item, which telescopes for ease of transport.

Pusher fan units have several different drive nut sizes, and the probes are normally specific to the fan unit. For both pusher and tractor probes it is necessary to apply a small amount of grease to the ball-driver or socket drive at regular intervals to prevent rapid wear of the drive parts. Almost any type will suffice, lithium based automotive types being commonly used.

There are a few instances where special probes are needed; on some jets they need to be longer than the fairly typical 500 mm (20 ") length, and for a few of the BVM sport jets they need to be especially slim to fit through a special hinged starting access flap. All the major fan manufacturers produce their own starter probes, and there are also some after-market types. One particularly novel tractor probe is the product from PMP which is telescopic, allowing the length to be reduced to only 300 mm for ease of storage in a fieldbox.

Constant Area-Ruling

Constant-area ruling is one of the factors that has dramatically improved the efficiency of ducted-fan propulsion systems in the last few years. In very simple terms it is the method of ensuring a constant

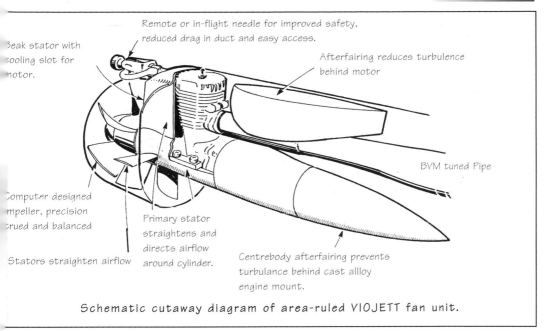

Beak stator with cooling slot for motor.

Remote or in-flight needle for improved safety, reduced drag in duct and easy access.

Afterfairing reduces turbulence behind motor

BVM tuned Pipe

Computer designed impeller. precision trued and balanced

Primary stator straightens and directs airflow around cylinder.

Centrebody afterfairing prevents turbulance behind cast allloy engine mount.

Stators straighten airflow

Schematic cutaway diagram of area-ruled VIOJETT fan unit.

cross-sectional area at all points throughout an object, producing the least possible drag on the airflow as it passes through the object, thereby maintaining the maximum possible pressure rise produced by the impeller.

Although this principle has been used in exhaust ducting design for several years, so far the only company to incorporate it in the design and manufacture of a model ducted-fan unit is Bob Violett Models. Their acclaimed Viojett was computer-designed by an aerospace engineer, the specially shaped shroud and stators compensating for the additional cross-sectional area of the centrebody and engine, and thereby eliminating pressure losses common in other units.

Contemporary Fans

More than 20 ducted-fan units have been produced commercially in the last decade, but the process of natural selection (ie: what works best!) during the last 3 or 4 years has reduced the ones that are commonly used, and therefore easily available, to those of just 5 or 6 manufacturers.

Nowadays, probably 90% of all ducted-fan models use one of the following fan units: Ramtec, Dynamax, Viojett, Thorjet 45, Turbax 1, Byrojet or Gleichauf. The first three tractor units are used in by far the largest majority of actively flown jet models, all being for the larger capacity (.65 - .100) capacity motors, with the Thorjet 45 and Turbax 1 tractor fans about equally used in the less common .45 sized models. For the pusher fan propelled jets only the Byrojet and Gleichauf units are still favoured, and are of about equal popularity. For the new, or aspiring, modeller who wants the greatest chance of success and the best possible performance the first three fans listed are the units to consider first. As stated in Chapter 5 the OS91VRDF motor is, without any doubt, the current industry standard in the ducted-fan arena, and all of these units are available for this engine, and produce excellent performance with it.

All of the five tractor units listed above are of nominal 5" (125 mm) diameter, but vary slightly in exact shroud dimensions. In some cases you can fit any of these fans into contemporary airframes, but usually jet kits are usually designed around a particular fan unit and may require slight modification for another unit. In particular the Dynamax and Ramtec fans are very similar, also being the most numerous, and can generally be interchanged quite simply. BVM kits are specifically designed for their Viojett and cannot easily be fitted with other units, due to the slightly smaller dimensions and design of the inlet and exhaust ducting systems. However it's possible to fit a Viojett into some models designed for other units, with some ducting modification. The shroud diameter of all Thorjet fan units is identical at 5.25", at making it possible to retrofit a larger capacity motor in an airframe at a later date. The Turbax 1 has a

slightly smaller shroud than other tractor units. The Byrojet and Gleichauf pusher fans have differen
diameters and mounting locations, and it is difficult to interchange them. All the above fan units weigl
similar amounts, varying between approx. 550 grams (20 oz) for the .90 sized tractor units, to just 40(
grams for the Turbax 1.

The list below summarises the main data for
these ducted-fan units, and the recommended
motors for use with each type, along with
benchmark rpm's achieved with a typical
motor and pipe combination motor, where
possible.

DYNAMAX

Produced by Jet Model Products (USA). Tractor
fan suited to .65 - .90 motors, particularly the
OS91 and K&B.82, but also available for
OS65 & OS77, and Rossi 65, 81 & 90. Pre-
balanced impeller (125.5 mm dia.) is injection
moulded from carbon-reinforced nylon with 11
individual blades. 16 moulded nylon stators.
Injection-moulded centrebody, with aluminium reinforcing, pre-configured for recommended motors. Requires some final assembly. Beam mounting with reversible aluminium flanges. Although designed several
years ago for the 4 bhp motors available then,
notably the Rossi 65 and OS77, the high
solidity ratio has proved able to absorb the
extra power of contemporary motors, producing reliable dynamic and static thrust.
Accurately manufactured with good instructions, rigid construction, well engineered and
widely available. It is simple to fit most after-

The Jet Model Products Dynamax unit is one of the
most popular, and best performing, tractor fans. Suited
to a wide variety of motors it fits many current kits
Shown here with OS91, latest JMP pipe, remote needle
valve and impeller pressure fitting.

market anti-vibration mounts to the reversible aluminium mounting flanges. The Dynamax fits the
majority of contemporary jet kits and is probably the most numerous fan unit in the USA, although
recently becoming slightly less common in Europe. (Benchmark - OS91 motor, with JMP or equivalent
pipe, peaks @ approx. 22,500 rpm.)

VIOJETT

Produced by Bob Violett Models (USA).
Tractor fan suited to .72 - .90 motors, currently pre-configured for the BVM91 or OS91,
but also still available for KBV72, KBV82 and
BVM81, although these motors are no longer
made. Pre-balanced impeller (117 mm dia.) is
injection moulded from carbon-reinforced
nylon with 7 individual blades. 4 stators, one
of aluminium, other 3 are injection moulded
from carbon-reinforced nylon, as is the
shroud. CNC machined aluminium centrebody.
Supplied fully assembled. Beam mounting.
Integral mounting flanges, with anti-vibration mounting system included. The only fan
unit designed around the 'constant area-ruled'
principle, and generally acknowledged as the
most efficient available, at around 85%.

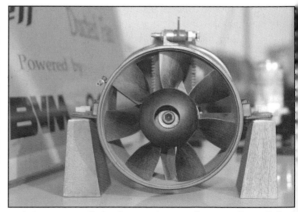

A front view of the famous Viojett fan unit from Bob
Violett Models. Note the lower solidity ratio than other
current types, the aluminium primary 'beak' stator in
front of the cylinder, and integral anti-vibration mounts.

Produces exceptional thrust, and highest exhaust air velocities. Fibreglass afterfairings also available to further smooth airflow behind BVM motors and tuned pipes. The Viojett is distinctive in both shape and superb manufacturing quality, and it's extremely rigid construction allows close tip clearances to be maintained. Fits all BVM kits and can also be installed in some other current jets with duct modifications. Popularity increasing world-wide, especially for scale and sport contest models where the maximum performance is required. (Benchmarks - OS91 motor & BVM pipe peaks @ approx. 23,000 rpm. BVM91R motor with BVM pipe reaches 24,000 rpm)

RAMTEC

Produced by Trim Aircraft (Australia). Tractor fan suited to .65 - .100+ motors, especially well matched to the OS91 and Rossi 90, and also available for OS65 & OS77, Rossi 81 & 105, K&B.82, K&B100, OPS80, KBV82, CMB85 and Webra 80. Pre-balanced impeller (127 mm dia) with 9 individual blades is injection moulded from carbon-reinforced nylon, as are the 10 stators, shroud and centrebody. Requires some final assembly. Beam mounting. Accurately manufactured with adequate instructions, gives outstanding dynamic and static thrust. Mounting flanges are integrally moulded with shroud, and permit fitment of optional extra Trim Aircraft anti-vibration mounts or similar after-market items. The most recently designed of the contemporary fans, the Ramtec impeller has quite a high pitch and is able to utilise the high power of the latest large capacity motors very well without exceeding their optimum rpm. Fibreglass afterfairings available to smooth airflow behind motor and centrebody. Took the European jet scene by storm in the 1990's and is totally predominant there today, and now also starting to become more common in the USA. The Ramtec fits the majority of current jet kits designed for .80+ capacity motors. (Benchmark - OS91 motor & Trim/BVM/PMP/Weston or JMP pipe reaches 21,700 rpm)

BYROJET

Produced by Byron Originals (USA). Pusher fan for .65 - .100 motors, available pre-configured for OS91, Rossi 90, and K&B100, and also for the OS77 and Rossi 81, although these two motors are no longer in production. All motors require enlarged heatsink cylinder heads for use in the byrojet. One piece injection moulded carbon-reinforced nylon 5-bladed impeller of 152 mm (6") diameter, which usually requires some balancing. 5 stators integrally moulded within injection moulded nylon shroud. Incorporates injection moulded glassfibre-reinforced nylon engine mount. Bulkhead mounting system. Limited assembly required. Although designed around the 4 bhp engines some years ago, it handles the current .90 size motors quite well, albeit with higher noise levels. A very simple fan unit which is known for producing large

Byrojet Pusher fan & Rossi 90 motor

amounts of static thrust, although lower exhaust velocities of approx. 200 kph. Still quite common in the USA, although becoming rare in Europe. (Benchmark - OS91 and byrojet pipe reaches 20,000 rpm)

TURBAX 1

Produced by Jet Hangar Hobbies (USA). Tractor fan designed for .45 capacity motors, available pre-configured for K&B7.5, OS46VRDF and Picco 45, as well as undrilled engine mounts to allow fitment of other similar motors. One-piece injection moulded nylon 5 bladed impeller of 120 mm (4.75") diameter, which requires balancing. Shroud and 6 stators of injection-moulded nylon. Machined aluminium centrebody. Assembly required, which is adequately explained in clear instructions. Beam mounting with bolt-on reversible aluminium flanges. Starting method is usually by 'V' belt, but a starter probe can be used if a smaller hexagonal ball drive is fitted to it. Although the Turbax 1 is an old design,

Turbax 1

based on the original Scozzi unit of the mid-1970's, it produces reasonable dynamic and static thrust for it's size and gives good performance in suitable airframes. Lighter weight than the Thorjet 45, and slightly less rigid, but otherwise comparable in performance. (Benchmark - K&B 7.5 with Weston UK pipe exceeds 22,500 rpm)

Note: A Turbax III fan unit was also produced for .65 motors but this was not generally favoured.

THORJET

Produced by Thorpe Bothers (England). A range of tractor fan units for most .45 - .90 motors, all having identically sized shrouds (133 mm dia.) which permit retrofitting of larger motors in the same airframe. Shrouds, impellers and stators are injection moulded from glassfibre-reinforced nylon. Aluminium beam mounting flanges. Different impeller configurations available with 5, 6, 7 or 9 individual blade segments, allowing power matching to specific motors. Impellers are all 127 mm diameter, and require balancing. All units have 6 stators. Engine mounts are CNC machined aluminium, supplied undrilled Recommended motors are;

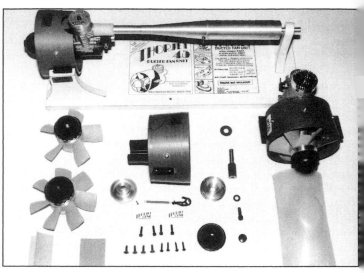

Several of the wide range of Thorjet fans, which can be configured for almost any D/F motor from .45 - 90 capacity, and are all based on the same shroud diameter and mounting dimensions.

OPS45, OS46VRDF, Picco 45 & K&B 7.5 for the 5 blade unit, Rossi 81, OPS80 and Picco 80 for the 6 blade unit, the 7 and 9 blade units suiting the OS91, Rossi 90, K&B100 and other larger motors. Also a finer pitch 7 blade impeller specially designed to suit the new OS46VXDF. All Thorjets are started by 'V' belt, or direct starter cone application, as the socket head cap bolt in the spinner is reverse threaded, not permitting use of a probe. These units were designed for sport models, rather than for contest types, but are well engineered and include fine instructions. The units for the larger capacity motors are less commonly seen now, but the Thorjet 45 is still popular. (Benchmark - OS91 in 7 blade Thorjet with PMP/JMP or equivalent pipe reaches 21,500 rpm. OS46VXDF in 7 blade Thorjet with Irvine 1040 pipe peaks at 22,700 rpm)

GLEICHAUF

Produced by Gleichauf Modellbautechnik, Germany. Three pusher fan units for .53 - .100 capacity motors, originally designed for Rossi but also commonly used with OS engines, and some others can also be fitted. All motors need heatsink cylinder heads. All have 5 blade one-piece impellers which require balancing, and 15 stators, injection moulded of reinforced nylon, as are the shrouds and 4-leg engine mounts. Gleichauf Mini shroud is 135 mm diameter, designed for the Rossi 53 motor, Maxi and Midi shroud diameters are both 165 mm with 137 mm impellers, suited to motors of .65 - .100 capacity. Units produce good static

Gleichauf Midi-Mix pusher unit & Rossi 90.

thrust, and manufacturing quality is adequate. Compatibility between some Maxi and Midi parts allows power matching. Bulkhead mounting. Assembly required. These units, particularly the Midi, were very popular in central Europe until the early 1990's, but have now been superseded by the Ramtec fan and are not commonly used. Good spares availability.

Other Fan Units

As well as the most common and popular units mentioned above there have been many other fan units produced over the years which are either not manufactured now, were inefficient, or are not favoured for various other reasons. However, some of these other ducted-fan units are worthy of mention, and still used occasionally, so a very brief summary is included below. Current production status and technical information should be obtained from the manufacturers, whose addresses are listed in Appendix I.

In particular there are only a very limited number of fans for motors of .25 capacity and less, these declining as it became easier to obtain success with larger units. The most well known are the range from Bob Kress, some of which are now out of production, although several similar units are made for electric power and this company has done a great deal of development in this new field.

MicroMold Impeller

Manufactured by Chart Hobbies (UK). Originated from the P.E.Norman design, which all Thorjet units are now based on. The only separate impeller that is commercially available, suited to .45 capacity motors, and used in many own-design lightweight jets. Economically priced 5" diameter impeller with 5 blades of injection-moulded nylon. Retention of the individual blade segments in the moulded nylon hub and spinner is not very positive, but can be upgraded with parts from Thorjet.

Kress

Produced by Kress Jets, Inc. (USA). A complete range of small tractor fan units, including: the 3" diameter RK-709 unit for Cox.09 up to .15 motors. RK-20 and RK-720 for .20 - .25 motors, of 4.1" diameter, most commonly used with the latest high performance R/C car engines. RK-740, now out of production, but designed for .40 - .45 motors and only 4.1" diameter. All units require substantial assembly. Anyone interested in small jet models would be well advised to investigate the Kress products.

Kress RK720 Mk.2, with OS25 VFDF motor, MACS Wizard 1/4 wave pipe and integral fuel tank.

RK-720 MK II

AeroJet

Produced by South East Models (USA). A tractor fan for .25 sized motors, almost identical to the Kress unit. Now believed to be out of production.

Boss

Manufactured by KB Lyco (Sweden). The first ducted-fan unit to be manufactured in Europe, originally as the Boss 601, then upgraded to the 602, and finally to the 901 Pro. Designed for .65 -.90 motors. All impellers are 135 mm diameter, with a very high solidity ratio of 12 individual blades and 24 stators in two rows. Unusually, the earlier versions were reversible to allow either pusher or tractor configuration. Required a great deal of assembly and the separate cast engine mount makes accurate alignment difficult.

Bauer

Produced by Bauer Modelltechnik (Germany). Originally designed for use at lower rpm , turned by standard 'sport' motors, but later versions designed for D/F motors. Available in both pusher and tractor configurations, several different diameters up to 175 mm, and various impeller blade numbers and solidity ratios. Almost extinct.

DYNAFAN

Produced by Pavel Bosak (Czech Republic). A nominal 5" tractor fan unit with 5 impeller blades and 14 stators, all of moulded nylon, designed for .40 - .45 capacity motors. Requires considerable assembly and balancing. Although of rather poor manufacturing quality, there is nothing wrong with the basic design of this unit and it produces reasonable thrust when turned at over 24,000 rpm by an MVVS pylon motor. The most economically priced tractor fan unit available, but not recommended.

Maintenance

As long as the ducted-fan unit has been properly assembled, and the impeller is well balanced, then little maintenance is required. However it is wise to periodically remove the fan unit from the model and check that all bolts are tight. Any damage to the impeller blades or spinner, however small, will cause the balance to be impaired resulting in vibration and the increased chance that the assembly bolts will become loose.

When removing bolts that were installed with a thread locking compound, make sure that you clean off all of the remaining compound from the threads before reassembling with fresh threadlocker. Acetone, cellulose and K&B thinners work well, combined with a small wire brush.

Check that engine mounting bolts are tight frequently, although this can normally be done without removing fan unit from model. Any increase in vibration levels, which can easily be felt by touching the outside of the shroud with your fingertips when the motor is running, indicates that there is a problem with either fan or motor. First suspect impeller blade damage, then check for engine bearing wear or failure.

Removing an impeller that has been on a crankshaft for some time can be quite difficult, especially if the retaining socket head bolt was installed with thread locking compound, as recommended by most manufacturers. The retention bolt is normally recessed inside the spinner, and it is important to use an accurately fitting allen key to loosen this, as it is also used as the starting drive on most fans and any damage will require replacement of the bolt. Actually this bolt should be replaced occasionally anyway, say every 100 starts - or more frequently if you have forgotten to lubricate the starter probe.

Puller to ease impeller removal from crankshaft cone, seen fitted to Ramtec. Similar items also available for Dynamax & Viojett.

Special tools are available from some fan unit manufacturers (included with Ramtec & Dynamax) to assist in holding the impeller stationary to allow the removal of its retaining bolt. In really stubborn cases, you can stop it rotating by inserting a piece of wood or plastic into the exhaust port of the motor, between the exhaust port and top of the piston - but this is only for emergencies as it can damage some pistons, or even bend the conrod of smaller motors if undue force is exerted.

Once the impeller retaining bolt is removed the impeller usually doesn't come off the tapered cone adapter or spool on the crankshaft, as it is an interference fit. Impeller pullers are made for some fan units (see photo) which eases this task. However if one of these is not available, then hold the impeller in one hand with the motor vertically below it, over a soft cloth or foam pad on the workbench. Place a soft aluminium tubular socket or small wooden/plastic block on the end of the crankshaft (to protect it and the threads) and give it a sharp vertical tap with a small hammer. This will normally free any stubborn impeller.

DUCTING

For the maximum efficiency, and therefore thrust, the design and installation of the inlet and exhaust ducting is very nearly as important at the ducted-fan unit itself. Not only must the fan unit receive enough air, but it should enter the shroud with as little turbulence, and exit the model with as much velocity and in sufficient volume, as possible.

In all the current kits produced by reputable manufacturers the ducting is supplied pre- moulded from fibreglass, making it almost unnecessary for the modeller to be concerned with the design of it, or the inlets themselves. However the design of some duct installations is far better than others, so it is useful to understand the basic aspects of it, especially if you wish to improve a kit that uses older technology.

Most of the principles of efficient inlet design explained below can only be applied to fully ducted installations, as normally used for tractor fan units. Many pusher propelled models don't have full inlet ducting, often none at all, the reduction in efficiency due to the turbulence caused by the motors location being partly recovered by having a 'bellmouth' shape to the front of the shroud.

Inlets

There are three common configurations; cheek inlets (eg: F4 Phantom), the chin inlet (eg: F16), and nose inlets (eg: F86 Sabre). The nose inlet fills the largest volume inside the fuselage, and can give problems with location of R/C gear, fuel tanks, nicads, and especially nosegear retracts as there is usually little space between the bottom of the inlet duct and fuselage, hence the use of twist-and-turn retracts.

Inlet ducts need to be very rigid to withstand the pressure drop applied to them, especially during full throttle ground runs and take-off, and if poorly designed they can collapse inwards. Inlet ducts can be strengthened, if necessary, by the addition of several hoops of glasscloth tape or carbon-fibre tows around the circumference, glued in position with either cyano or laminating epoxy. If noise absorption hush-kits are applied to the inlets these have the same stiffening effect.

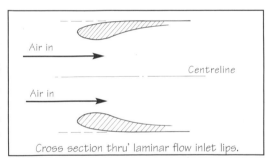

Cross section thru' laminar flow inlet lips.

Much experimentation and development was done by the early pioneers (Kress, Scozzafava, Violett, Norman, etc.) into the sizes and shapes of inlets required to give the best compromise between static and dynamic thrust, and their findings still apply today. The most important factor is that the airflow must not separate from the internal surfaces as it enters the duct, as this causes vortices and therefore turbulence, which decrease the efficiency of the ducted-fan unit. This 'laminar flow' effect is achieved by using a smoothly rounded aerofoil section at the inlet lip, with a perfectly smooth surface on both internal and external surfaces. The worst case is to have sharp inlet lips with angular corners. Any ridges, bumps or roughness inside the duct or around the inlet lips will also causes vortices, so it is important to make an absolutely perfect job of filling and sanding these areas for best performance. Most contemporary kits have properly shaped inlet lips moulded as part of the fuselage or duct, and no attempt should be made to reprofile them.

The other major consideration is the total area of the inlets which, for tractor fans, should generally be a minimum of 80% of the area swept by the impeller; pusher fans normally requiring at least the same area as the shroud. With current jet kits you won't need to worry about this aspect either, as the inlets are already moulded for you and cannot be altered.

Once the air has passed the inlet lip and entered the duct the same principles apply to prevent airf[?] separation; ensure that the inner surface of the duct is perfectly smooth and that the air reache[?] impeller blades with as little turbulence as possible. The shrouds of most tractor fan units fit insi[?] inlet ducting, and this causes a small step for the air to pass over, which creates turbulence. Bob

Models addressed this problem some years ago, and their Viojett has a shallow rebate around the inside of the shroud lip, which the ducting fits inside, thereby minimising turbulence. Other ducted-fan manufacturers have been slow to follow this idea, although the latest 1997 version of the Ramtec also features a similar system.

In older designs of models (with cheek inlets) the spinner is enclosed inside the inlet duct, which is a completely circular shape to fit over the shroud. This caused turbulence around the impeller spinner, but the most up-to-date jet designs use a split inlet system

Typical BVM 'split' inlet duct type, with hush-kit fitted.

(sometimes called 'full flow'), where each inlet is a separate duct that extends right up to the spinner, eliminating this deficiency. Split inlet ducts have another benefit in that they allow easier starter probe access.

Engine Cover Caps

In fully ducted tractor fan systems access to the motor is obtained through a small removable hatch in the exhaust ducting, just behind the fan unit. This is commonly called the 'engine cover cap', at least that's what I call it! This cap allows easy access to the motor, fuel feed to the carburettor, the tuned pipe connection to the exhaust manifold, throttle linkage and the carburettor itself. During normal motor starting you don't need to remove it, as a small hole in the cover cap permits the power connector to be attached to the glowplug. To ensure the minimum air leakage and disturbance of the accelerated air the shape of the cover cap must blend properly with the exhaust duct, and be retained by a reliable and strong system to withstand the air pressure. Different kit manufacturers have their own methods of attaching the cover cap, some providing a better airtight seal than others, but all being a compromise between efficiency and ease of removal.

The pressure losses through the hole in the cap for glowplug access are minimal, but it is advantageous to seal it after starting the motor, also preventing fuel and oily deposits getting out of the duct. A simple method is to glue a small piece fibreglass on a balsa framework on the underside of the main hatch, which lines up with the hole, but a better option is to use a small fibreglass fairing (eg: BVM 'Coolcap' # 5877) which also aids cooling of the plug.

Exhaust Duct

The exhaust duct, also called the 'Thrust' tube, used to be just a simple convergent tube from the back of the fan unit to the exhaust nozzle, normally made from a rolled sheet of lightweight fibreglass or polycarbonate. However since the early 1990's the principles of 'constant area-ruling' have also been applied by the leading kit manufacturers, producing a definite and worthwhile performance increase. The diameter of the duct is slightly enlarged around the motor and centrebody to maintain the same cross-

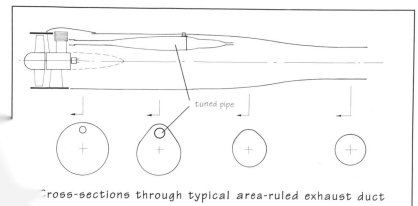

sectional area as the efflux of the fan unit, thereby eliminating pressure loss. In most cases the cross-sectional area of the duct also takes into account the tuned pipe, resulting in the shape seen left.

The reduction in diameter of the exhaust duct towards the back of the airframe increases the

tuned pipe

Cross-sections through typical area-ruled exhaust duct

velocity of the air flow, but also it increases the induced drag. Cont̲ ̲ ̲porary exhaust ducts maintain the cross-sectional area of the exhaust duct for as long as possible, before reducing the diameter, to diminish this effect. The final outlet (efflux) diameter of the duct at the jet nozzle has an important effect of the velocity and pressure of the exhaust air, and therefore the overall performance of the model. If it is too small the air cannot exit the model quickly enough, in severe cases causing the impeller blades to stall; if it is too large then the efflux velocity will be decreased but static thrust will usually increase. The optimum jet nozzle diameter varies for each fan unit and duct configuration, also depending on shape and length of the duct, and these are a compromise between static and dynamic thrust. As the exhaust ducting is pre-moulded in current kits this diameter is already set for you, but typical efflux diameters for commonly used fans are as follows: Ramtec = 95 mm, Viojett = 86 mm, Dynamax = 92 mm, Byrojet = 110 mm, Thorjet 45 = 93 mm, Turbax 1 = 90 mm. As explained in Chapter 9 there are also several commercially produced adjustable jet nozzles, which allow the diameter of the efflux to be fine-tuned during flight to give different thrust characteristics.

The inside surfaces of exhaust ducts need to be as smooth as possible, for the same reasons as inlets, but they don't need to be as strong. However it is important that they are totally impervious to fuel and oil, as any leakage through the duct walls will eventually collect in the rear of the model and affect the Centre of Gravity. Pay particular attention to the seal between the back of the shroud, and around the engine cover cap, to minimise air leakage.

Particularly for newcomers to the ducted-fan environment, my advice is simple; go to a jet meeting, watch to see what propulsion system is used in the models that are actually flown consistently and reliably, and gives the performance you require - and use it!

4 - Motors & Pipes

The ducted-fan units described in the previous chapter produce hardly any thrust until they are turned at about 16,000 rpm, the amount rising from there onwards at an exponential rate in relation to increased rpm. To produce enough thrust to fly a ducted-fan model with jet-like performance most of these fans need to be spun at a minimum of 21,000 rpm, and therefore the motors must be capable of turning these high speeds, and produce their maximum power (bhp) at this level.

Suffice to say that it isn't possible to meet these requirements using conventional 'sport' motors, which develop their maximum power at a much lower rpm. It is imperative to use a motor that was specifically designed for ducted-fan applications, and to achieve the optimum performance it must be matched with a tuned pipe exhaust system, and a suitable fuel and glow plug. In the past it was a matter of experimentation to achieve a reliable and efficient ducted-fan propulsion system, but now there are many well proven combinations using off-the-shelf products that ensure success.

DUCTED-FAN MOTORS

Just as in the case of fan units, the number of motors that are now commonly used has reduced considerably since the early 90's, again due to natural selection. All the motors mentioned below are specifically designed for ducted-fan use, many of them having evolved from marine or pylon racing engines. There are two main capacities of ducted-fan motors in common use, .80+ and .45 sizes, the various motors in between these (eg: OS65 and Rossi 65) becoming increasingly rare as there are few fan units ideally suited to them and they offer little weight advantage, and less power.

All contemporary D/F motors have rear exhaust and rear carburettors, most .45 and larger types using drum valve induction, and all must be fitted with a tuned-pipe exhaust system to release their designed maximum performance. The majority have ringless pistons, utilising AAC or ABC cylinder liners, relatively high compression ratios, and exhaust timings of 165° - 180°. All motors are available with a 'normal' cylinder head for use with tractor fans, and some also with an optional enlarged 'heatsink' head, which is necessary to provide extra cooling for use in pusher fan units.

Heatsink heads are available for the following: Rossi 65, 80, 90 & 105, OS 65, 77 & 91, K&B82, K&B100, CMB85, Picco 80 & 90, and OPS80. The majority of the today's D/F motors don't require high percent-

Without any doubt the OS91VRDF is the most popular ducted-fan motor in the world. It has a power output of nearly 5 bhp at 21,700 rpm, simple handling, excellent reliability, and worldwide parts & service availability. It suits most of the current fan units and fixed-length pipes, and requires 20% oil and 5 - 7% nitro for best operation. Shown inset is the heatsink head version for pusher fans.

ages of nitromethane in the fuel, typically between 5 and 10% being sufficient for good throttle transition and idling in .65+ capacities, and most .45's being happy with 10 - 15%, although some of the Italian engines, .25's and the micro-motors of .10 and smaller often use up to 20%.

The maximum rpm's turned in the common fan units vary a little depending on the actual motor and fan combination, but generally the .45 - .100 sizes peak between 21,000 - 24,000 rpm, the .25 sized motors at about 23,000 rpm, and the micro motors of .049 - .10 usually around 19,000 rpm. As a guide ducted fan models require a thrust to weight ratio of at least 1:2 to give realistic jet-like performance. Typical static thrust produced by a .90 motor in a tractor fan is about 5.5 kg, a .90 motor in a pusher fan around 6 kg, and a .45 motor in a tractor fan approximately 3.6 kg. Although static thrust is not the most important factor for sparkling flight performance, as explained in Chapter 4, these figures give an indication of the maximum model weights possible with current technology.

As already mentioned, the bulk of present jet models are powered by motors of .80 capacity or larger, and there are only a small selection of these that the ambitious beginner should consider. They are the OS91VRDF, Rossi 90, BVM 91 and K&B 82, these proving by far the most popular and reliable, and probably accounting for at least 75% of all jet models actively flown. Less prevalent are the Rossi 80, Rossi 105, K&B100, KBV82, OPS80, OS77, Picco 80 and 90, some of which are no longer manufactured, and the two largest engines only having been released recently, and therefore being relatively unproven at this time.

In the medium .45 capacity motors the choice is more limited, the most favoured are the OS46VRDF and K&B 7.5 (# 9101), with the Picco 45 and OPS45 being less common. Production of the OS46 VRDF stopped in 1996 but a replacement, the OS46VXDF, will be released towards the end of 1997.

There were several specialised motors produced for the smaller fan units, most popular being the OS25VRDF, K&B 3.5 and .21, but all have now been discontinued. Nevertheless considerable success has been achieved by the few modellers interested in the smaller models, mostly using the very powerful motors developed for contest R/C cars. One motor that has shown great promise is the NovaRossi .21, combined with a Kress RK-720 Mk.2 fan unit and Macs Wizard pipe, which produces 1.9 kg of static thrust at 29,000 rpm. However the cost of these motors is disproportionate in relation to the larger engines, being almost identical, and a great deal of experimentation is needed for good performance.

(Above) The K&K45 #9101 drum valve motor is a solid performer. Earlier versions were disc valve induction..

The few micro-fans still available, predominantly the Kress units, mostly use the Cox range of motors, in particular the TD.051 and TD.09, neither of which are designed for the fitting of tuned-pipes, therefore proving rather raucous.

(Above) The new IRVINE 46R ABC D/F is an economically priced entry level motor, and will be released in 1997.

Newcomers to the jet scene should be especially wary of purchasing a second-hand motor without being completely certain of it's internal condition, and having checked that the type is currently being manufactured. Spare parts and service for the less popular motors, and those that are no longer produced, are becoming increasingly difficult to obtain, and the choice of fixed-length pipes is also more limited. The exceptions to this latter recommendation are the OS77, OS46VRDF, KBV 82 and BVM 81, as these reputable manufacturers are likely to be able to supply spares for some time. The availability of some of the Italian motors and spares for them, especially the OPS and Picco ranges, also tends to fluctuate greatly, although spare parts for Rossi engines are quite easily obtainable.

Contemporary Motors

Below is a brief summary of the most established and reputable ducted-fan motor manufacturers and their product ranges.

OS ENGINES

The range of ducted-fan motors from OS are the most widely used, all being orthodox in construction and design, having good power-to-weight ratios and low vibration levels. Known for being extremely reliable and simple to operate, it is imperative to use at least the percentages of oil recommended in the instructions. First becoming generally available in 1989, the OS91 is definitely the 'industry standard' motor to which all others are compared, and it performs extremely well with 20% oil content, between 5% and 8% nitromethane, and a McCoy mc9 glowplug. All the published tests show that it reaches it's peak power of 4.8 bhp between 21,500 and 22,000 rpm, and most of the current fixed-length tuned pipes mentioned below allow it to reach this with

(Above) The latest ducted fan motor from OS is the new 46 VXDF, which replaces the OS46VRDF. Power output is now increased to 2.5 bhp @ approx. 23,000 rpm, and it will be available in 1997.

ease. Motors, spare parts and service are the most easily obtainable world-wide, and almost all of the contemporary fan units can be purchased pre-configured to suit it. Early motors had a woodruff key and slot in the crankshaft to locate the impeller, but current motors use the normal tapered cone or spool fitting, and this method can be used on all OS91's.

The OS25VFDF, OS46VRDF, OS65 and OS77 are no longer in production, but spares are still available for them. Pre-production versions of the new OS46VX-DF motor tested by several fan unit manufacturers have already proved it to be potent and reliable.

ROSSI MOTORS

The wide range of ducted-fan motors manufactured by Rossi Motors and Electronics, in Italy, are well known for their high power output and strong construction, usually being a little heavier than the OS equivalents. Current motors come complete with a remote needle valve assembly. The exhaust manifold is cast as part of the cylinder and care is needed to fit the correct size and type of 'O' rings to ensure a good seal with some makes of tuned pipe. All the Rossi range require a little more care in mixture adjustment than the benchmark OS motors, and often a slightly longer tuned pipe to prevent overheating. However some of the larger volume pipes have proved well matched to the Rossi 90, which is the most popular motor from this company. Generally tend to perform best using Rossi glowplugs, the instructions recommending a much lower oil content than for all other motors, often as low as 14% by volume. The Rossi 80 and 65 are no longer in production, and the Rossi 53 is very rarely seen, although it does turn a Thorjet .45 unit very quickly indeed. In 1996 the massively constructed Rossi 105 was released, supposedly designed for the Ramtec fan unit, and manufacturers figures indicate it to be extremely powerful, producing a quoted 6.57 bhp @ 23,000 rpm. However several very experienced modellers that have used it have found it rather temperamental, negating the performance advantages.

The new Rossi 105 motor was designed for the Ramtec fan, and is very powerful, but has not proved popular so far.

BOB VIOLETT MODELS

BVM are the only jet kit manufacturer to produce their own motors, which are specifically suited to their Viojett fan unit. Early engines, the KBV72 & KBV82, were made by K&B to Violetts design, but the current units are manufactured by Nelson Engines and assembled at the BVM factory. Today only the BVM 91 motor is produced, available in either 'sport' or 'race' versions which differ a little in port timing, both turning the Viojett at about 24,000 rpm. Using specially designed castings and bearings, and a unique carburettor, with a distinctively shaped cylinder to minimise the cross-sectional area presented to the airflow, the BVM 91 is acknowledged as the smoothest running and most powerful ducted fan motor available. Instructions recommend 23% oil content in the fuel, either a McCoy mc9 or K&B 7300 glowplugs, and only BVM pipes should be used for maximum performance and reliability.

This motor is a real thoroughbred, and requires a little more care and understanding to obtain the best reliability, but is almost as easy to operate as the OS91. Experience has shown that the BVM 91 is not suitable for use in other fan units.

Although not now produced, the KBV82 and BVM 81 motors are still highly sought after, and have similar fine characteristics as the 91.

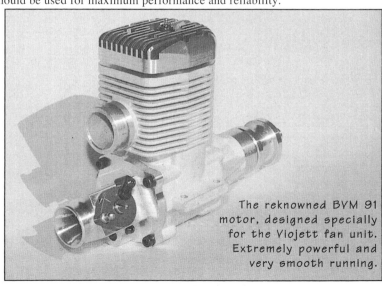

The reknowned BVM 91 motor, designed specially for the Viojett fan unit. Extremely powerful and very smooth running.

PICCO MOTORS

Picco Micromotori, a well known Italian racing motor manufacturer, released a complete range of ducted-fan motors in the late 1980's, which were very economically priced. The range originally included P40 & P45 motors well matched to the Thorjet and Turbax 1, as well as P67 & P80 motors that were used in Dynamax fans and several of the pusher units common at that time. Subsequently a Picco 90 was produced, developed directly from their marine racing

The Picco P45 D/F motor. Rugged & inexpensive, but availability is often poor.

motor, which came with an enlarged 'heatsink' cylinder head as standard although some of the Picco dealers offered a modified head for tractor fan use. Although extremely powerful, it proved temperamental and difficult to match with any available tuned pipe.

All the Picco range are ruggedly constructed, being a little heavier than most equivalent units, but the 45 in particular is a nice performer and, to the best of my knowledge, is the only motor still available. It runs very happily on 16% oil content and 10% nitromethane, but requires a relatively cold glowplug, such as the OPS300. Some Picco motors were supplied with nylon-bodied carburettors, which occasionally give trouble. Currently the supply and spares service for these engines is rather poor.

OPS MOTORS

OPS, another very well known racing motor company, have manufactured several specific ducted-fan motors since 1984, with capacities of .40, 45, 60, 67 and 80. All are disc valve induction, rather than the more common drum valve, especially finely engineered and capable of very high rpm's, probably due to their pylon racing parentage. For many years the OPS45 fan motor was the choice of many pilots who required the maximum performance in this size category, being especially well matched to the 5-bladed Thorjet 45 unit in conjunction with a Weston UK or Macs pipe, and fuel with 17% oil and 10% nitro.

OPS 45 FAN motor. Powerful and well suited to Thorjet fan.

The new OPS 120 FAN motor, designed for the Ramtec fans. Talked about for 3 years, but will it ever be available?

The other motor sizes have never been very common, although the OPS80 gives quite good performance in the Dynamax and larger Thorjet units. Currently only the 45, 67 and 80 motors are manufactured, unusually the latter two having needle roller main bearings. Since 1994 OPS have been promising the release of their OPS 120 motor, now utilising drum valve induction and a completely revised crankcase compared to the original prototypes, which has been developed specifically for the Ramtec fan unit. Current information suggests that this motor, together with a matching fixed-length tuned exhaust system, will finally be available at the end of 1997. The OPS range, like several other Italian motor manufacturers, has suffered badly with fluctuating supplies of motors and parts availability.

K&B M**FG**, I**NC**.

K&B motors are highly respected in the ducted-fan scene, and they were the first major company to fore-see, and invest in, the future potential of jet modelling way back in 1978. Since then they have manu-factured 5 ducted-fan motors; the K&B 3.5, K&B 7.5 (# 9100 disc valve), K&B 7.5 (#9101 drum valve), K&B.82 and the K&B.100. The only motors currently in production are the 7.5 (# 9101), the .82 and the latest .100 engine, both of the latter also available with optional heatsink cylinder heads. The 7.5 is a lovely little motor, being tractable and powerful, and still popular for Thorjet and Turbax 1 fans. Although the .82 is hugely outnumbered by the dominant OS91, it is still a very smooth running, light-weight and powerful motor. It is quite content turning in excess of 23,000 rpm, and an ideal partner for the Dynamax fan. It performs very well with the majority of the fixed-length pipes listed below, being most commonly used with the older type JMP pipe.

The recently released K&B 100 was the first motor of over .91 capacity to be available, and has been mostly used in Ramtec fans so far.

The K&B 82 D/F motor, although an old design, is still in common use today.

Released in 1995, and with several major revisions since then, the K&B100 has not proved popular. Even considering it's larger capacity, most modellers have not found any significant performance increase over the OS91 in either the Dynamax or Ramtec fans. Carburettor problems, connecting rod failures and the lack of any really well matched fixed-length tuned pipes have combined to slow it's acceptance in the jet community so far.

Glow Plugs

There are five commonly used glowplug types for the .45 and larger capacity ducted-fan motors, these being the McCoy mc9, the range from Rossi, the range from OPS, the K&B7300, and the OS No.8 plug that is often supplied with their motors. None have 'idle bars', and this type is not recommended as they can separate from the plug body at high rpm, causing instant destruction of the motor. To the best of my knowledge, all current .45 and larger motors use long-reach plugs.

Although the glow plug used does influence outright motor performance, different types affecting maxi-mum speeds by up to 500 rpm, the main difference between them is most easily noticed in the lifetime, idling reliability, and the smoothness of acceleration. The temperature range of the plug is an important factor; colder types with thicker elements being more resilient at high rpm's and temperatures, but sometimes giving poorer transition.

The instructions with most motors usually recommend the glowplug type to be used, if one is not included, normally the plug made by the engine manufacturer. In the case of most of the Italian motors, which tend to have high compression ratios and run at higher temperatures, a relatively 'cold' plug is ypical, such as the Rossi R8 or OPS300. The vast majority of other popular D/F motors perform very well with McCoy mc9, which is certainly the most commonly used world wide, and has proved extraordinarily reliable and durable. K&B's recently released 7300 glowplug is also gaining popularity, especially for use in their own, and BVM motors.

Glowplug life is governed by the temperature and the amount of vibration it is subjected to. Nowadays, using contemporary motors and fixed-length tuned pipes which are slightly conservative, it is not uncommon to exceed 15 flights before needing to change a plug, either because the platinum element has distorted, or failed. However if you run a motor with a too lean mixture or insufficient oil content in the fuel, both resulting in higher temperatures, then you will need to replace it much more frequently!

The steel body of the popular McCoy plug is unplated, this having a useful side-effect as the colour of it after each flight gives an indication of operating temperature. At normal cylinder temperatures the body remains light brown, but if it turns blue or very dark grey - then it's running too hot.

TUNED PIPES

In very simple terms a tuned-pipe has a supercharging effect on the motor. What it does, in effect, is to suck out the 'used' fuel & air mixture, and enable the engine to suck in a larger than normal charge of fresh fuel & air for the next compression stroke, and combustion. To do this it must be set at the correct length so that the resonance of the pipe produces internal air pressure waves that efficiently control the movement of the air & fuel mixture inside the pipe and motor.

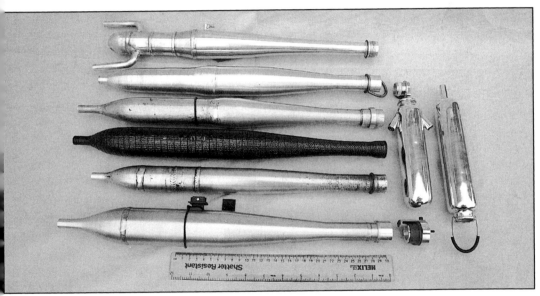

A selection of current fixed-length tuned-pipes for tractor motors. All are held onto the motor by the spring method, unless stated. (Top to btm.) Twin outlet Rossi 90 pipe, lightweight but quite noisy. The new Trim Aircraft pipe, specifically suited to OS91 motors in their Ramtec fan, shown with manifold and sealing ring. Bob Violett Models pipe with retention collar, designed for BVM & KBV motors in Viojetts, but also quite often used with OS91 motors in Ramtec fans for top performance. Bolly Products pipe for .80 - 90 motors, manufactured from carbon fibre. Extraordinarily lightweight, but not very popular. The 'old' style of Jet Model Products/Tom Cook pipe, one of the first fixed-length types available, lightweight and still well suited to many 65 - 90 motors, especially K&B82, Rossi 65, OS65, OS77 & OS91. The new JMP pipe, released in 1994, is much larger than the rest, and slightly heavier, but gives excellent noise reduction and very smooth throttle transition. Note the unique moulded connection gasket and retention bracket. Also shows typical location of pipe mounting bracket. The two pipes on the right are from Weston UK, and are very short (175 - 220 mm), and lightweight. Both these are for 82 - 90 capacity motors. The left pipe has twin outlets at the front, and the other has a single rear outlet. All their range are supplied complete with buffer rings and twin springs. Exceptional noise reduction and good performance.

All contemporary pipes for ducted-fan motors also include a noise absorption chamber, and the design of these are carefully calculated to give the maximum noise reduction without compromising the performance increase. Although unsilenced pipes are still occasionally available, mostly for pusher fans, they really are no more powerful than a properly silenced pipe and their only advantage is a minuscule weight saving. Do not use them under any circumstances, as you will only harm this hobby, which has made such strenuous efforts in the last 10 years to reduce the noise signatures of our models.

However, as with most of the components of today's ducted-fan propulsion systems, you don't need to understand tuned-pipe theory for success, as the major manufacturers now produce a range of pipes that are pre-tuned to the correct length for the majority of current D/F motors. There are many different shapes and types of fixed-length pipes, some more successful than others, and some best suited to specific motor and fan combinations. The types that are most common are listed below and shown in

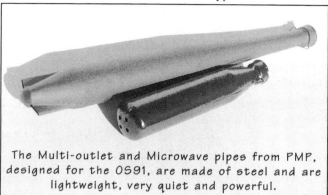

The Multi-outlet and Microwave pipes from PMP, designed for the OS91, are made of steel and are lightweight, very quiet and powerful.

nearby photographs. In some cases the motor manufacturer recommends a particular pipe in the instructions, usually his own, but if this is not of the fixed-length type then you should strongly consider using one of the products shown here that is already in common use with this motor.

All of the currently available fixed-length tuned pipes are designed for the .80 - .90 capacity motors, but also useable for sizes down to .65, unfortunately there being none available at present for smaller engines. However Weston UK will be releasing a fixed-length pipe suited to .45 capacity motors as this book is published (see advertisement). Most tuned pipes are made of alumnium, the steel items from PMP being the exception and proving especially quiet and less susceptible to fracturing due to vibration.

Pipe Connections

Tuned pipes need to be firmly connected to the motor's exhaust manifold so that no leakage of gases can occur, but also allowing some flexibility to cater for thermal expansion, vibration and the torque reaction of the motor. On most current .65+ motors the gas-tight seal is achieved by using one or two high temperature silicone gaskets or rings around the manifold stub, usually located in shallow grooves, which are a tight fit inside the boss at the end of fixed-length pipes. Motor manufacturers use a variety of slightly different methods to achieve the seal, some longer lasting than others, usually being a compromise between ease of installation and seal efficiency.

The most commonly used pipes of the fixed-length type suited to the majority of motors of .65 - .100 capacity are those supplied by JMP, BVM, Trim Aircraft, PMP, JHH, Yellow Aircraft and Weston UK, all designed for use with tractor fans. All of them (except the latest JMP and BVM pipes) use a single large silicone ring to give the seal, and many of these sealing rings are also compatible with the other pipes. The exceptions are the BVM pipes which use dual viton 'O' rings, and the current JMP pipe that utilises a uniquely moulded high temperature silicone gasket. If properly fitted all of the above systems should last for between 15 - 20 flights before replacement of the seal is required, assuming normal vibration and temperature levels. If the pipe is allowed to become loose on the seals, they are very quickly degraded by the hot exhaust gases, and the seal is destroyed in just a

(Shown left) Buffer ring and glassfibre pipe protector from PMP. (Shown right) JMP exhaust manifold with c'sunk bolt holes achieves the same result. Both suited to OS91 and similar motors.

couple of minutes. When this occurs in flight it is recognisable by the change in exhaust note and a loss of power, and you should land immediately to prevent wear caused by the metal-to-metal contact between the pipe boss and exhaust manifold. If using a tuned-pipe, or puffer pressure, system for fuel tank pressurisation the motor sometimes stops altogether when the pipe seals fail.

Of course there are minor performance and noise level differences between the various fixed-length pipes mentioned above, some proving more suitable to particular motor and fan combinations than others. However the permutations are almost endless, and would fill at least 3 pages! The weights of all the equivalent length pipes are fairly similar, with the new steel types being a bit lighter and quieter than the aluminium ones. The most recently developed pipes mostly have a very slight performance advan-

tage, but often only with a particular motor, and the vast majority of these were developed around the OS91. The newcomer will notice little difference between any of these pipes, all having been proved throughout many thousands of flights.

Latest pipe retention system from BVM, also showing an OS91 fitted in the Viojett, with BVM in-flight needle on top of shroud.

Pipe Retention

Tuned pipes must also be prevented from coming off the manifold under the pressure of the exhaust gases, yet be easily removable for maintenance. The most common system of pipe retention uses a spring attached to a pair of small holes or eyelets at the front of the pipe, pulled tightly around the cylinder, a simple and well proven method. However the high tensile steel used for the springs eventually fractures under the effects of vibration and temperature, and it is recommended to use two springs for additional safety. The latest pipe from Jet Model Products is retained by a unique steel clip that is bolted to the special JMP exhaust manifold and locates behind the pipe collar, which works extremely well. All BVM pipes are held in place by either an adjustable collar that is tightened around the pipe boss, or a more complex system that combines this with a steel hoop around the cylinder in the same manner as a spring. Both give excellent security, but are a little more time-consuming to fit or remove than some others.

It is also important to ensure that the front edge of the tuned pipe cannot touch either the motor or the manifold, or the bolts that retain removable exhaust manifolds, as this will rapidly destroy the lip on the front of the pipe boss, making it impossible to achieve a good gas-tight seal. This problem is particularly common with the OS motors as the bolts that retain the manifold project from the surface of the flanges by several millimetres. Several companies (eg: PMP and JMP) produce economical accessories to prevent this problem, consisting of either a large silicone buffer ring to insert between the front lip

of the boss and the motor, or a replacement bolt-on manifold with recesses to accept the heads of the bolts.

Adjustable Pipes

On the older or smaller motors, for which fixed-length pipes aren't generally available, it is necessary to use a standard tuned pipe (designed for the motor capacity), normally in conjunction with a manifold extension tube, or

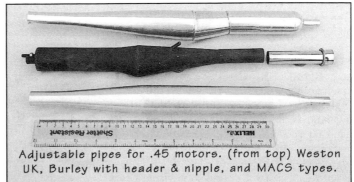

Adjustable pipes for .45 motors. (from top) Weston UK, Burley with header & nipple, and MACS types.

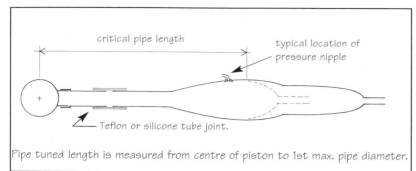

critical pipe length

typical location of pressure nipple

Teflon or silicone tube joint.

Pipe tuned length is measured from centre of piston to 1st max. pipe diameter.

header. The header is normally sealed to the exhaust manifold using a short length of heat-proof silicone tube, with a wall thickness chosen to give a tight fit between the manifold and header boss. The header either slips inside the pipe, allowing easy length adjustment, or if of similar diameters they are joined using another length of heat resistant silicone tube, or a teflon connector. Teflon connectors are much preferred as they are far more resistant to the hot gases. The parts are held together either using jubilee clips, or equivalent, but preferably with proprietary swage clips. Connections using these methods require more regular inspection and replacement than the systems used for fixed-length pipes.Often the motor manufacturer will advise on correct pipe length in the instructions, or an approximate length can be sourced from another modeller using a similar set-up, but if neither of these are possible then you must calculate the length yourself. A very simple, but reliable, formula for finding an approximate pipe length is as follows:

$$\text{Pipe length (in centimetres)} = \frac{3660 \times \text{Exhaust timing (in degrees)}}{\text{rpm}}$$

The 'pipe length' is measured from the glow plug location (centre of piston) to the 'first maximum pipe diameter'. The required rpm is that corresponding to the maximum power output (bhp) of the motor, assuming that it is capable of turning the impeller at this speed. This formula gives slightly conservative figures (ie: too long), but is safe point to start at. Small reductions in this initial length, say in 5 mm increments, will allow you to optimise the performance. As the pipe length is shortened the rpm and operating temperature of the motor will rise, and eventually smooth throttle transition will suffer, the motor rpm rising very suddenly as the throttle is increased. At this point the pipe is too short.

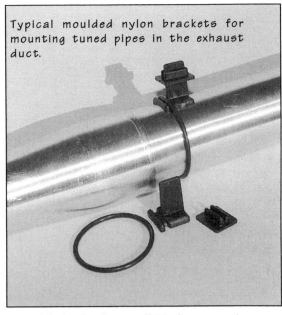

Typical moulded nylon brackets for mounting tuned pipes in the exhaust duct.

Pipe Brackets

As well as the pipe being fixed to the exhaust manifold it also has to be supported at another point, usually at a position of about two-thirds of it's total length. This can be achieved using several methods, but most popular is the use of commercial pipe brackets available from several companies. These are injection-moulded from reinforced nylon, the pipe being held onto the foot of the bracket using a single large diameter 'O' ring, allowing easy pipe removal. The top of the bracket is glued into a slot in the exhaust ducting (in the case of tractor fans), and the duct wall should be reinforced at this location with a glasscloth patch to spread the imposed loads. It is necessary to protect the foot of these brackets from the high temperature of the tuned pipe, normally with a small self-adhesive silicone pad which is included. Popular pipe brackets are manufactured by BVM, JMP and Trim Aircraft, all being of similar design and type, and proving equally suitable.

Operation

The differences between current ducted-fan motors and standard sport motors are almost comparable to those between the engine in your family car, and the ones used in Formula 1 motor racing. OK, perhaps this a slight exaggeration - but it is important to recognise that D/F motors do require considerable care to maintain their reliability and long life.

At the higher temperatures, internal loads and pressures imposed on them, even one flight with a too lean mixture setting can cause expensive motor damage, and with the ample power provided by current motor and fan combinations it really isn't necessary to screw the last possible rpm out of them. When setting the mixture you could think of the needle valve as a temperature control - the more you screw it in, so the temperatures, pressures and stresses increase inside the motor. As well as the air passing around the outside of the motor, a large proportion of the necessary cooling is done by the cool unburned fuel, and especially the oil, passing through the crankcase. This understanding is the reason for the generally increased oil percentages that are now common in ducted-fan fuel. As well as the amount, the quality of the oil used is also extremely important, and in the last 3 or 4 years there are a couple of new synthetic lubricants that have proved especially beneficial to motor life and reliability (see Fuel Systems chapter).

Most fuels will give a slight smoke trail when the engine is set a little rich, but some of the latest synthetic oils produce very little visible smoke. Although a very crude guide, with the motor at full power, holding your hand behind the models exhaust nozzle for just 5 seconds should result in a very obvious oily deposit that will confirm that some unburned fuel is passing through the motor - indicating a rich setting. Newcomers are strongly advised to get the assistance of an experienced jet modeller when adjusting the motor in their models, as the art of getting this just right is not quite as simple as with conventional sport motors.

Running-in

The running-in process for new motors allows the moving parts, especially the connecting rod, to mate together to give the minimum possible friction levels for normal operation. In effect, any minuscule defects or high spots are abraded until the fit is perfect, and this process causes extra heat to be produced. Therefore it is necessary to provide the motor with as much cooling as possible during this procedure, which has an important bearing on the eventual lifespan of the motor.

If the manufacturer's instructions state a particular procedure for running-in, then you should follow it, but generally modern D/F motors do not require much running before they are flown. In the absence of conflicting recommendations from the manufacturer, running-in should always be done with the motor installed in the fan unit, and preferably fitted into the model, where it will receive the maximum amount of cooling air flow over it. All that is normally necessary for a new motor is to run about 2 or 3 tanks of fuel through it, the first with the mixture set very rich, and the second and third a little closer to the normal operating mixture - but still rich enough to ensure plenty of extra cooling effect by the surplus fuel passing through the motor. The mixture should be set a little richer than normal for the first 4 or 5 flights as well, with full throttle only used for short periods, allowing the motor to cool off in between, using half or three-quarter throttle.

Special fuels are not usually necessary for running-in, a normal fuel mix being quite adequate, perhaps with an extra 2% or 3% oil added if you want to be really careful. However you cannot use a fuel based on Aerosave or AeroSynth oils for running-in, as the extraordinarily low wear rates that this oil gives will not allow the internal surfaces of the motor to bed in. There is a special Aero Run-in oil available, or alternatively just use a standard sport model fuel, with sufficient oil content, for the first few runs and flights before reverting to AeroSave based fuel.

If carefully run-in, installed and operated, many of the current ducted-fan motors will give reliable service of many hundreds of flights - often more than 150 without any replacement parts at all.

Maintenance Tips

Day to day maintenance of ducted-fan motors is little different to that of sport motors, common sense being the most important aspect. Generally the same principles apply to ducted-fan motors, although they are a little more complex and it is recommended that they are returned to service agents for parts replacement.

If rust is allowed to form on the bearings during periods when the motor is not in use, then they will self-destruct very quickly the next time it is run - requiring replacement. The use of a good quality After-Run oil after every flying session is recommended.

Each time the fan unit is removed from the airframe all engine bolts should be checked for security, as they are subject to the most vibration. In particular the bolts retaining removable exhaust manifolds are prone to loosening, and often need threadlocking compound.

With new motors the cylinder head bolts should be checked for tightness after the first few runs as these often loosen. Be careful to tighten all bolts equally, in a diagonally opposing sequence, to prevent distortion of the head. In most cases it is best to do this with the motor at working temperature, just after it has stopped running. Be sure to use a good quality, or new, allen key for the cap head socket bolts, as it is quite easy to 'round' the sockets in the bolt heads.

The throttle arms on the carburettors of some motors, notably the OS range, are stamped from thin steel and can fracture if subjected to excess vibration. Several companies make better replacements, the item from JMP being highly recommended.

Occasionally the bolt that retains the barrel in the underside of OS carburettors has been known to come out, but if the threads of this are properly cleaned and it is replaced with one drop of threadlocking compound this doesn't occur.

5 - Fuel Systems

Due to the high power output and rpm of ducted-fan motors they consume a much larger quantity of fuel than the equivalent sized motors of most conventional, propeller driven, models. Therefore it is necessary to pay extra special attention to the fuel system to ensure that an adequate supply reaches the carburettor at all times. Most jet models also tend to have higher wing-loadings than conventional models, and consequently don't have such a good glide capability, so it's doubly important to have a motor that runs reliably.

By far the most common reason for motors stopping in flight is a fuel system related problem, either due to simple fuel starvation, or because of a fuel or air leak (or blockage) resulting in a 'lean' mixture, and subsequent overheating followed by eventual mechanical failure of the motor. Of all the hundreds of crashes and hard landings I've seen, by far the greatest percentage can be directly attributed to the fuel system causing the motor to stop or lose power, inevitably ending with an early return to earth - sometimes with disastrous consequences.

FUEL PRESSURISATION

It is fair to say that just about all contemporary ducted-fan models use a pressurised fuel system to ensure a constant supply to the carburettor, and there are many reasons why this is necessary. Compared to conventional models jets normally have much longer lengths of fuel tubing between the fuel tanks and carburettor, due to the tank location outside the ducting, and often multiple tanks to give sufficient capacity. In addition the large 'G' forces during high speed manoeuvres, which act on the fuel in the tanks, and the constantly changing attitude between the tanks and the carburettor in these aerobatic models puts additional stress on the fuel system. Lastly, as ducted-fan motors tend to have large carburettor venturis to give increased power, they have less natural suction effect on the fuel supply, due to the reduced pressure differential in the carburettor. All these reasons combined make it imperative to have a slightly positive pressure on the fuel in the tanks to maintain an adequate fuel supply.

There are four methods of providing this pressure to the fuel; tuned-pipe pressure, impeller pressure, puffer pressure, and pump pressure. The latter method, pump pressure, is very rarely used nowadays except in special circumstances with very remotely located fuel tanks, for instance in an A-10 Thunderbolt or Learjet where the tanks are sometimes located inside the rear fuselage and the engines are in separate pods at a higher level. Until the late 80's jet modellers believed that it was necessary to use highly pressurised fuel delivery systems to obtain adequate performance in most types of ducted-fan models, to the extent that separate fuel pumps utilising crankcase pressure (such as the 'Robart' and 'Perry' pump) were almost 'de rigeur'. These pumps were a constant source of problems, and frequently proved unreliable at the high rpm's turned by D/F motors. However, in the light of experience, this has proved to be a total fallacy and now almost all jets use a relatively low-pressure system.

Before I explain the three remaining 'real' options I should also mention the fuel 'regulator valves' that have become increasingly popular on conventional propeller powered models in the last few years. I've tried several of these, in an effort to obtain an even more constant fuel mixture, but though the manufacturers claim wonderful results I haven't found one that seems to supply enough fuel to a high-revving ducted fan motor in flight, so my recommendation is to steer clear of them.

Impeller Pressure

Impeller pressure, sometimes called 'pitot' pressure in the USA, collects high velocity air in a small scoop (or pick-up) from immediately behind the impeller and feeds it to the fuel tanks via silicone fuel tubing. It is relatively low pressure system, producing only between 0.035 to 0.05 bar (0.5 - 0.75 psi), but it's quite sufficient in most models where the fuel tanks are relatively close to the motor and don't have unnecessarily long, or small diameter, tubing. It works especially well with tractor fan units, although it can also be used with 'pushers', and has few disadvantages. The power loss, compared to tuned-pipe pressure, is minimal at about 200 - 300 rpm at most, and this is favourably offset by the many advantages. It is by far the most commonly used system world-wide, and in my experience a properly installed impeller pressure system is the best method for most conventional ducted-fan models, having the fewest disadvantages and being extremely reliable.

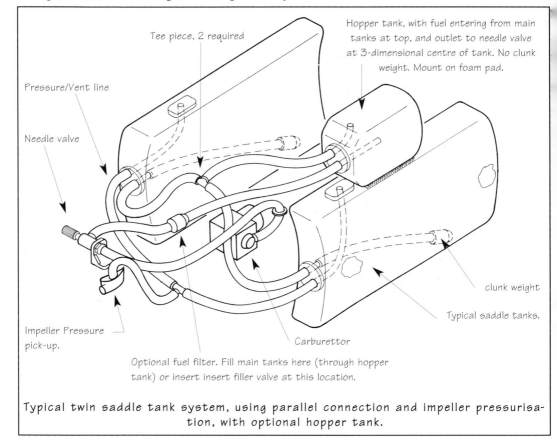

Hopper tank, with fuel entering from main tanks at top, and outlet to needle valve at 3-dimensional centre of tank. No clunk weight. Mount on foam pad.

Tee piece, 2 required

Pressure/Vent line

Needle valve

clunk weight

Typical saddle tanks.

Impeller Pressure pick-up.

Carburettor

Optional fuel filter. Fill main tanks here (through hopper tank) or insert insert filler valve at this location.

Typical twin saddle tank system, using parallel connection and impeller pressurisation, with optional hopper tank.

This system normally requires the shortest length of tubing in the model, reducing both pressure loss and weight, and there is no tubing inside the exhaust duct where it can flap around and get damaged. Perhaps the most beneficial result of using impeller pressure is that there is no recirculation of burnt fuel residues, which contain nitric acid, to corrode the internal parts of the motor and generally gum up the fuel system. If you don't believe that this happens, just look at the discolouring of the tanks and tubing in a tuned-pipe pressure fed model after 50 or so flights, and remember that all this is also going back into the motor! Due to the low pressure the fuel tanks don't need to be reinforced, and motors don't suffer from 'flooding' when the throttle is closed quickly and then reopened - which often causes the motor to stop with tuned-pipe pressure.

The only real disadvantage with this system is that if you overfill the tanks then the excess fuel comes out of the impeller pick-up fitting in the fan shroud, allowing fuel into the ducting, which can then leak into the inside of the fuselage, so some care is needed. In flight, even after rapid transition from low to high, or high to low, throttle settings this leakage out of the pick-up does not occur.

Several companies manufacture special impeller pressure fittings for you to install in the shroud of your fan unit, and in particular the items from JMP, Trim Aircraft and UEI are recommended. Each manufacturer gives adequate instructions for fitting them in the shroud, but generally they are located midway between a pair of stator blades, with the inlet hole about 5 mm behind the trailing edge of the impeller blades. The angle of the pick-up relative to the impeller blades is important to give adequate pressure, and normally they point about 10° towards the back face of the impeller blades.

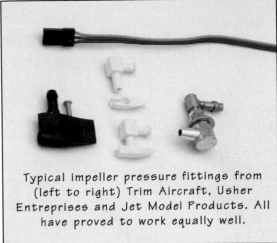

Typical impeller pressure fittings from (left to right) Trim Aircraft, Usher Entreprises and Jet Model Products. All have proved to work equally well.

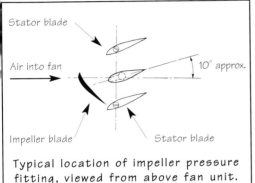

Typical location of impeller pressure fitting, viewed from above fan unit.

I have also seen some impeller-pressure installations which have utilised the plastic or metal scoops that are meant for cooling water pick-up in model boats, and these seemed to work quite well, are very inexpensive and easily obtained.

It is necessary to use large bore fuel tubing for both the air pressure feed to the tanks, and from the tanks to the carburettor, to reduce pressure loss. Normally a minimum internal bore diameter of 3 mm is sufficient, but if you find that the main needle valve is very insensitive this can be increased to 3.5 or 4 mm to improve flow. The needle valves supplied with some motors, and also a few of the 'remote' needle valves, have a very fine taper on the needle, which makes them a little insensitive with low-pressure systems but, as before, larger bore tubing is usually the solution.

Note: Bob Violett Models do not recommend the use of this system with their Viojett fan as, due to the constant area-ruled shroud, there is a much reduced area of localised high pressure in front of the motor, and therefore the pressure available could be insufficient. However I have seen it used successfully in a Viojett on a couple of occasions, most impressively on the huge 25 lb own-design F86 Sabre of Dick Rotkosky which certainly performs extremely well. He used a very large internal bore (Ø 4 mm) length of brass tube, bent into a shallow 'S' shape and inserted it through a hole in the shroud at the side of a stator blade, pointing at the impeller blades at a shallow angle.

Puffer Pressure

This is the name given by Bob Violett Models to their system of tapping air pressure from just behind the outlet of the tuned pipe, using a small alloy pick-up which is already welded onto their Puffer Pressure pipe. It was developed specifically for use with BVM's Viojett fan unit, and is not in common use with other fan types. However there is no reason why it shouldn't be used with others, and my Spectre used a BVM puffer pipe combined with an OS91 & Ramtec fan to win several high speed awards, proving 100% reliable.

View on the aluminium pressure pick-up which is welded onto the end of the BVM Puffer pipe during manufacture. Note the use of a short aluminium tube where the pipe passes under the tuned pipe retention 'O' ring to prevent it getting squashed.

It is a low pressure system, although slightly higher than impeller pressure at around 0.05 - 0.06 bar (0.75 - 0.85 psi), and avoids most of the disadvantages of tuned-pipe pressure. However there is a small amount of recirculation of burnt fuel residues, and it does need a considerable length of large diameter silicone tubing inside the exhaust duct. This tubing needs to be secured properly to the tuned pipe, to prevent it flapping around in the exhaust air flow, and it requires regular checking for condition.

The special pick-up on the end of the pipe doesn't restrict the exhaust outlet and the power loss, compared to tuned-pipe pressure, is negligible at 200 - 400 rpm. No reinforcing of the fuel tanks is necessary, and in use there is no flooding after rapid throttle changes, or during aerobatic manoeuvres. If you overfill the tanks you still get fuel inside the ducting, but as you can normally see the fuel level in most jets this is a rare occurrence anyway. Only BVM offer a tuned pipe with this 'puffer' fitting on it.

Tuned-Pipe Pressure

This system taps off a small amount of high pressure air through a nipple on the tuned pipe to pressurise the tanks. It gives the highest pressure of the three systems, at about 0.07 - 0.1 bar (1 - 1.5 psi), permitting the use of smaller tubing (internal Ø 2mm) if necessary, and it is therefore the most suitable to use with a very remote fuel tank location.

Pipe pressure has several disadvantages compared to impeller pressure. The worst is that it recirculates the residues of the burnt fuel, which contain Nitric acid if you use any Nitromethane in the fuel, and this promotes extra corrosion and rusting inside your motor. To protect against this corrosion it is necessary to use a good after-run oil (ZAP After-Run is highly recommended) after every flying session. This same residue also discolours and attacks the fuel tubing and tanks, and if you use a fuel with any castor oil in the lubricant then the gummy deposits from the burnt castor also get recirculated, coating the insides of the tubing, tanks and carburettor.

There is also the increased maintenance aspect of tuned-pipe pressurisation. The silicone tubing from the nipple on the tuned pipe is inside the exhaust duct, which can cause it to flail around when the motor is running, and the tubing is also degraded much more rapidly by the hot residues than by clean, cool fuel, meaning that it requires more frequent checking and replacement. Finally, if the tubing should puncture or come off the pressure nipple in flight the difference in pressure usually causes the motor to stop, whereas with impeller or puffer pressure it just causes the motor to run badly - normally allowing you to make a safe landing under reduced power. You may have gathered, by now, that I'm generally not in favour of tuned pipe pressurisation! However there are instances where it is still the best system, bearing in mind the points above.

As in all cases where silicone tubing passes through the duct walls it should be protected from chafing with a rubber grommet, and it is a good idea to shield it further with a second sleeve of larger tube pushed over it to give a tight fit in the grommet. This helps to prevent air losses and also limits the amount of slack tube in the duct that can flail around.

Most of the established tuned-pipe manufacturers either supply pipes with a pressure nipple already fitted, or include one for you to fit - often there is a large spot of weld on the outside of the pipe to show the correct location, and also to give some extra thickness to thread the nipple into. You can also buy nipples separately (either straight or angled)to fit most pipes, and I recommend the sort that is fitted from the inside of the pipe and secured with a nut on the outside; OPS make an excellent pressure nipple of this type. Although it is a fiddle to get the nipple inside the pipe and through the hole (use a piece of bent wire) this is the safest type, and after the nut is tightened it should be secured with a blob of heat-proof epoxy to prevent the nut slackening. If no location for a nipple is indicated on the pipe, then the nipple should be fitted just in front of the first maximum diameter from the engine end of the pipe.

In the late 80's and early 90's this was by far the most common system, although it has now been largely superseded by impeller and puffer pressure. Nevertheless there are still a considerable number of modellers using tuned-pipe pressure very successfully, especially in the smaller diameter fan units and motors, where impeller pressure is not always adequate.

FUEL TANKS

Fuel consumption depends mainly on the motors capacity. Based on a typical flight profile of about 7 minutes, using both full and part throttle settings, an .80 - .100 size motor uses about 500 ml (16.5 fl. oz), a .45 size motor about 350 ml, and a .25 motor around 250 ml.

Most popular single-engined jets have twin main fuel tanks, one located on each side of the fan unit or ducting, as close to the model's Centre of Gravity as possible to reduce trim changes as fuel is consumed during flight. These are normally the specially shaped 'saddle' tanks (supplied in pairs) which make it easier to install them around cylindrical ducting, and there are currently two manufacturers that supply them.

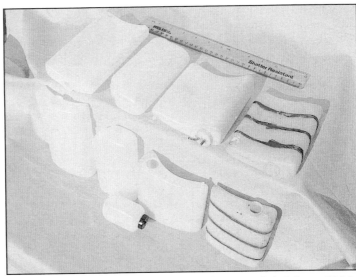

The most commonly used are the #380 tanks from Sullivan, which are the largest at 325 ml each, and Yellow Aircraft also make a saddle tank which has a capacity of 290 ml (approx.10 fl. oz). Until 1995 BVM also produced it's own saddle tanks, and although of slightly smaller capacity (270 ml each) they are of excellent quality and worth obtaining if you can. The oval cross-section 'Pylon Brand' tanks are also used occasionally as they are relatively narrow, but most current and new jet model

View of the most popular saddle tanks. (left to right) Sullivan #380, Pylon Brand oval type (available in various sizes), Yellow Aircraft's own saddle tanks, and discontinued BVM tanks. Below is a typical hopper tank, in this case a standard 60ml(2 oz) Dubro type.

designs are based on the Sullivan items. The normal system is to connect these main tanks in parallel, as in a series configuration there will always be a change in the mixture when the first tank has emptied.

Many of the older model designs, and some current types with unusual ducting configurations, use a single main tank of the normal rectangular shape (approx. 600 ml/20 fl. oz capacity) located below the cockpit area and this works fine, although it benefits greatly from a Hopper tank adjacent to the motor. Of course there is more trim change as the fuel is consumed, tending to be nose-heavy at take-off and more sensitive to the control inputs at landing, and you should check on the manufacturers plans whether the Centre of Gravity should be determined with the tank full or empty. A single main tank system often has a greater length of fuel feed tubing and therefore the use of at least 3mm internal Ø tube is recommended, possibly also benefiting from tuned-pipe pressurisation. Twin-engined models also tend to have restricted space between the ducting and the fuselage sides, and therefore these sometimes utilise a single main tank for each motor, maybe specially shaped to fit between the inlet ducts, and almost always in combination hopper tanks.

A rarely seen tank configuration is that used by some of the smaller D/F units, like the Kress RK720 for .20 - .25 sized motors, which have a specially manufactured 'bullet' shaped tank that fits directly behind the motor, and also increases the aerodynamic efficiency of the fan unit.

Tank Reinforcement

The Sullivan and Yellow Aircraft tanks mentioned above are sufficiently strong enough to handle the slight pressurisation induced by either Impeller or Puffer systems. However if Tuned-pipe pressure is being utilised with motors of .60 or larger capacity it is prudent to reinforce them to prevent fluctuations in the fuel/air mixture. This occurs because when full throttle is selected the increased pressure expands the tanks by a substantial amount, which also initially reduces the response from the motor.

Then, when low throttle is selected, the increased pressure in the tank causes a slightly rich mixture, and as the excess pressure reduces the mixture becomes leaner before eventually stabilising. In rare cases tuned-pipe pressure can even cause the tanks to split if they are not reinforced.

The normal method of reinforcing the tanks is to apply a couple of wraps of carbon-fibre tow around each fuel tank in locations at one-third and two-thirds of their length, and then saturate them with thin cyano to make a stiff 'belt', which prevents most of the expansion and hence the mixture fluctuations. It is only necessary to reinforce the main tanks; hopper tanks do not need this treatment.

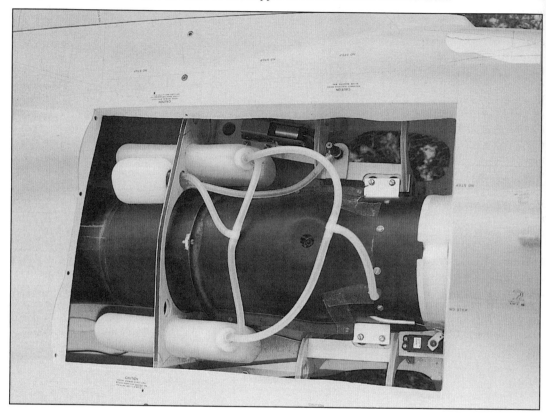

This view of the engine bay of a Philip Avonds F-15 Eagle shows a typical twin tank layout with parallel connections and impeller pressurisation. Notice the small hopper above the main tank, and the standard OS remote needle valve mounted on a plywood plate. Feed to carburettor from bottom of needle goes into duct through a rubber grommet. Tank filling is accomplished by removing the tube to the hopper tank from the back of the leftmost 'Tee', but a small brass tube inserted into the line, or a fuel filler valve would be better. Cover cap is retained by plastic bolts, as these are lightweight and less likely to vibrate out, and hole in the centre is for glowplug access. Throttle servo (btm. right) gives very direct actuation, through a hole in the shroud, but is also likely to suffer from vibration eventually. Location of impeller pressure fitting is clear in this view.

Tank Assembly

Pay particular attention when you assemble fuel tanks, especially new ones which often have small slivers of loose plastic inside them, sometimes caused by fitting the stoppers for the first time. Wash them out with clean filtered fuel to remove all particles and dust, and don't tighten up the screw in the stopper too much; it is only necessary to expand the rubber bung enough to make an airtight seal.

With high 'G' manoeuvres, and sometimes hard landings, one problem that occasionally occurs is that the clunk weight on the end of the fuel feed tube gets trapped at the front of the tank by the vent or filler tubes - especially in saddle tanks with their narrow widths. To prevent this you should always install a 'clapper' clunk system in all main tanks. This is simply a length of brass tubing (about half the tank length) soldered onto the existing clunk, which should be located so that can't get closer than about 12mm from the end of the tank. Note that the silicone tubing from the stopper to the clapper clunk should be replaced every year, as it is constantly immersed in fuel and subjected to a lot of movement from the clunk weight.

Anti-vibration mounting of the tanks themselves is not usually needed, but it is beneficial to make some effort to isolate them, which is easy to do using small bits of medium-density foam. Off-cuts of acoustic foam from 'hush kits' are useful for this, and they're self adhesive! A pair of large rubber bands around saddle tanks that are in direct contact with the insides of fibreglass fuselages prevents chafing, and also provides a small degree of isolation from the airframe.

Fuel foaming is very rarely encountered with modern fuels and the low vibration levels from current well-balanced motors, but it is unwise to mount the tanks rigidly. The normal method of wedging tanks in place with pieces of soft foam, or sticking them to the structure with a couple of blobs of silicone sealant is fine. However foaming, and an increase in the number of air bubbles in the fuel, can still occur in multi-engined models due to sympathetic vibration. There are some specially manufactured clunks that are designed to prevent these small bubbles being ingested into the fuel system, and they look like they've got a blob of metal sponge on the end. They are generally quite rough to the touch, but work well, although you should be aware that they will eventually cause wear on the inside of the fuel tanks.

If you start to get problems with fuel foaming, or a lot of air bubbles in the system, then the first thing to check is whether there is more vibration than usual from the motor or fan unit. If there is then this could be an indication of either a damaged impeller, or advance warning of imminent bearing failure.

Hopper Tanks

Hopper tanks, also called 'bubble' tanks, are normally of small capacity (60 ml/2 fl. oz) and located in the fuel feed line between the main tanks and the needle valve, and are now standard practice in the majority of ducted-fan models. The main reasons for using a hopper tank are that the small size enables location close to the main needle valve, and it also removes any bubbles that may have travelled in the fuel from the main tanks which reduces the chances of the engine 'coughing', or even stopping, during violent manoeuvres. Both of these give improved engine reliability - which is very beneficial to the pilot's heart rate during flight!

The connections to a Hopper tank are slightly different than main tanks, and therein lies the secret of its ability to supply bubble-free fuel to the motor. The fuel enters the tank at it's highest position, using the normal 'vent' tube, and fuel is taken from it and supplied to the motor by a brass tube which ends at the 3-dimensional centre of the tank - not from a clunk feed. Any bubbles that enter it from the main tank(s) go to the top, bottom, sides or front (depending on the orientation of the model and 'G' forces), but never to the middle where the feed tube always collects bubble-free fuel.

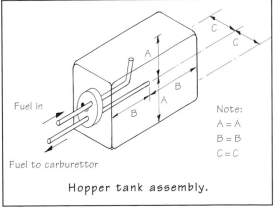

Hopper tank assembly.

The fuel level of a Hopper tank does not reduce during flight until the main tanks are empty, and at this point the mixture tends to become noticeably richer - providing an indication that you have only a minute or so of fuel remaining, which is a useful warning. Note that the Hopper tank can only be half emptied by the motor, due to the pick-up location. Assuming that you have not run out of fuel in the main tanks, then the amount of air in the hopper tank after each flight will also give you a good indication of the overall state of your fuel system, and whether it is producing a lot of bubbles or leaking air. The only small disadvantage of this system is that it isn't easy to completely de-fuel the model (as the hopper tank always remains at least half full), so it is recommended to use either a haemostat between it and the motor, or one of the quick-filler valves that comes with a blanking plug to prevent fuel reaching the carburettor. Lastly, as there is no clunk in a Hopper tank, it's not important which way it is oriented, unlike the main tanks which must always have their clunks towards the back of the model.

Fuel Tubing

The biggest single contributing factor in the efficiency of the fuel flow is the total length of the tubing as the internal surface area of the tube causes 'drag' on both the fuel and air as they pass, and the amount of drag is greatly increased by small diameter tubing. This drag, and hence pressure loss, can easily be counteracted by using a larger diameter tube, and as a general rule all motors of .45 and upwards perform best with an inside diameter of 3mm throughout the whole plumbing system - especially when using either impeller or puffer pressure systems.

The quality of fuel tubing varies, but you generally get what you pay for and you should chose a type that has thick walls and is resilient to both heat and nitromethane. With multi-tank systems it helps to use two different colours of tubing; one for air pressure and the other for fuel feeds, preventing mistakes when reconnecting tubes after maintenance or servicing. In the case of the Viojett fan system the fuel tube from the remote needle valve (located on top of the shroud) passes through a small hole in the top of the shroud, and alongside the cylinder and crankcase to the carburettor at the back of the motor.

Make sure that you install rubber grommets at every location where tubes pass through ducting walls, or any other structures that may damage it. They are easily obtained from any car accessory shop in a multitude of sizes. The tubing inside fuel tanks should be replaced every year, as it is constantly immersed in fuel and subjected to considerable number of movements by the clunk weight.

Tube Connections

When using the larger diameter tubing one of the problems is how to ensure a good seal onto the relatively small (normally 3mm or 1/8" O.D) brass tubes commonly fitted in the tank stoppers, and other fittings such as 'Tees'.

There are several ways to ensure a good seal; the simplest is to slip small rings of fuel tube over the main tube at every fitting, using the jaws of fine-nosed pliers to expand the ring for fitting. Another way of preventing fuel tubing from slipping off the tubing is to slightly roughen the outside surface with a piece of 80 grit sandpaper, ensuring that no metal particles remain to be sucked into the fuel system. You can also enlarge the brass tubes by removing them from the stoppers, and soft-soldering the next larger size over the top of them. However the best method is to use the special 'fuel barbs' manufactured by Dubro (Part # 512), which are designed specifically for this application, and only need to be soft-soldered over each brass tube. These will retain even 4 mm I.D silicone tube and are highly recommended. Don't use wire ties to hold tubing on, like those supplied with the Sullivan tanks, as they slowly cut into the silicone tube.

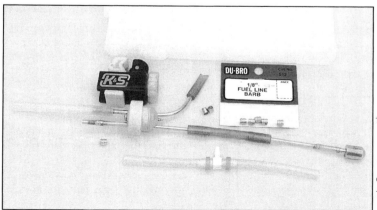

Shown left is the proper way to assemble the fuel tank, with a clapper clunk and short length of silicone on top of the pressure/vent tube to ensure complete filling, but no chafing of the tank. Cut a small notch in the top to make sure it doesn't get blocked against the tank. Also seen are a K&B tube cutter, and various good methods of retaining large diameter fuel tube onto standard 1/8" diameter brass tubes and 'Tees'.

Normally the brass tubes for the tanks need to be cut and bent, and care is needed so that the, already small, inside diameter is not further reduced. The old standby of inserting a short length of braided metal cable inside the tube to prevent it crushing when you bend it is OK, but if it's of smaller diameter than the inside of the brass tube it inevitably leads to some restriction. Several companies make suitable pipe bending springs, which are slipped over the outside of the tube to prevent any deformation, and the ones from K&S and Dubro are excellent. Likewise K&S also make a great little tube cutter, although this slightly swages the ends of the tube which reduces the inside diameter. Therefore my preferred method is simply to roll the tube on a flat non-slip surface under a sharp straight-edged modelling knife blade, which cuts through cleanly in a couple of seconds. Whatever method you use make sure that no burrs or rough edges remain that could damage the soft silicone tubing.

Right is shown the fuel system used in Byron models, where the motors are often mounted inverted. A special valve is supplied that allows the tanks to be filled without flooding the engine, and it is then moved to the 'run' position just before starting.

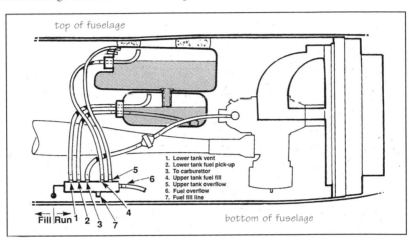

top of fuselage

1. Lower tank vent
2. Lower tank fuel pick-up
3. To carburettor
4. Upper tank fuel fill
5. Upper tank overflow
6. Fuel overflow
7. Fuel fill line

Fill | Run 1 2 3 7

bottom of fuselage

Fuel Fillers

Refuelling operations are simplified by the use of one of the many 'quick-filler' valves, most of them also providing some method of shutting off the supply from the tanks to the motor, normally with a blanking plug. This can be particularly useful when the centreline of the main tanks is slightly higher than the carburettor, as is often the case with many installations, as it prevents fuel siphoning into the carburettor when the motor isn't running.

When the refuelling tube is inserted into this type of filler valve they also shut off the line to the carburettor, ensuring that the motor isn't flooded during refuelling. The correct location for these filler valves is between the hopper tank (if installed) and the main needle valve. Several typical examples are shown on the right.

Fuel Filters

The decision on whether to fit an in-line fuel filter in a model is really based on personal choice. The extra connections in the fuel line are another possibility for a fuel or air leak, but they could also prevent debris reaching the carburettor which would cause the same symptoms, and maybe even damage to the motor. If you use impeller pressure and regularly fly from dusty strips or grass fields, where debris can occasionally be sucked into the fuel system through the impeller pick-up, then it is wise to install a filter in the model.

If you do fit a filter in the model then make sure it is the type that can be taken apart easily, and that it has a good 'O' ring seal at the joint. Clean it out regularly, and if you find that it is necessary for the needle valve to be richened more than usual, then this is the first place to look for dirt particles restricting the flow of fuel. Most fuel filters have an arrow on them to indicate the normal flow direction, but if they haven't then make sure you don't reinstall a used one the wrong way round - or the particles in there will be washed into the carburettor.

All fuel should be filtered between your fuel container and the models tanks during filling anyway, but this doesn't get around the problem of filler nozzles left dragging in the dirt - a common sight in many pits areas! The solution is to fit a 'return' connection into the cap of your external fuel container and store the filler nozzle there when not in use, this also making it easy to drain fuel from your model at the end of the flying session.

Remote Needle Valves

Many ducted-fan motors still come with a standard needle valve as an integral part of the carburettor on the rear of the motor, but it is inconvenient to adjust when the motor is running as it is inside the ducting. Even in pusher-fan powered models, where there is often no inlet ducting, it can still be difficult to get at the carburettor, and dangerous as well - as your fingers get close to the rotating impeller blades. Although it is possible to fit wire extensions to some needle valves, which makes adjustment a little easier, they still have their disadvantages - the vibration usually resulting in either broken extensions or increased wear on the needle valve itself. Therefore most jet models use remote needle valves, positioned outside the duct in a location that is easy to reach.

OS remote needle & blanking plug for carburettor.

The actual position of the remote needle valve is up to you; it's only important to mount it securely and ensure that you don't have an unnecessarily long supply tube between it and the carburettor. Normally lengths of up to about 225 mm (9") are OK for impeller and puffer systems, with a little more being possible if tuned-pipe pressure is used. Some manufacturers include remote needle assemblies with the motor, and most others supply them as an optional accessory. In some cases, like the popular OS range of motors, the original needle valve can be unscrewed from the carburettor body, and replaced with a small blanking plug, allowing it to be remotely located. There are also a number of standard after-market needle valves which can be used, it is only necessary to ensure that it's suitable (large enough to allow sufficient flow) for the motor. Most high quality needle valves use one or two 'O' rings in them for an efficient seal, and although these usually last for a considerable length of time they should be replaced every couple of years as preventative maintenance, as the fuel does slowly degrade them. These 'O' rings should also be checked if you start to get uneven runs or mixture variations and everything else checks out OK.

Apart from making adjustment convenient and safer, remotely mounted needle valves have another benefit in that they don't suffer as much from vibration and wear as when they are on the carburettor.

In-Flight Mixture Controls

These are needle valves that can also be controlled by a separate servo which allows the mixture to be adjusted from your transmitter during flight. They are normally of the 'remote' type, located in a convenient position (not more than 225 mm from carburettor), although some early Rossi motors and current versions for the Byrojet, actually have an arm on the carburettor for in-flight adjustment. Most types consist of a normal remote needle valve with the addition of a control arm which rotates the whole needle assembly on a coarse thread - allowing the short throw from a servo to adjust the mixture by a sufficient amount. Several companies make these, but the most commonly used items are those from Bob Violett Models and Jet Model Products; the latter available in two versions, with a fine taper for tuned-pipe pressure or a coarse taper for impeller or puffer pressure. OS also supply a separate control arm that bolts onto to their standard needle valve assembly, but normally there is insufficient adjustment from the limited throw of a servo, even if tuned-pipe pressure is used.

There are several other types of in-flight mixture controls. One consists of a tube with a metering slot in it, which is rotated inside a barrel, a bit like the main fuel jet in a normal carburettor, and these are used instead of any other needle valve. Examples of this type are made by Innovative Products (USA) and Schulze Technisher Modellbau in Germany. Another sort simply uses a lever with an eccentric lobe on it that squashes the fuel tube that passes through the body of the unit, and these also work well, the product from Atlantic R/C being quite common.

3 of the commonly used in-flight mixture needles. (from left) BVM, Atlantic R/C and Jet Model Products types.

Since the early 90's in-flight adjustable mixture controls have become quite common, and can be very advantageous on some models, especially speed and multi-engined types, but are not really needed in most instances - as the mixture should be set correctly before take-off! However they can also be useful in some emergency circumstances if they have enough adjustment, for instance if a tuned pipe breaks, or even in the case of a broken throttle linkage, as by setting the mixture very rich it can be possible to make a safe landing under power - instead of waiting to run out of fuel. A tip is to set the control on your transmitter so that the motor cannot be adjusted too lean in flight, as it is often difficult to hear your motor properly when other models are in the air. If using a rotary knob to control the mixture on your transmitter, use the servo reverse facility to ensure that it adjusts in same direction as a normal needle valve (ie: anti-clockwise for 'richer').

Fuel

Because of the increased internal stresses and loads in a D/F motor, compared to conventional model motors, it is even more essential to use a high quality fuel to give longevity and reliability. Needless to say, the fuel must also be clean and free from any dirt particles, as these will eventually find their way into the needle valve or carburettor, resulting in fuel starvation.

Ducted-fan motors run on a mixture of Methanol and oil, usually with a small percentage of Nitromethane included to enhance the combustion properties and/or improve the performance. The largest component percentage in the fuel is Methanol, which is hygroscopic, meaning that it absorbs water from the atmosphere. This characteristic is what causes much of the corrosion and rusting inside the motor (aided by the nitric acid in the residues of burnt fuel) and, although it is accentuated in conditions of high humidity, it always occurs to some degree. When a motor is cooling down after running the moisture present in the air will be absorbed by the remaining Methanol, which then condenses on the internal parts and causes rust.

The most important fuel component is the oil - not just the quality and type, but also the percentage of it. As explained in Chapter 5 the motor is cooled not only by the airflow over the external surfaces of it but, perhaps more importantly, by the flow of cool fuel and oil mixture internally. Most D/F motors require 17 - 20% oil content by volume for satisfactory operation, but there are exceptions to this wide generalisation, notably some of the Rossi motors which seem to run better on 12% - 15%. In the last couple of years the general trend has been to increase oil content slightly, many jet modellers now using 22 - 23% in .90 and larger capacity motors, and I have no doubt that this the main factor in the increased lifespan and reliability obtained.

It is unusual for modern ducted-fans motors to need high percentages of Nitromethane, the amount required generally being inversely proportional to the capacity. The majority of current .45 - .100 capacity motors only require about 5 to 10% by volume, most .20 - .25's will perform quite happily on 10 to 15%, but the very small motors such as the Cox .051 and .09 normally need at least 20% to run satisfactorily. The relatively small percentage of nitromethane used in the larger motors makes little difference to the maximum power output, it is required more to improve the combustion process and hence the tractability and throttle transitioning characteristics. Of course, as with the oil content percentages, you should always follow the manufacturers recommendations on the nitro content required, at least as the initial basis for your fuel mixture.

Most commercial fuel manufacturers include various additives (eg: 'Metalon', 'Snake-oil' and 'Teflon') to reduce wear rates and provide protection from acid attack and corrosion. To the best of my knowledge none of these have proved detrimental and, although I'm sceptical about the advantages of a few of them, any extra defence against rusting and corrosion has got to be beneficial to motor life.

Synthetic Oils.

In respect of the fuels used now, jet modelling has progressed considerably in the last few years, especially with the fairly recent introduction of very high grade synthetic oils that are specifically designed to lubricate and protect high performance two-stroke motors - but the pro's and con's of castor versus synthetic oils are still a constantly debated subject amongst modellers.

Until the mid-80's there was little choice of lubricant in the fuel, the majority being based on natural castor oil, occasionally with a small percentage of synthetic oil as well. The majority of the fully synthetic oils at this time were not really designed for the high rpm's and stresses in D/F motors, and were often blamed for the fairly common engine failures. This was probably quite justifiable, but the lower total oil content used at this time was also an important factor in the breakage's and unreliability. However synthetic oils have improved greatly since then, and the vast majority of jet modellers now use fuel which is based either on fully synthetic oil, or at least includes a large percentage of it.

Almost certainly the two most commonly used lubricants now are Klotz Super-Techniplate KL100 (which contains 80% synthetic and 20% refined castor), and the range of totally synthetic Aerosave/Aerosynth oils from German manufacturing giant Fuchs Mineroelwerke GmbH. Both were specifically formulated for high performance two-stroke motors, deteriorating less under the high pressures and temperatures than pure castor, and therefore giving enhanced protection. The Aerosave/Aerosynth range is extremely popular in Europe and it's properties neutralise the acids caused by up to 20% of Nitromethane in the fuel and protect against rusting, making it unnecessary to use any after-run oil. Unfortunately it is not available in some countries, notably the USA, in sufficient quantities to be used in commercial fuels - but it can usually be obtained in small amounts to allow you to mix your own. Of course no oil will protect a motor against gross misuse but in my personal experience, and that of a large majority of jet pilots world-wide, nothing else matches these two and they are highly recommended.

The most important thing is to ensure that there is a sufficient percentage of whatever lubricant you use in the fuel. When buying commercial fuel make sure that you know the true oil percentage in it, and what type it is. I mix my own fuel so that I'm absolutely sure what it contains, and several of my motors have over 4 years of use and several hundred flights on Aerosave based fuels - with no failures, negligible wear, no bearing replacement, and no carbon deposits .... Enough said !

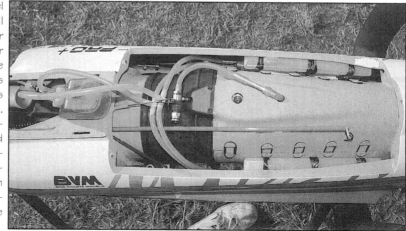

A tidy engine bay & fuel system installation will reward you with better reliability and lower maintenance. A large engine hatch also makes life easier, as in this BVM Maverick Pro. Notice the carbon fibre-tow reinforcement around the main tanks, the hopper tank system & in-flight needle located on top of the shroud for convenience. Plastic snake contains Rx antenna.

INTERNATIONAL JET MODEL COMMITTEE

By Jet Modellers - For Jet Modellers

Many scale jet model competitions have been held during the last two decades, some of these (eg: 'Deutsche Impeller Meisterschaft' in Germany, and 'Top Gun' in the USA) having considerable international participation - however they were all based on very different rules, making it confusing and difficult for those who wished to enter. In April 1992 two jet enthusiasts, Winfried Ohlgart of the DMFV (German modellers association) and Mike Cherry, came up with the concept of a new international competition class for scale jet models, with a universal set of rules. The important thing about these rules, they decided, was that they should be what the jet modellers wanted - and not what was dictated by any single modelling federation or association with little current experience of this type of model.

To carry this idea to fruition a new organisation was formed, named the 'International Jet Model Committee'. Towards the end of 1992 the IJMC met with CIAM (the modelling section of the FAI) at their headquarters in France, to seek official recognition as the 'Special Working Group' for scale jet modelling competitions, and this was granted at the FAI Plenary meeting in Paris in March 1993.

The main purposes of the IJMC are twofold. Firstly to compile the F4J competition rules, modify them as proves necessary in the light of contest experience, and to provide support and advice to organisers of events held to these rules. Secondly, to promote jet modelling internationally and obtain improved recognition from national modelling federations - and eventually to seek full FAI/CIAM competition class status, which will permit 'official' World Championships.

The F4J rules can be briefly summarised as follows: The contest consists of three parts, each of which is worth a maximum percentage of the total marks as follows; Static judging (40%), Flying judging (55%) and Noise judging (5%). Judging is carried out by an international panel of judges, selected by the IJMC, of 3 persons for the static, and 5 for the flying and noise parts. Each competitor has the opportunity to make three flights, with the lowest scoring flight being discarded. Apart from the mandatory take-off, level pass and landing each competitor must attempt 5 other manoeuvres - with a wide choice of aerobatic, non-aerobatic and technical options listed in the F4J rules to chose from.

Currently the IJMC has 38 members representing 21 countries, each having equal voting rights, and a main council of 4 members, who are democratically elected at each bi-annual general meeting, normally held at the Jet World Masters. Currently the council members are:

Winfried Ohlgart *(Chairman)*	-	Germany
Reto Senn *(Secretary)*	-	Switzerland
Ralf Ploenes *(Treasurer)*	-	Germany
Mike Cherry *(Press Officer)*	-	England

For more information on the International Jet Model Committee, or copies of the F4J rules, you should write to the Chairman at: Stauffenbergstrasse 42., D-5308 Rheinbach., Germany.

6 - Airframes

With the mammoth expansion of jet modelling in all three disciplines (electro-impeller, ducted-fan and gas turbine) in the last four or five years there has been consequential growth in the number of jet kits available. Of course, just as in the case of fan units and motors, some of these have proved better than others, and I have attempted to include photographs of, or mention, the most popular and successful types somewhere in this book.

At a rough count there are over 150 commercially produced jet kits available at the moment, nevertheless if you attend a typical jet event (if there is such a thing) then it is likely that you can easily count the types being flown consistently on your fingers. There are usually a handful of own-design or scratch built models, these adding much needed variety and interest to the events, but the huge majority are kit designs from ten or so major manufacturers. The best way to enter the hobby successfully is by choosing one of these, and investing your money in a model that has proven construction techniques and flying characteristics, and knowing that there are other modellers that can advise on any particular building, setting-up or flying aspects of it, if required. The opportunity to diversify into successful own-design or scratch-built models comes later, after a certain amount of experience has been gained with 'standard' jets.

Probably the earliest scale ducted-fan jet with decent performance was Bob Violett's famous A4 Skyhawk, first flown in 1976. With a fibre-glass fuselage, built-up wings and powered by K&B 7.5 & Turbax fan, it set the pace for others to follow. Seen here at the 1978 USA Nationals, where it earned 2nd place overall, with Bob Violett and John Brodbeck (right), of K&B engines. Three A4's produced by other kit manufacturers today are all based on the same fuselage moulding.

The overriding trend in the last 4 or 5 years has been for larger models, these normally having lower wing-loadings, which make them easier to fly and give nicer slow speed characteristics, as well as allowing more internal space for installation and maintenance. I can remember the battles I had trying to keep some of my earliest small jets in the air at slow speeds, landings in particular being fraught with anxiety! Therefore, if your budget will allow it, I can assure you that choosing a larger model, or one with a bigger wing area, will generally be rewarded with a more stable flying style.

Most of the delta planform jets are particularly suitable for newcomers, having a very wide speed range and extraordinarily stable landing configuration. The most commonly seen certainly include the Philip

Avonds single-engine F15 Eagle and Rafale, Jim Fox Models Saab Viggen, Aviation Design Rafale, and Top Gun Aircraft 'Ultra-Eagle'. Others that are proving especially popular for beginners in recent years are the BVM Maverick, JMP Starfire, Yellow Aircraft single-engine F18 and Trim Aircraft Spectre. Some of the swept-wing scale jets are also remarkably easy to fly, for instance F86 Sabres and Mig 15's. The ageing Byron F16 has also brought success to many over the last decade, even though the pusher fan system itself has several disadvantages and is now not popular.

Another famous jet model is this F15 Eagle, with which Philip Avonds (seen here) became FAI Scale World Champion in both 1988 & 1990, the first and only jet to achieve this to date. Originally powered by a pair of K&B7.5 motors and Turbax 1 fans, this well proven model is available as a very comprehensive kit for both twin and single engines.
The single .91 engined version has a fully moulded fuselage and foam wings and tails, excellent instructions, is extremely simple to construct and fly, and has become one of the most popular models for newcomers to this fascinating hobby.

Personal preference, and financial resources, will determine which model you choose start with, and the cost can be anything from as little as a few hundred pounds for a second-hand model or semi-kit, to several thousands of dollars for the latest state-of-the-art multi-engine or gas turbine powered super scale jet aircraft. To a certain extent you get what you pay, the more costly kits are quicker to build, and often more durable, and the less expensive will require more time and effort from you. Whether you chose a sport or scale model for your first jet is also unimportant, many of the contemporary scale jets being nearly as easy to handle as the sport types, and they are often bigger with lower wing-loadings.

Before choosing a model, I strongly advise newcomers to go to at least two jet events and watch what types of jets and equipment are being flown regularly, and reliably. Don't listen to the guy in the pits who spends all day fiddling with his model, which may look superb - but does it really fly? Ask questions from the pilots that are actually flying their jets consistently. It would be easy to summarise the simplest way to get into the hobby by telling you to buy an OS91 motor combined with a Ramtec, Dynamax or Viojett fan, and latest technology complete kit from a reputable and established manufacturer (eg: Philip Avonds, Jet Model Products, or Bob Violett models), and if you want absolutely guaranteed first time success this is a good way to do it - but it isn't cheap!

Airframe choices

There are five main choices for your jet airframe, own-design or scratch built, plan-pack, semi-kit, or full kit. The final option is to buy a second-hand model that is already completed. Of course I wouldn't recommend that you consider the own-design or scratch-built route if you are a newcomer to the jet hobby, but all the other possibilities are viable options.

Plans & Scratch-Building

The number of current plans available for 'scratch-building' of jet models is limited, at least those from reputable designers, and seems to be decreasing every year as modellers require quicker and easier building procedures so that they can spend more time flying. Many of the model aircraft magazines have their own plans lists, and most include a few ducted-fan types, but be aware that many of these are very old designs. In particular you could look at the available plans from Model Airplane News (USA), Traplet Publications (GB), R/C Modeller (USA), Nexus Publications (GB) and Radio Commande Magazine (France). Both Thorjet in the UK, and Bertella in Italy, also have a range of plans for sport and scale jets.

Plan Packs and Semi-Kits

Although they are becoming rarer, there are a few reasonable plan-packs available for building traditional balsa and plywood jets, and if you are an experienced builder and have spent some time examining jet models, then it is possible to start this way. You are much more likely to succeed if you have the assistance and advice of an experienced jet modeller, as many of these leave a great deal to be determined by the builder and usually include no instructions, only drawings. However I can endorse some of the range from Thorjet, which are of built-up construction from balsa and plywood and proven flyers, and also the Hawk 45 from Jim Fox Models which includes fibreglass ducting and pre-cut bulkheads.

Semi-kits are a better option, although some have pitiful or non-existent instructions, and they still need a considerable amount of construction skill and forethought to complete them to a standard where they will approach the performance and lifespan of a proper kit. Generally semi kits include a basic fibreglass fuselage and foam wing set (or occasionally plans for built-up flying surfaces), fibreglass inlet and exhaust ducts, drawings and brief instructions, and a clear cockpit canopy. It is necessary for the builder to supply the plywood, balsa, linkages, fuel tanks and other materials, and cut out all the bulkheads and other parts. Ownership, or use, of a bandsaw or jigsaw makes this a simpler task, but the overall cost saving due to the labour time is substantial compared to a full kit. Beware that some semi-kits are little more than out-of-date jets that are not manufactured in their entirety any more, and are either designed

This single engined 1/10 scale F/A-18 Hornet kit, from Yellow Aircraft, is also suited to relative beginners and is quite easy to build and fly. Seen here with its designer, Canadian pilot Martin Lefebvre at the '95 Jet World Masters, the model is 1720 mm long, and designed for Dynamax or Ramtec fans and motors of .82+ size. The full kit includes a fibreglass fuselage and foam wings, plan and good instructions.

for pusher fans or still include 'cheat' inlets, which will likely require modification, and again help from an experienced jet pilot will be very useful. A few of the more specialised scale jets, especially twin engine models and others that are likely to have low volume sales, also fall in to this semi-kit category, but if they are fairly recent designs then the instructions and information provided is usually sufficient. Of course you shouldn't even consider multi-engine models until you have experience of at least half a dozen single engine types first.

One of the most recent composite moulded kits is this nice F5B, which can also be built as a T38 Talon, from Air Magic in the USA. Designed for Viojett propulsion and .82+ motors, it is 1805mm long, with a 1090mm wingspan, and weighs about 6.5 kgs ready to fly. The kit is very complete, and includes mainly BVM accessories and ancillaries. Although not suitable for beginners, it would make a good 3rd or 4th model after some experience.

Full Kits

Full kits should really be divided into two separate categories, the 'basic kit' and the 'complete kit', and the differences between these can be very great indeed. I regard a complete kit as the type that includes fully detailed instructions, comprehensive drawings and all the necessary hardware (all parts pre-cut to shape, linkages, fuel tanks, etc.) required to complete the model, excepting perhaps the undercarriage system. Most of the manufacturers of basic and complete kits can supply hardware packs, suitable retractable undercarriages and wheels, etc., as optional extras, but you should remember to check exactly what is included, and what other items are required, before you purchase any jet kit. Some of the established companies also list other options, especially for scale jets, these commonly consisting of such things as scale undercarriages, drop tanks, cockpit detailing kits and gear door packs.

The majority of current kits, say those released since 1990, use the latest techniques for moulding fuselages and other parts, often including carbon-fibre or kevlar reinforcement, which increases the strength in high load areas - whilst reducing the overall weight of the airframe. All the best types are moulded using epoxy, rather than polyester resins, and come with a gel-coat finish on the outside (usually white or grey) which reduces the amount of finishing and painting required, therefore also saving weight. In the last couple of years some of the larger companies have started producing fully moulded wings, and sometimes even stabilisers, which further reduces build time and makes the models more damage resistant in the case of minor accidents.

For a beginner purchasing a full or complete kit is the most likely to give success, although it is also initially the most expensive. Don't forget that when you buy a kit from one of the reputable manufacturers you are not only paying for the design and constant development time taken to keep their products in line with current technology and performance, but also to ensure that they are still around when you require assistance, spares or product support. Therefore, in the long term, purchasing a complete kit may not actually be more costly than the other approaches.

Second-hand Models

Another course is by purchasing a second hand model that is already built, and this can be an excellent way of entering the hobby. The best way is to buy a complete model that you have seen flying, and often there are models for sale at jet events that give this opportunity. Even if the owner wishes to keep

some parts (usually the motor, fan unit and receiver), you will be assured of a proven airframe which eliminates most of the possible pitfalls, and offers a beginner the chance to experience the thrill of flying a jet immediately.

If you decide to buy a used or ready-built model that you haven't seen flying, for instance through a magazine advertisement, then always take an experienced jet modeller with you to check it over before parting with your money. There are a considerable number of newcomers who bought second-hand gear, hoping to save time and money, that have been lost to the hobby forever as the equipment they purchased was either so out-of-date that the performance was awful, or it just plain didn't work at all. Of course, if you are not seeking a jet at the upper level of current performance, then some of the older types are an economical way to get into the jet scene, but great care is needed to select the right model.

Fanjets owner, Peter Nye, and his superb 1/6 exact scale own-design BAe Hawk, which is designed for single engines of .91 capacity & larger, or turbine conversion.
With a wingspan of 1525mm and length of about 1900mm this is an impressive model in flight. Originally produced by Fanjets as a semi-kit, it is believed that this model will eventually be available as a complete kit from Yellow Aircraft.

CONSTRUCTION

Construction of jets is not much different from propeller driven airframes, and any reasonably competent modeller who has built a couple of fibreglass-and-foam models should have no trouble, providing they choose a kit with adequate instructions. The main difference is that the propulsion system is located inside the fuselage, meaning that the majority of the construction is also internal. In the case of low-end, or semi-kits, this requires some forethought in determining the building sequence, although full kits usually have adequate instructions to guide you through everything in the correct order.

Linkages and control systems need to be carefully planned so that they will not interfere with the ducting, and often some of these are difficult to access after the model is completed so they must be built or installed correctly first time. One point to remember is that any fuel leaks inside the model will quickly penetrate any bare wood parts, and can even seep through some fibreglass mouldings. For this reason it is good practice to seal all bare wood inside the fuselage during construction, either by applying a very thin coat of laminating epoxy, or using 2-pack paint. Extra care is also needed to make sure that the airframe will withstand the generally higher speeds and flight loads, although this is really down to accurate joints and good gluing techniques, as these factors have already been taken into account by the designers and manufacturers of contemporary kits.

Even with the more than adequate power output of the current motors and propulsion systems it is still important to construct a jet model as lightly as possible to give the best performance. Light models are not only easier to fly, but less stress is placed on the major structural components of the airframe during flying manoeuvres. The biggest weight increases are usually made by using too much glue, and applying too much paint. Unfortunately there is not sufficient space for a detailed chapter on finishing techniques - but the most important thing to remember during the finishing process is that you should rub down to a achieve good finish, not build up to it by applying more paint!

Adhesives

Just as with all other aspects of a high performance jet model, it is imperative to use high quality adhesives to ensure structural integrity. Most jets consist of composite moulded parts, normally using epoxy resins, and therefore the best bonding of the main structural parts is made using similar adhesive types. 5-minute epoxies should be avoided for all high-stress areas, and slower setting types used instead. Most of the 30-minute and 1 hour types are quite sufficient for many parts, but all major bulkheads, undercarriage supports, motor mounts and wing fixing points should be made with a 24 hour epoxy, these often also requiring reinforcement with strips of glass tape.

Epoxies can easily be modified to produce different characteristics. The addition of micro-balloons makes them easy to sand, but more brittle and less strong, and by adding a small amount of very short milled glassfibre strands the strength can be increased dramatically. This latter mixture is often used in high-stress areas, such as wing mounts, and is highly recommended where maximum strength is required without increased weight. It is available from fibreglass moulding companies, usually only in large quantities, or from BVM in a handy 120 gram (4 oz) jar which is sufficient for several kits.

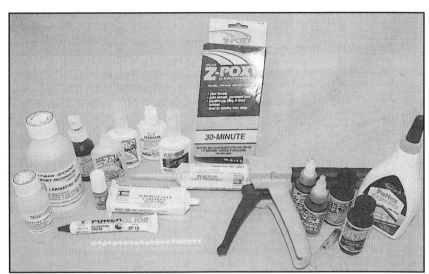

The advent of cyanoacrylate adhesives for modellers has speeded up construction processes immensely in the last few years, and these are excellent for most other parts of the building process and saving weight. However it is important to make tight, close-fitting joints, as otherwise the excess glue used to fill the gaps reduces the bond strength and eliminates any possible weight saving. There are several specially formulated cyano's

High quality adhesives are required for jets. A small selection of products that I personally recommend are: Westbury Laminating epoxy, ZAP cyano's & 30 minute epoxy, BVM Aeropoxy for structural bulkheads etc., DeLuxe Materials heatproof epoxy & Super-Crylic adhesive, & a 5 minute PVA such as Pattex express.

for bonding to carbon-fibre and some plastics, and also for gluing to polystyrene foam which is normally melted with these types. These can be very useful when building some of the latest jet kits that include a lot of moulded nylon accessories and brackets.

PVA and Aliphatic types are also commonly used for balsa to balsa joints, for example adding leading and trailing edges to balsa sheeted foam wings, and some of the rapid drying types are hard enough to allow further work after only a couple of hours. These glue types are also considerably less expensive than cyano's or epoxies. Two-part acrylic adhesives are also becoming popular, and are especially good for bonding dissimilar substances, for instance aluminium to fibreglass, and most of them have a rapid setting times.

Tools

The tools and equipment needed for building the latest moulded composite jet kits is little different from building a traditional balsa and plywood model. However a miniature high-speed rotary drill or grinder, such as the well known Dremel, is a very big advantage, and the use of these with suitable cutting discs is the easiest and fastest way to cut fibreglass mouldings.

Likewise normal sandpaper and wet-or-dry is not very effective on fibreglass mouldings, and I highly recommend that you invest in a few of the specialist tungsten-carbide grit sanding tools to ease the building process. These tools are extremely hard-wearing, lasting for many years, and will cut and sand wood, fibreglass, ceramics, plastics and non-ferrous metals. The best known, and certainly the favourite of a great many jet modellers, are the fabulous range from Permagrit, which include every conceivable shape and type of tool from 600 mm long sanding blocks, through special shapes for forming complex profiles, needle files and a superb range of rotary bits and cutting discs.

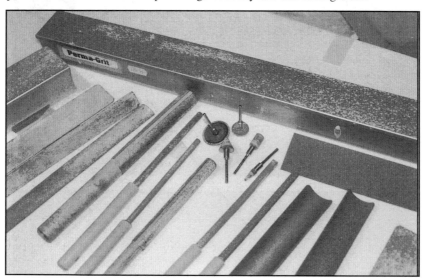

The absolutely brilliant range of sanding and cutting tools from Permagrit make jet construction easier, faster and more accurate, and are highly recommended. They are made of tungsten-carbide grits in various grades, which are permanently brazed to metal profiles, are almost everlasting, and can be cleaned with paint stripper if they get clogged.

Hinging

Again due to the higher flight speeds of jet models, the control surface hinging needs to be done very c Not only should the axis of all the hinges on each surface be exactly in line with each other to ensure smooth movement, but they must also be of a strong type and properly glued into place. Many of the complete kits include the correct type of hinges for jets, but some others leave this choice up to the builder. I can highly recommend the Robart 'Hinge-points' which are very strong, extremely easy to install, and if glued in place with 30 minute epoxy they will never pull out. There was a fine article published in the April/May 1995 issue of R/C Jet International magazine on this subject, which gives some excellent guidelines and tips, and this issue is still available from Traplet Publications.

Glassclothing

Almost all jet models have balsa sheeted or veneered wings and other flying surfaces, and covering these with the common heat-shrink plastic films is not usually sufficient, due to the high flight speeds and loads. The most common finishing process is glass-clothing, which involves covering all bare wood surfaces with a lightweight glasscloth (usually about 30 g/m2 or 1 oz/yd2) and laminating it in place with one or two extremely thin coats of slow setting (24 hr) epoxy. When cured it is sanded smooth with diminishing grades of wet-or-dry sandpaper to give a perfect finish for the application of paint and markings. Glassclothing adds a great deal of extra strength to these parts, giving a hard and durable skin all over, which also spreads the induced loads. Although glassclothing is not a difficult technique, it does require some practice to ensure that there is no unnecessary weight gain. Therefore I recommend that you get some experience of this on at least a couple of other models before using it on your first jet.

Airframe Maintenance

The maintenance of a jet model is quite different from a conventional model, the major reason being that many of the parts are deep inside the fuselage and the ducting fills most of the remaining space. Therefore it is often a little difficult to get at them - and sometimes it can a bit like self-taught amateur gynaecology! For this reason it is even more important to regularly inspect the airframe, as small cracks around bulkheads and other important parts can easily go unnoticed until it is too late, maybe even causing a potentially dangerous failure in flight.

The latest complete kits are manufactured using state-of-the-art techniques, and usually include carbon-fibre and kevlar in the epoxy mouldings to give added strength & reduced weight. These production processes are not cheap, but do result in a very rigid airframe capable of handling the power of gas turbines, and reduce the finishing and building time considerably. The 2180mm wingspan T-33 Shooting star seen right, from Jet Model Products, is typical of the 'high-end' kits now available, and hardly has any balsa wood in it ! Notice that even the wings & control surfaces are fully moulded.

Other leading companies, like Bob Violett Models, Philip Avonds Scale Jets and Trim Aircraft, manufacture complete kits using similar levels of technology.

It is usually either impossible, or a major task, to remove the exhaust ducting in most contemporary jet models, but there are normally few structural parts hidden by this anyway, excepting for the stabilisers and their control linkages. So, apart from ensuring that they are constructed and installed properly during construction, there is little you can do in this area. However it is normal for there to be some seepage of fuel and oil from ducted-fan systems, and this collects in the back of the fuselage, not only soaking into any unsealed wooden parts, but also eventually altering the Centre of Gravity. A simple solution to this is to drill a couple of minute holes in the bottom of the fuselage just in front of the exhaust nozzle to allow it to drain out as it accumulates.

Wing fixing points should be checked carefully before every flying session, especially on the types with plug-in or removable wings, as well as the bolts and retention plates or similar methods used to hold them on during flight. Probably the area that requires the most frequent examination is the undercarriage mountings (especially in the case of beginners!), but these are normally easy to access anyway.

All control surfaces should be given a good tug before every flying session, to ensure that the hinges are secure, and at some of the larger jet events the organisers will even come around and check items like this before allowing you to fly! Any loosening of the fan or motor mountings will be obvious by increased vibration when the motor is running. Fuel systems are one of the most common items to fail, either due to blockages or leaks, and the maintenance of these is dealt with in an earlier chapter.

Finally the security of all the servos, extension leads, receiver and nicad should be verified, and a regular range-check is a wise procedure to undertake, especially after any repairs or accidents.

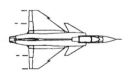

7 - R/C Installation

ets represent a far greater investment in time and money than the majority of conventional propeller powered models. With the higher flight speeds and 'G' forces, vibration levels and weights of most contemporary jet models it is imperative to use high quality R/C equipment, and install it properly, to ensure safe and reliable operation.

Quite a number of newcomers to the jet scene damage their models during early flights, not due to poor piloting skills - but because of inadequate care taken over the R/C installation. The best advice I can give is to strongly recommend that all new models are checked over by a really experienced modeller before they are flown, the first flights also being undertaken by a competent jet pilot.

Transmitters

It is not necessary to have the latest all-singing-and-dancing computerised transmitter to fly a jet model successfully. There are many hundreds, probably thousands, of jet pilots that use standard transmitters, and often 6 or 7 channels is sufficient. Of course if your model has extra functions, perhaps including flaps, wheelbrakes, in-flight mixture control and ordnance release, then you will need a more sophisticated transmitter, and most that have six channels or more are 'computerised' anyway. Even the basic computer sets, for example Futaba FF7 and JR X347 have model settings memories, and include several 'free mixers', allowing you to program one function to adjust or control another.

Computerised transmitters do make the setting-up of such things as servo throws, end points and exponential movements etc., a lot easier than having to do all this manually - especially as the servos, linkages and control horns are often more difficult to get to in a jet model. However they are not a substitute for poor mechanical linkage geometry, and the indiscriminate use of such facilities as throw limits and subtrims can reduce the efficiency of the servos to the point where they can't cope with the loads imposed on them by the control surfaces.

Whether you use a transmitter tray is a matter of personal preference. Nevertheless many of the top contest pilots do use them, especially in Europe, and having converted to this mode a couple of years ago I can say that it improved my flying considerably. A tray allows you to rest your wrists on the sides of it, supposedly giving slightly more accurate finger tip control of the sticks, and I certainly found that it smoothed out some of the minor wiggles in flight due to nervous fingers !

For the most complex models with many extra functions, one of the top computer sets (eg: Futaba 9ZAP, Multiplex 3030, Graupner mc20 or JR pcm10) is a considerable advantage. Not only do these generally have 10 channels, but the sophisticated mixing and trimming facilities allow you to alter almost any parameter, and can make it much easier to control an extremely

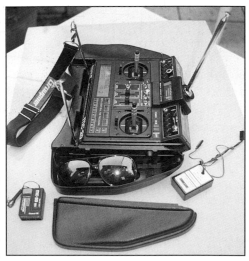

An expensive computerised transmitter isn't necessary to start with, like the Graupner mc20 above, but for the more complex and valuable models it's false economy and dangerous to use sub-standard equipment

A Turbomin T-100 installed in a Fiber Classics F-86 Sabre, which is complete with removable rear fuselage for motor access - exactly as on the full size aircraft! The 1:6 scale kit is completely moulded, including wings, & features working leading edge slates on the wings, speed brakes on the rear fuselage and scale undercarriage. At 1920mm span, 1850mm length and weighing around 11 kgs this is quite a large model. The quality of the surface detailing on the mouldings is exceptional; all rivets, panel lines and access hatches faithfully duplicated. It is also available for ducted-fan propulsion, but really needs a turbine for convincing performance.

Yellow Aircraft's 1/10 scale F4 Phantom is a complete kit, & includes fibreglass fuselage and foam wings & stabs. and good instructions. Dimensions are 1730mm length, 1100mm span, and it is suited to .82 motors and larger, &5" tractor fans. Flies quite nicely, & simple to build.

Superb twin-engined F4E Phantom, built from BVM kit, on final approach. Powered by twin Viojett ducted-fan units & BVM .91R motors this super-scale model is capable of over 300kph, but will happily fly on a single motor in the event of one stopping. A great deal of experience is needed before flying one of these powerful twins.

The venerable Byron Originals F-16 Fighting Falcon, although now a little outdated(mostly due to the pusher fan) flies well & has been the first successful jet model for thousands of newcomers since 1984. Slightly larger than other single engined F16's, at 1/8th scale, it is 1900mm long, with a 1200mm wingspan, and normally weighs in at about 6 kgs. Simple building, operation and flying still ensure some sales of this kit.

Beautifully finished F-104 Starfighter by Wim Reynders, who designed it jointly with Philip Avonds, who manufacturers the very complete kit. Powered by an OS91 & Ramtec fan this model is surprisingly easy to fly, although not a 'first' jet. Very light at less than 6kgs, but with a length of 2390 mm and a narrow span of just 990mm wingspan it is also quite large, but the fuselage separates easily into 2 pieces for transport. Based on the Avonds principle of 'simple is best' it follows the easy assembly of all of this range of high quality kits, which have made them so popular for newcomers to the jet hobby.

The sport-scale A4 Skyhawk from Jet Hangar Hobbies includes a fibreglass fuselage and built-up wings, has a length of 1440mm, a 1200mm span, & weighs only 4.3 kgs with a .45 motor, or approx. 5kgs with an .82 size. Designed around the Turbax 1 fan it still retains some outdated concepts, such as cheat inlets under the wing but is economically priced & flies quite well. Some of the other JHH kits have been successfully modified by experienced modelers for GWM FD3/67 gas turbine propulsion, giving good performance.

complex and difficult flying model. However I guess that most jet pilots don't use even 25 percent of the facilities available! As this book was compiled Graupner and Multiplex both released 12 channel transmitters, which will permit even more functions to be built into the most detailed scale models, for instance opening cockpit canopies and drogue parachute releases.

Receivers

The location and mounting of receivers in jets is little different than for conventional models, but extra care should be taken to isolate them from the high frequency vibration that is present in all i.c. powered ducted-fan models. The further away from the propulsion unit they are, the better it is, although the most common location in the nose of the model has the disadvantage that it is usually the first area to get damaged. In the past, due the high vibration levels caused by poorly balanced impellers, some of the Europeans went to extreme lengths to isolate the receivers - even suspending them in the fuselage by 4 elastic bands! However, with current fan units, surrounding the receiver in 12 - 18 mm of foam (soft rubber water-pipe insulation is excellent) is all that is necessary.

Nicads

Even with the best R/C gear in the world, and perfect installation and linkages, your model is only as safe as the batteries that power it. It is the most important part of the flight system, so don't economise on the quality or size of the nicad pack.

The capacity of the nicad pack is governed by the number and type of servos installed. Jets have more servos than sport models, usually one close to each control surface, and often more powerful types, therefore requiring long extension leads which also increases the electrical resistance. For these reasons larger capacity nicad packs should be used, at least 1200 mAh being common in jets with 7 to 9 servos, and 1700 or 1800 mAh packs in more complex models. The additional weight of the larger packs can often be useful in obtaining the correct Centre of Gravity, and it is better to use a bigger nicad in the nose than a useless lump of lead.

Regularly cycle your nicads - especially if they aren't used very frequently. The type with a visual capacity readout gives peace of mind, like this modular set from SMS, which has given excellent service most probably saved me a model. Don't fast-charge except when absolutely necessary.

Nicad batteries accept their maximum capacity when regularly exercised, and jets usually aren't flown as often as sport models, so it is advisable to use a nicad cycler regularly to maintain the performance of the pack. Nicads are less susceptible to vibration than servos and receivers, but should still be protected by wrapping them in foam, paying particular attention to the routing of the wire to the switch to ensure that it cannot be damaged if it passes through bulkheads or close to sharp items.

Antennas

Receiver antennas are normally installed inside the model, usually inside a snake outer tube that runs backwards from the receiver position. If possible, adjust the length of the tube so that the antenna protects from the end by a few millimetres where it can be fastened to the inside of the fuselage with a short piece of tape, or a plastic clip. This prevents it from creeping back up the tube, and reducing the effective range of the radio system.(see photo of Maverick engine bay in Chapter 5)

The antenna should be kept as far as possible from any substantial steel parts, large areas of carbon-fibre, and all other materials that are electrically conductive, as these can also reduce the range of the equipment. If is impossible to avoid these items completely, then try not to position the antenna so that it is parallel to them, and complete proper range checks with the Transmitter antenna retracted before flying the model. Generally there is no problem with models that are covered in aluminium or 'chrome' coated plastic films, but extra care should be taken if large areas of lithoplate or aluminium tape are used for model covering.

When electrical interference cannot be avoided with an internally mounted Rx antenna, then an external 'whip' aerial will have to be used. You should consult your R/C supplier for advice on this, but usually any of the types used for R/C boats or cars will suffice. It is only necessary to ensure that the total length of the remaining antenna wire connected to the receiver, and the length of the whip antenna total the same as the original length. Do not shorten receiver antennas under any circumstances.

If you've ever had trouble re-threading an antenna through a snake outer on the airfield you'll know how frustrating it can be! A simple solution is to keep a length of inner snake coiled up in the lid of your transmitter case, and simply fit the end of the antenna wire into the small hole in the end of snake and then push it through the outer tube. Works every time !

Switches
As with nicads, you should use the best quality switch available from your radio supplier, bearing in mind that with extra servos the current drawn through it will be greater than for a conventional sport model. Some of the main R/C manufacturers offer switches with gold-plated contacts and these give lower electrical resistance and better connection. Many also have integral charging sockets in the switch bodies, which is neater and saves a loose wire dangling around in the model. Just like other electronic equipment the switch is sensitive to vibration and should be kept as far as possible from the source. If you are really paranoid about switch failure, then you could mount it on rubber pads, but this shouldn't be needed.

Extension Leads
Due to the remote location of the servos in jets it is usual to have several long extension leads, some of these often being 1 metre in length in a typical .90 size scale jet. Some R/C manufacturers recommend, and will supply, ceramic chokes to prevent any possibility of interference, although I have not found them necessary with the latest R/C equipment - so far. Installation of these is normally simple, the receiver end of the extension lead usually being wrapped around the small circular chokes. Some types of chokes are fitted in line, using a normal plug and socket.

Long servo extension leads also have a greater electrical resistance, and the reputable radio manufacturers use larger diameter wire and gold-plated plug and socket connector pins to counteract these losses. Many of the top R/C manufacturers are now starting to use bigger diameter wire for all nicad connections and servo extension leads anyway, as the typical sizes of all models increases. The electrical resistance is also increased substantially by each plug and socket between the receiver and servo, so it is not wise to join several short extension leads together. It is better to either to buy a single extension lead of the correct length, or to extend the leads you already have, using the correct cable type and diameter, always ensuring that the soldered joints are perfect.

It is extremely rare for plugs and sockets connectors to come apart in normal use. Nevertheless it is a wise precaution to use some method of preventing this possibility on the major flight functions, particularly as it is usually difficult to check these joints frequently as they are deep inside the model. There are several types of lightweight plastic proprietary clips available that hold the socket and plug together firmly, or a short length of heatshrink tubing over each plug and socket does the same job. The heatshrink tube method has an advantage in that it helps to stop the ingress of fuel or water into the connectors, but it is not as easy to undo.

Servos
It is often necessary to use special servos in jets, either due to size and weight constraints, or because extra power is needed for a particularly large control surface, such as flaps or all-flying tailplanes. A very few jet kit manufacturers advise on the servo types suitable for each function of the model, but normally you need to use some common sense.

Probably a world 'first' was achieved when these 4 gas turbine models were flown together at Top Gun UK in 1994. (from left) John Palmer/John Franklin & Sagittario, Jacques Buchoux of JPX Propulseurs, Ian Stockdale & JFM Saab Viggen, Eric Rantet & Rafale from his own Aviation Design company, and David Gladwin and another sagittario. All four were powered by the propane fuelled JPX T-240 motors, and it was quite a feat to get them all off the grass strip at the same time!

The Saab Gripen, designed & kitted by Paul Gray's Performance Model Products company, is becoming more common in Europe. Close to 1/8th scale, it is 1705 mm long, and weighs around 5.8kg with an .80 - .100 motor & Ramtec or Dynamax fan. Typical fibreglass fuselage & foam wings, fin & canards, good plans & instructions. Reasonably priced, easy to build, & superb performance from grass or tarmac.

The BVM Ultra Viper has dominated the jet speed contests for several years. Often achieving in excess of 360kph (225 mph) in level flight, powered by a Viojett & BVM 91R, the model is 1700mm long and has a wingspan of 1300mm. A considerable amount of carbon fibre reinforcing and specially designed parts ensure that this model can handle the loads at these velocities, and more, with ease. A real rocket!

Englishman Alec Cornish-Trestrail (right), and pilot Paul Leighton prepare their latest own design 90" span Gloster Meteor. Powered by a pair of Dynamax fans and Rossi 65's, the model weighs about 20lbs and flies extremely well. It is completely scratch built, and includes many fibreglass mouldings and composite materials. No kit available.

Hans van Dongens immaculate replica of the famous F-15A 'Streak Eagle' aircraft, built from Philip Avonds Scale Jets kit, which placed 2nd overall at the 1995 Jet World Masters. High quality fibreglass mouldings and foam core wings & stabs. Many scale options also available. A single OS91 & Ramtec fan adequately power this 2160mm long scale jet, which has achieved so many competition success. The reason - It's so easy to fly !

The author's F-80 Shooting Star, built from the BVM kit, and powered by an OS91 & Viojett fan. 1830 mm span and 7.7 kgs weight, with all the scale options, including flaps, gear doors, drop tanks & wheel brakes.

(photo P. Allsop)

You can save precious space, weight and money by using low power mini-servos for less important, such as in-flight mixture controls and retract valve operation, but the type with only three wipers on the potentiometer are more susceptible to vibration failure. Coreless servos are excellent for the main flight controls, offering increased speed, power and resolution with slightly less weight in an equivalent sized servo case. The latest ranges of 'Super-servos', which use high frequency control pulses, are also highly recommended for main flight controls (elevator, rudder, ailerons) as they give the best response to stick movements, and full power even at small deflections from their neutral positions.

Several manufacturers make servos with special mounting lugs which allow the servo to be mounted flat (on it's side), especially useful in thin wings etc., a particular favourite being the excellent JR/Graupner 3321 which is commonly used for aileron control.

Use a high quality servo for throttle control, although it doesn't need to be very powerful, as it is subjected to direct vibration transmitted through the throttle linkage from the carburettor.

Servo Mounting

Servos should always be mounted using the supplied rubber grommets and ferrules to provide isolation against vibration, as even with the latest surface-mount-technology they are still adversely affected by it. It amazes me how many experienced modellers incorrectly insert the ferrules from the top of the rubber grommet, totally neutralising the isolation effect. The ferrules should be inserted from the bottom, and servo screws tightened just enough to give a firm but slightly flexible mounting, and the servo case should not touch the mounting plate or airframe at all.

In many models some servos are mounted in a fairly traditional servo tray, often made from 'light-ply', and in this case you should always glue extra plywood 'doublers' on the underside of it (with the grain at right angles to the tray) to provide sufficient depth for the screws to hold into properly. Some of the bigger R/C manufacturers, and several jet companies, make moulded brackets for side-mounting individual servos to the insides of fuselages, or to permit them to lay flat in wingboxes, and these are very useful. Zone 5 and BVM make neat examples of both types which are adjustable to suit most servo sizes.

It is common for aileron, and some times flap, servos to be installed in balsa or plywood lined boxes in the wing, where they must be laid flat. As already mentioned there are several servos available with lugs to allow side mounting, but if you want to use a standard servo type it is difficult to get at the securing screws when the servo is mounted on blocks in the base of the box. A better solution is to use a stronger material (2.5 mm plywood or fibreglass sheet) for the cover to this box, and secure the servo to it instead. Multiplex, Robbe, Futaba, Graupner and JR, amongst others, also make moulded plastic boxes for installation in wings which are designed to accept various servo sizes, and some of these have the servos mounted to the covers. The mounting of servos using double-sided tape is not sufficient in a jet, and sticking them to the fuselage with silicone adhesive is not recommended as the acetic acid could attack the electronic conductors inside.

Servo-Slows

The ability to slow down the operation speed of one or more servos in a model can be advantageous, and many of the current computerised transmitter systems have this facility built-in, normally with the end-to-end transition times programmable from about 1 - 30 seconds. This can be very useful for retarding the operation of functions like retractable undercarriages, gear doors, speed brakes or opening cockpit canopies, and it is also commonly used for slowing down the deployment of flaps or speedbrakes, thereby reducing any sudden trim change and generally smoothing the transition between flight modes.

This facility can also be used on the throttle channel in ducted-fan models, and by setting the servo speed to about 2 seconds it prevents the motor quitting in the case of a 'panic' full throttle command - for instance during an emergency 'go-around' after an aborted landing attempt. After a few flights you won't notice the short delay in throttle response, and it also smoothes your flying and protects the motor from unnecessary stresses.

If your transmitter doesn't have this ability, or only allows it to be used on a single channel, then there are a multitude of small electronic add-on modules that accomplish the same effect, which are inserted between the receiver channel output and the servo to be controlled. The speed is normally adjusted using a small potentiometer on the servo-slow module itself, and then sealed in position with a drop of wax. Beware that some of the older and less expensive units move the servo in small steps, and have to complete their whole cycle before the servo direction can be reversed, and this type should definitely be avoided. The current types that incorporate microprocessor control to operate the servo in a smooth movement, even when set at 30 seconds between end points, are much more reliable, and reverse direction instantly. Nevertheless I still don't recommend the use of add-on servo-slows on any major flight functions.

Servo Reversing Modules

When two servos are connected by a 'Y-lead' and plugged into a single receiver channel, you can't reverse the direction of one of them from the transmitter. Yet this is often required to give absolutely identical linkage geometry, for example to control a pair of flaps. In this case the best option is to purchase a reverse rotation servo, or to have the motor and potentiometer connections in a servo reversed by an authorised dealer. However this isn't always possible with the latest types as the motors are soldered directly to the SMT circuit board, and the motor connections are usually offset from the centreline, preventing it from fitting inside the case if it is rotated through 180°.

The other solution is to use an add-on electronic servo reversing module, and several companies make these. They are generally small, lightweight and quite inexpensive, some of the latest types being built into a standard extension lead, and only the size normal plug and socket connector. Occasionally they also include a tiny potentiometer, which allows the centre point of the servo to be adjusted, a very useful feature, this being sealed in place after use with a small blob of wax. The types I have used from the reputable manufacturers have all proved reliable so far, yet the same recommendations apply as with add-on servo-slows, don't use them on any of the major flight functions.

Wire Management

Because of the increased number of servos, as well as all the air tubing for the retracts and other functions, the inside of a jet fuselage can begin to look like spaghetti! The routing of all of these connections is important, not only to protect them from chafing and damage, but also to simplify maintenance. All the adjacent extension leads should be bundled together, with the pneumatic tubing if possible, and held together with miniature cable-ties or short lengths of elastic band glued to the nearby structure. If these bundled services are close to the location of the starter probe, they should be further protected using a length of plastic spiral cable wrap (available from electronics stores), or better still the plastic expandable mesh tubing used for wiring looms.

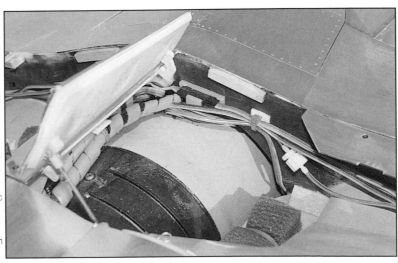

It is worthwhile protecting servo extension leads & pneumatic lines with spiral wrap or plastic conduit where there is any chance of chafing or damage. This is especially inportant in the retracts area, near fan units or turbines, and near starter probe access. Bundle wires together and use mini cable-ties where possible. Notice the plastic safetyclip on the servo lead plug/socket connections & quick-disconnect on pneumatic brake tube.

Wolfgang & Helmut Klühr with one of their own-design Sukhoi Su27;'s, after winning the German Impeller Masters for the third consecutive time. This massive model, available as a semi-kit from Modellbau Klühr, is just under 2500mm long, and weighs 10 kg. Propulsion is by a pair of Ramtec fans, OS91 motors and BVM tuned pipes, with impeller fuel pressurisation, which gives extraordinary performance in this jet. A similar sized Mig 29 Fulcrum is also manufactured.

The latest high performance sport jet released by BVM is the BANDIT, designed specifically for JPX turbine propulsion, but also available for the Viojett fan. Its slightly larger size, compared to other current sport jets, makes it easier to see in the air, & the lower wing loading allows very slow and stable landings. The model is 1860mm long, has a span of 1640mm and weighs between 7.3 & 8.5kgs, depending on motor. Easy motor and equipment access due to large engine and cockpit hatches, make operation easy, and the performance is also more than adequate with at around 320kph. The extremely comprehensive kit is fully composite moulded, including the wings, and the modular construction allows it to be completely disassembled for transport. As with all the BVM range, the product quality and instructions are unrivalled.

The recently re-vamped Century Jet Models F4 Phantom is 2450mm long, and suited to Dynamax or Ramtec fan units and .90 - 100 motors. Weight is around 14.5 kgs, and although he model is not exact scale it seems to be a stable performer. It is sold as a basic kit, with various extra options available, including a set of scale retractable undercarriage, wheels and brakes.

The totally redesigned Starfire IIc, from Jet Model Products, replaces the original Starfire kit that was so popular around the world. The wings, fuselage & stabilisers are completely composite moulded to a very high quality, and most major parts are factory asembled to speed building. The Starfire is designed for JMP's own Dynamax fan & a .91 motor, wieghs 6.5 kgs, has a length of 1650mm & span of 1400mm. Kit instructions and product quality are very good.

This F20 Tigershark is one of a small range of sport-scale basic kits from Thorjet, in addition to their plan packs. Designed around their .90 size Thorjet fan unit, it is a one-piece model of 1020mm span & 1680mm length, and weighs approx. 5.5 kgs. Fibreglass fuselage & foam wings. A proven flyer, and quite economically priced.

Always use a rubber grommet, or similar protection, where wiring passes through holes in hard substrates or adjacent to fan units, this also applying to fuel and pressure lines as well. It is a great help to number all the extension lead plugs close to the receiver; the simplest method being to write the channel numbers on a small patch of white typing correction fluid on each plug. A superlative product that has recently become available from RPM is small heatshrink sleeves pre-printed with numbers for achieving this same result.

Tidy equipment installations and connections inside jets aren't a pre-requisite, but they definitely make operation and maintenance easier, helping to give a safer and more dependable model.

Gyro s

Gyros offer auto-stabilisation on the axis (pitch, roll or yaw) that is operated by the control surface or function to which the gyro is connected. The rotation of the model around the axis stabilised by the gyro generates a signal which is fed to the relevant servo to counteract the sensed movement.

By adjusting the sensitivity ('gain') of the gyro the amount of stabilisation in relation to stick movement can be set, thereby varying the authority that the pilot has on the controlled function. For example, with the gyro on the aileron channel and the gain set to maximum, any roll inputs on the transmitter stick would be almost totally resisted by the corrective signal of the gyro, severely limiting the pilots control authority. Therefore the gain setting is important, but can be set automatically using a transmitter mixer so that the stick can directly control the gyro control gain. This is arranged so that if there is movement of the stick demanding, say, a roll, then the gyro gain is reduced so that the required roll is not opposed.

Although not normally necessary for today's jet models, gyros can be useful on the nosewheel steering channel of models with short-coupled or narrow track undercarriages to keep it tracking straight during take-off, especially in crosswinds. They are also occasionally used on rudder functions, particularly on swept-wing models such as the F86 which have a tendency to fishtail. Dutch-Rolling, a combination of yaw-roll coupling exhibited by some models, can also be completely eliminated by the use of a gyro on the rudder function.

If properly configured a gyro can tame a tricky model and make much it much more stable and enjoyable to fly, but if incorrectly set up it can also make it more difficult. For more detailed information on gyros I recommend that you read the article on them that was published in the June/July 1997 (issue 24) of RC Jet International magazine.

Electronic Mixing

The electronic mixing facilities in the latest generation of computerised transmitters makes the setting-up of the control systems in jet models much easier than it used to be. Thoughtful use of these mixers allows almost endless possibilities, either for decreasing the pilots workload during flight, or increasing the number of functions that can be controlled with a limited number of receiver channels.

The most commonly used is probably Flap > Elevator mixing, where deployment of the flaps automatically makes a small adjustment to the elevator trim to counteract the pitch change that normally occurs. On most low-wing jets the deflection of flaps gives a slight nose-up attitude, and the amount of mixing required is usually equivalent to about 3 or 4 clicks of 'down' elevator trim.

Another popular mix is Retracts > nosewheel steering, where the nosewheel steering is switched off when the gear is up. This particularly beneficial if using the common type of pneumatic retract that is steered with a single pushrod from the servo to a tiller arm on the leg (eg: Spring-Air #205 & #107), as the movement of the wheel in the retracted position can jam the wheel in the fuselage or stall the servo. A variation on this mix is when separate servos are used for rudder and nosewheel steering, on different channels but controlled by the same transmitter stick. In this instance 3-way mixing is necessary using a 'dummy' mix channel, so that the rudder is still active when the gear is retracted, but the nosewheel servo is inactive.

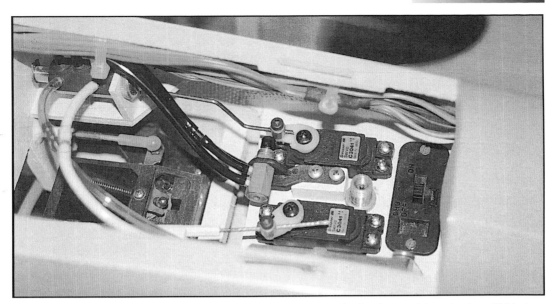

Notice that the servo that operates the pneumatic retract valve is also used to actuate a BVM air microswitch that controls the wheelbrakes, by mixing it with a dummy channel to allow it to go over-centre when the undercarriage is extended. Neat wire & tube management in this Aggressor,

Other favourite examples are the slight upward deflection of both ailerons during landing to reduce any tip-stalling tendencies (usually mixed with flaps 'down'), and 'over-centre' deflection of servo output arms to actuate secondary functions from a single servo. This can be used to operate a pneumatic micro-switch for wheelbrakes from the same servo that operates the retracts.

Linkages

It makes no difference how accurate the resolution of your radio system, or how good the quality of the servos installed, if the linkages are badly made or have unnecessary play in them. Bearing in mind the higher loads on the main flight controls of most jets there are several guidelines that should be born in mind.

• Make all the linkages as short as possible to increase the rigidity of them and counteract the possibility of the pushrods bending under load.

• Make the linkages as straight and direct as possible. This is especially important when using long 'snakes' for control of remote surfaces (eg: elevators & rudders) where the servos are often located some distance away. If the outer tube of the snake can be installed exactly, or very nearly, straight then you can increase the stiffness of the linkage by replacing the braided metal cable with a similar diameter piano wire.

• Be extra careful when installing linkages to all-flying tailplanes. The reputable jet kit manufacturers provide special pushrods or linkages for these, and have tested them properly before the kit is released - so don't modify them at all.

• Throttle linkages are especially subjected to high frequency vibration. Keep them lightweight, and mount the servo as far away from the motor as possible to reduce the vibration transferred to the servo. The use of a ball link on the carburettor throttle arm is very common, making disconnection simple when the fan unit is removed, and the Sullivan "ball-connector with locking sleeve" (# 560) is very suitable for this.

• Control horns must be firmly fixed into place. Screwing or gluing them onto the surface of balsa control surfaces is not good enough. Reinforce the area on both sides with small plywood patches let into

The 'Spectre' sport-jet from Trim Aircraft (Ramtec manufacturer) is very popular due to low cost, simple construction & easy flying style. It is also quick, regularly achieving 320 kph in level flight. Kit consist of good quality moulded fuselage & area-ruled ducts, foam wings & stabs, pre-cut parts & adequate instructions for modellers with some experience. Designed for Ramtec fan & motors of .82+. Extremely stable at slow speed, making landings simple & good take-offs from grass strips. Length 1775mm, span 1270mm, weight 5.3 kgs.

Joe Grice's immaculate F4 Phantom. At 2035mm long & 1450mm span, this large model is extremely fast powered by twin Viojetts and .91 motors. Full scale landing gear set is a work of art, & operates in scale manner. Built from BVM kit, which includes fully composite moulded fuselage, wings and stabilisers, and all parts needed to complete.

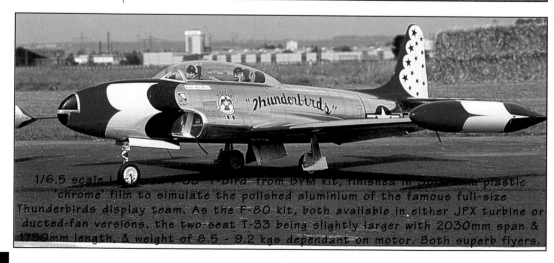

1/6.5 scale Lockheed T-33 'T-Bird' from BVM kit, finished in Sig plastic 'chrome' film to simulate the polished aluminium of the famous full-size Thunderbirds display team. As the F-80 kit, both available in either JPX turbine or ducted-fan versions, the two-seat T-33 being slightly larger with 2030mm span & 1750mm length, & weight of 8.5 - 9.2 kgs dependant on motor. Both superb flyers.

The large T-33 Shooting Star kit from JMP has fantastic performance when combined with one of the 10 kg thrust range turbines, such as the AMT Pegasus which is the most commonly used in this model. 2180mm wingspan, 1950mm long, weight 9 - 11.5 kgs dependant on motor. Probably the most highly prefabricated scale kit available, very accurate scale shape, & good instructions. Both D/F and turbine versions available.

The Aviation Design Mirage 2000 is large at 2110mm length & 1340mm span, yet lightweight at 10 kgs with the recommended AMT Pegasus turbine. Like all Aviation Design kits, construction is simple & fast, this kit having moulded fuselage, wings and fin. Scale undercarriage option. Delta planform makes it easy to fly with a wide speed range. Aviation Design were the 1st company to make kits for gas turbines, and currently the only one making a twin turbine model - the big Rafale.

Austrian pilot, Peter Cmyral, with his massive own-design RFB600 Fantrainer, an accurate replica of one of the few full-size true ducted-fan aircraft. Model features scratch-built scale undercarriage, landing lights, split speed brakes on shroud & even working trim tabs - a wonderfully stable performer & a real work of art. 2050mm wingspan and 7kg weight are reliably hauled around the sky by his own-design 5 bladed pusher impeller, moulded from carbonfibre, turned by an OS108 motor - one of the very rare instances when a sport motor has been successfully used in a jet model.

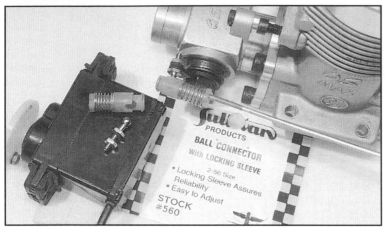

The Sullivan "Ball-connector with locking sleeve" (part # 560) is excellent for throttle connections, and other similar linkages, being lightweight, and durable,yet easy to remove.

the surface, sand flush with the surrounding balsa, and glasscloth over them during the finishing process to ensure a firm base that won't be squashed by the bolts or screws.

• Closed-loop linkages are excellent for giving accurate control with no possibility of 'blow-back', and are commonly used for elevator and rudders when the servos are remotely located.

• Most of the common clevises are a very tight fit in holes in standard servo output arms, causing unnecessary friction, and sometimes binding at large deflections. Enlarge the holes in the servo arms with a correctly sized micro-drill held in a pin vice to ensure a good fit on the clevis pins, but without any slop.

• Always use a safety retainer clip on all the clevises and quick-links used for major flight functions, such as the type included with Sullivan snakes. A short length of fuel tube slipped over the jaws of the clevis will also do almost as good a job.

• Don't use soft plastic ball-links, clevises or quick-links on any important functions.

• Don't use brass threaded extenders for soldering onto pushrods and cables, as they will fracture under vibration. Always use the hardened steel types, available from many companies (eg: JMP and BVM).

• If you have an in-flight mixture control, then adjust the manual needle valve (or servo end points) so that it is impossible to make the motor too lean using the rotary knob or slider on the transmitter. It's often difficult to gauge how rich the motor is running when the model is in flight, especially when there are others in the air as well, and this makes it impossible to damage the motor inadvertently.

• When soldering threaded extenders or quick-link connectors onto piano wire, pushrods or braided metal cables be sure that the joint is really strong. Abrade both surfaces first with wet-and-dry or a metal file, clean with a degreasing agent (Acetone, K&B thinners or similar), and make the joint as quickly as possible with a soldering iron of adequate wattage. I highly recommend the use of a low-temperature silver solder for these connections (eg: Stay-Brite), rather than the soft resin-cored electrical type, as it is much stronger. If you want to be really sure about the connection then, after the solder has cooled completely, you can lightly crimp the metal fitting onto the wire as well.

• During construction, and once each year thereafter, remove all unplated metal pushrods from their snake outers or guide tubes, clean lightly with 3M scuffpad or equivalent, and lubricate lightly with after-run oil. This will prevent rust and corrosion that could increase friction in the controls, and this is especially important in humid countries. All metal actuating linkages, hinges, torque rods etc., should also be treated the same way, although they are usually more difficult to get at.

8 - Undercarriages

There are 4 choices for jet undercarriages; no gear (hand-launch), fixed gear, 'dolly' cradles, or retractable systems. However the majority of contemporary jets use retractable gear of some description, & these often seem to cause problems - not only to beginners & inexperienced jet modellers !

HAND-LAUNCH

Almost exclusively used for electric jets and very small ducted-fan models, which are hand-launched and landed on their bellies on grass surfaces. Sometimes specially formed hand-grips or skids are located on the bottom of the fuselage, and usually they are lightly reinforced with epoxy & glasscloth to protect them from damage during landings.

FIXED GEAR

Fixed undercarriage gear on a jet model is exactly the same as for a conventional propeller powered model, normally consisting of wire legs that are bent to shape, fixed to the airframe using slotted bearers or similar, with the wheels held onto the axles by washers soldered either sides of the hubs. Fixed gear increases the drag by a large amount, as well as detracting from the aesthetics of the model in flight, and therefore it is not commonly seen on jets.

DOLLY CRADLES

Dolly systems are still used occasionally, mostly for the smaller sized jets when weight saving is of great importance and space inside the airframe is at a premium, and on prototype or experimental models where the extra time and effort needed to install retracting gear is not justified. They usually consist of a triangular wire frame (cradle), made from piano wire soldered together, with the wheels attached to three axles in a conventional tricycle ('trike') layout. The cradle has 3 or more upright posts in strategic positions to prevent the model from leaving the cradle horizontally, only allowing it to rise up off the dolly when sufficient airspeed has been attained for take-off. Uprights are normally located in front of the wing leading edges, with a third slotting into a tube in the nose of the model. Of course the cradle can only be used for take-off, and the model must then make a belly-landing - preferably on a grass or other soft surface.

View of a dolly undercarriage cradle system on an F-104 Starfighter. The model is of all built-up balsa/ply construction from the Thorjet plan-pack and flies quite nicely on a Thorjet and OPS45 motor. It is 1825mm long, with a 915mm span, and weighs only 3.8 kgs when ready to fly with dolly gear. The use of flaps makes this model easier to fly, but it's not suitable for a complete novice, and requires a considerable amount of building.

(below) A JPX T260P turbine powered Starjet, from the Aviation Design kit, seen in the pit area with all equipment necessary for starting; Propane tank, compressed air cylinder & fire-extinguisher - a necessary safety precaution. The Starjet is one of the most popular turbine sport models available, and has incredible performance with over 380kph maximum speeds being commonly achieved. A wingspan of 1620mm, length of 1770mm and weight ready-to-fly of about 7 kg - with over 6kg of static thrust make it a hot performer.

(above)

My German friend, and technical adviser, Ralf Ploenes, with his BVM Aggressor II - seen here just after winning the Top Gun UK high speed contest in 1995. Aerosave fuel, with Viojett and BVM.91R propulsion.

The renowned BVM Maverick is a good choice of model for the newcomer to jets with some experience of fast models. Extremely comprehensive kit, with the best instructions of any company. Wide speed range with very stable and slow landings with flaps. Span 1525mm, length 170mm, weight apprx.6 kgs. Designed for a Viojett fan unit, and either a BVM, KBY or OS91 motor.

Japanese jet pilot, Takashi Komuro, with his immaculate T-33 Shooting Star, built from the fully moulded Jet Model Products kit. All up weight of the model is just 12 kgs, and with an AMT Pegasus Mk.3 gas turbine motor installed the performance is simply awesome.

Stunning scale colour scheme on this F-86 Sabre, with performance to match and easy flying characteristics, although not suited to a raw novice. Wingspan and length 1475 mm, and all up weight just 6kgs (BVM kit).

A few modellers have developed the cradle system to higher levels, incorporating steerable nosewheels using a servo mounted on the cradle framework and connected to the wiring harness in the model by a plug and socket - which disconnects itself when the model rises off the dolly at take-off. Dolly Cradles can be cleverly disguised with the addition of lithoplate gear doors etc, and with a little effort it can be made difficult to notice the cradle from a few metres.

RETRACTABLE GEAR

Retractable undercarriages can be split into three separate types, categorised by the method by which they are operated; Pneumatic, Mechanical and Electrical.

Pneumatic Retracts

There is no doubt that pneumatic (air-powered) retracts are by far the most predominant type, and they have many advantages over mechanical and electrical types for the majority of contemporary jets. Usually they are powerful and lightweight, reliable, simple to install, and obtainable in a huge variety of types, configurations and sizes to suit most types of jet models. In addition there is no possibility of stalled servos draining your flight nicad in the case of a jammed undercarriage, few linkage geometry problems, and the same air system can be often be utilised for other functions in the model, such as gear doors and wheel brakes etc. All commercial types are similar in that they consist of an air storage tank, filler valve, operating valve, air tubing and connectors, and the retract units themselves, many also including wire legs, and usually adequate instructions. The air valves used to control them can be installed in any convenient location, as can the air storage tanks, and only require a mini or micro servo for operation, saving weight and space. The commonly used 'standard' types mentioned below are relatively inexpensive, but costs increase proportionately for the special units designed expressly to suit some of the scale jet kits.

There are two operating systems for pneumatic retracts, the type that uses twin air lines - one to extend the gear and the other to retract it, and the single-tube type that only requires air pressure to retract the wheels, which are spring-loaded for extension. In the latter type if air pressure is lost for any reason the undercarriage automatically extends, allowing a safe landing. All require an air storage tank to be pressurised for operation, normally to about 6.5 bar (100 psi), either using a hand-pump of the type available from many of the manufacturers (often with integral pressure gauges), or with a 12 volt mini-compressor. On a simple trike gear system where the storage tank is only powering the retract units this pressure will normally allow about 6 or 7 complete cycles of the undercarriage, with respectively less operations if complex gear door systems are also controlled.

Without any doubt Spring Air retracts are the most commonly used in jets, giving almost unrivalled reliability, combined with wide availability & economy. Shown here are the 1/5th scale units and the new 500 series, which retract in the opposite direction to the air ram, and accept either standard 3/8" oleos (eg: Robostruts) or 3/16" wire legs.

Currently the most commonly used units in jets are 'Spring-Airs', which use a single tube air system, and a return spring that automatically extends the gear if air pressure is lost. They are easily identifiable by the gold coloured anodising on the T6 aluminium alloy frames, are very simple to connect and install, lightweight, durable and extremely reliable. Several types and sizes are available; the Slimline, 100, 200 & 300 series are suited to models weighing up to about 7 kg, and these retract the gear to the same side as the air ram. Three different mounting configurations of steerable nosegear unit are made; #106 belly mount, #107 bulkhead mount and #205 top mount, steering being accomplished by a pair of cables to a bellcrank on the #106, and by a single wire linkage onto a tiller arm on the latter two. The latest 500 series, which have 50% thicker aluminium frames and bigger diameter air cylinders, are designed for models up to 8.5 kg (19 lbs), and retract the leg or oleo to the opposite side from the air ram, making installations easier in thin wings and restricted spaces. These can either be fitted with 3/16" wire legs, or with contemporary oleo legs (eg: Robostruts) directly into the wider pivot blocks. The 500 units also have a 2nd air nipple on the cylinders, giving the option of using a twin air-line system to enable controlled extension speed & to facilitate operations with sequencing gear-door systems.

There is also a much larger 1/5th scale set for airframe weights of up to about 15 kg. Main units are available in either 85° or 90° retraction angles, and the larger units are also obtainable with a 74° retraction angle. Several different sizes of air tank are available, and the operating valve is in the style of a toggle switch, only requiring a simple wire linkage to a mini servo. Due to the spring loaded air ram system it is difficult to slow down the extension of the smaller Spring-Airs (slimline, 100, 200 & 300 series), which come down instantaneously, although it can be done either by using several in-line restrictors, or a specially designed adjustable valve like the fine Ultra Precision UP5 unit.

Also quite popular, particularly in the USA, are the wide range of retract units from Rhom-Air, and although these haven't been generally available in Europe for some years they were reintroduced in 1997. These are similar in configuration and sizes available to the Spring-Air range, differing mainly in that they use a twin air line system for operation on all units. Construction is of aluminium, with T6 pivot blocks, stainless steel shafts and trunions, and bronze bushes on the larger sizes. They are reliable, lightweight and easy to install and are also available in a wide variety of styles, some with varying retraction angles. The current 3000 series units are designed for models up to about 6 kg in weight, but are often used in slightly heavier models, and the recently released 500 & 750 series units are suited to larger airframes of 14 kg and 20 kg respectively. Most of the Rhom units retract the leg or oleo to the same side as the air ram, but there is also an FAI range with reversed air rams that push the leg away from the rams, useful for installing in thin wings etc. Twist-and-turn 500 & 750 series units for rotating main and nosegear systems are also a stock item, as are several different retraction angles and custom units for special applications. The operating valve is of the 4-way 'shuttle' type, which can also be used to control simple gear door mechanisms if connected to additional air rams. Several sizes of air tanks are obtainable, and each set comes with two colours of connection tubing to differentiate between 'up' and 'down' lines, as well as all connectors, valves, and full instructions.

Recently the famous Rhom Air retract range has been completely updated, the old standard size being replaced with the new 3000 series, which are of high quality & feature good up and down locks. Each set comes complete with all parts required for the complete system, including 3/16" wire legs, air tank, filler, tubing and shuttle valve. Suited to models up to 7 kg.

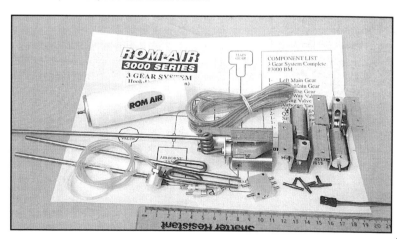

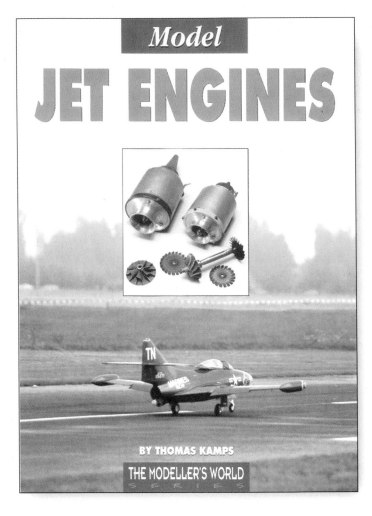

Jet Model Products manufacture two sizes of pneumatic retracts specifically designed for jets, the Mk.10 and the Mk.20, suited to airframe weights of about 6.5 kg and 11 kg respectively. The air-rams are fitted with U-cup seals, instead of the more commonly used 'O' rings, and they are well-known for being strong and durable. The units follow similar manufacturing methods, configuration and operational reliability as the types above, are lightweight, and use twin air-lines for operation. Retraction angle is infinitely variable and all sets come complete with everything necessary for installation.

The well known Mk.10 pneumatic retracts, from Jet Model Products, are suited to jets up to 6.5kg. They have been available for several years and have proved very durable. Featuring fully adjustable retraction angles and positive mechanical 'down locks' they come as a complete set with instructions, tank, valves, legs and tubing. A Mk.20 set is also produced for jets up to about 11 kgs. Also shown are the new lightweight JMP sport jet wheels.

Robart released a new range of pneumatic retracts in 1997 that look suitable for the popular sized jet models in the 7 - 9 kg range, these also being based around very strong aluminium alloy frames of a dark grey colour. All use a twin air-line system and are operated by either of Robarts excellent 4-way shuttle valves, either the standard blue unit #RB167, or the new red #RB167A valve which also features an integral adjustable speed control facility. Although I have only recently had a chance to examine these retracts, they seem to be of outstanding quality, and Robart's reputation for excellent products leads me to assume that these will be very durable, and will therefore become popular with jet modellers.

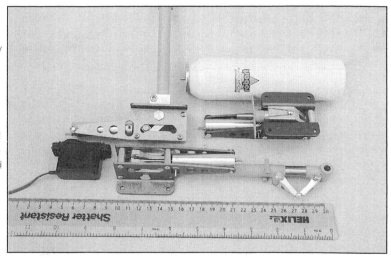

The new Robart 630/640 series 'Jet' retracts are very strongly made, and should be suited to model weights of up to about 10 kgs. They come ready machined to accept 7/16" diameter Robostruts (also shown) and will be perfectly matched to many of the new larger sized ducted-fan and gas-turbine powered jets. A full air support package is also available as a separate item. Standard servo shown for size comparison only.

One tip to remember about some of the pneumatic retracts described above (notably Spring Airs) is that when the 'extend' command is given, each leg goes up by a very small amount before travelling to the down position, due to the locking geometry of the units, so allow a few millimetres clearance above the wheels in the retracted position for this to occur.

Several other companies make high-quality retracts suitable for jets, but the above 'standard' types are the most numerous. One in particular that deserves a mention is Hawe of Germany, who manufacture a wide range of twin air-line retracts in various sizes and styles, as well as a custom building service, and these are frequently seen on the European jet scene. Bob Violett Models also manufacture a standard pneumatic retract unit system, which is specifically designed for their range of kits, but occasionally used in others up to about 9.5 kg weight. The main frames are manufactured from carbon-fibre reinforced nylon with metal moving parts, can accept either wire legs or oleo struts, and are extremely durable. Various retraction angles, as well as rotating nosegear units, and individual spare parts are available. Until the mid-90's these BVM retracts were mechanically operated, but they are now powered by 14mm diameter individual air rams which give excellent power and reliability - totally overcoming the old tendency of noselegs to collapse during landing.

Bob Violett Models manufacture their own unique retracts, especially designed for their kits. The frames are injection moulded from carbon-fibre reinforced nylon, with metal bushes and operating parts. Very lightweight & reliable they will accept either 3/16" wire legs, 3/8" Robostruts, or BVM's own Durostruts (shown). Also seen are nosegear 'Flexarms' (btm) & main gear 'Flexplates' (right) which are sacrificial in case of hard landings, & easily replaceable to get you back in the air rapidly. The wheel is also from their wide range of sport & scale types, which are all very well manufactured, durable, and have optional brakes.

By fitting the retracts recommended above, or the specialist units below, reliable undercarriage operation is almost guaranteed - assuming proper installation and maintenance. Of the multitude of other small and medium sized retract units available, only a few are of an acceptable standard, generally the plastic framed types not being strong enough for contemporary jets, and the majority of the units with cast aluminium bodies (especially those of Italian origin) are usually of low quality and poorly engineered.

Specialist units

Apart from the standard systems described above several of the established jet manufacturers make specific undercarriage systems for their own scale jets, mostly for the larger models and those with special undercarriage configurations, like the F-16 Falcon. Some of these can be adapted to fit other marques, and almost all are pneumatically operated, sometimes with the air rams in the correct locations to represent the hydraulic cylinders used on the full size aircraft. The list below, although by no means complete, represents a sample of some of the complete systems currently available, and should give an idea of the levels of scale realism and complexity that are possible. However the range of scale jets is constantly increasing, and most established manufacturers offer complete undercarriage systems to suit their new scale kits shortly after they are released - especially if they have unusual geometry.

Yellow Aircraft have complete scale gear and wheel sets for their 1:9 scale F-14 and 1:7 scale F/A-18 models (both twin-engined), as well as their 1:9 scale F-16, and also a set of semi-scale undercarriage and wheels for the single-engined 1:10 scale Hornet.

The pneumatically operated main gear for the 1:10 scale F-16 from Yellow Aircraft. A twist & turn nosegear retract is also available, & both come complete with wheels.

Century Jet Models have a complete scale gear set, including wheels and brakes, for their own 1:7.6 scale twin-engined F-4 Phantom.

Jet Hangar Hobbies, who manufacture the 1:9 scale twin-engined Philip Avonds designed F-15 under licence in the USA, have a complete set of scale gear for this kit, which includes the retracts, scale oleo legs, wheels, tyres & brakes.

Fiber Classics make a complete scale undercarriage set for their 1:6 scale F-86 Sabre, consisting of a twist-and-turn nose retract unit, main retract units, oleo legs, wheels, tyres and brakes.

Jim Fox Models offers a complete set of undercarriage for the 1:10 scale Saab Viggen, including retract units, oleos, sprung trunions and scale wheels, which may be operated either mechanically or by using air rams (eg: Robart #RB165).

Bob Violett Models stock a very accurate scale undercarriage system for their 1:8.8 scale twin-engined F-4 Phantom (seen left) which includes retract units, oleos, drag links, air rams, wheels, tyres and brakes. They also have a complete scale gear set for their 1:9 scale F-16, and a twist-and-turn nosegear retract unit for their Sabre.

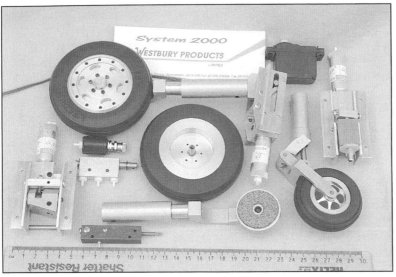

Westbury Products have a complete set of scale undercarriage (shown left) for their very accurate 1:7 scale gas turbine powered Hawker Hunter, which includes pneumatic retracts, oleos, scale wheels & tyres, operating and fill valves, proportional brake operating valve, and pneumatic disc brakes. Already well proven during flight testing of the prototype Hunter, this gear set is finely made and very strong indeed.

Trim Aircraft manufacture a twist-and-turn nosegear retract unit (seen right) for their new 1:7.2 scale F-86 Sabre which can either be operated pneumatically by using a standard air ram (eg: Robart #166), or mechanically using a dedicated retract servo. It is machined from an aluminium casting, and features precision ground steering mechanism, which is extremely innovative and works well. Designed to accept a standard 3/8" Robostrut or BVM Durostrut this unit looks to be well made and durable.

Connections

If properly assembled pneumatic systems should be expected to retain their air pressure for several hours, and sometimes a few days, the amount of time depending on how carefully the tube connections are made and the quality of the retract units. However the small diameter plastic tubing is notoriously difficult to push fully onto the 'Tee' fittings to ensure an air-tight system, most especially the plastic types, without damaging the tube or fitting - or hurting your fingers! A couple of good methods of temporarily softening or enlarging the diameter of the ends of the tubing are either to dip it in hot water, or push a tapered spike into the tube - a old (blunt) crosshead jewellers screwdriver works very well. Don't use a naked flame to soften the tube as it permanently deforms it, and using a pair of pliers to force it over the connectors or nipples can also damage the tubing and cause future leaks.

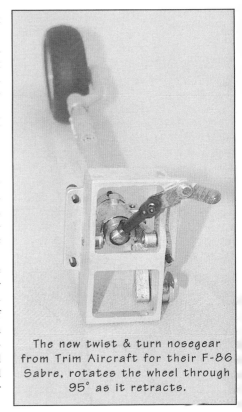

The new twist & turn nosegear from Trim Aircraft for their F-86 Sabre, rotates the wheel through 95° as it retracts.

Some manufacturers supply small threaded circular clamping sleeves (eg: the JMP item seen on the tube connected to the air tank on the opposite page), which can be used to retain the tube on the nipples - but normally if the correct size & type of tube is used these are unnecessary except for pressures above 7 bar (110 psi). Likewise cutting the plastic tubing to length with side-cutters or pliers should be discouraged, a sharp modelling knife is less likely to damage the remainder of the tube.

Accessories

There are several accessories available from many of the major pneumatic retract manufacturers and after-market companies. The most useful are 'quick-disconnect' fittings, most of which include 'O' rings to ensure a leak-proof seal. By installing a set of these in the supply tubing close to each retract, or other pneumatic system (brakes etc.) individual units can be removed easily for repair, without having to remove the tubing from the 'Tee' connectors.

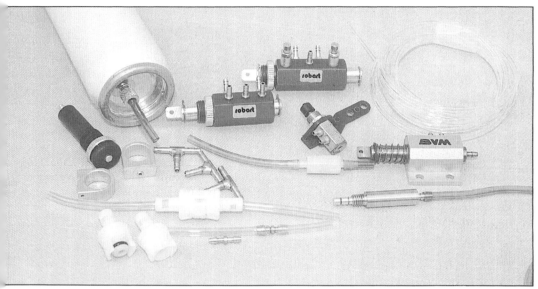

A selection of recommended pneumatic accessories in common use in jets, all having been well proved. (left to right) From Robart: 3/8" dia. alloy collars (RB#655) for attachment of gear doors to oleos, on-board air pressure gauge (RB#173) and, in front, airline quick-disconnects (RB#190). Also in foreground are the small brass airline restrictors, available from most retract suppliers and Robart dealers. Behind these are brass 'Tee' pieces for tubing connections & also an airline clamp on the airtank tube, both from Jet Model Products. At the back, centre, are the standard Robart shuttle valve (RB#167) & the new type with adjustable air needles (#157VR), both of which are especially fine. In front of these are a BVM air microswitch, most useful for operating brakes & sequencing gear door systems, and the new dual-rate brake valve - also a BVM product. Centre & front/right are the Spring Air combined restrictor and air filter (SA# 131) for pneumatic systems, & the Spring Air on-board air pressure 'Monitair"(SA#126). Finally, top/right, is a coil of the very small clear tubing used for wheelbrake systems, from BVM.

In-line restrictors are small tubular fittings inserted into the air tubes which have microscopically small airways in them which restrict the volume of air passing through, and therefore reduce the operating speed of the item that they are connected to. The most commonly seen are the brass types from Bob Dively in the USA. Spring-Air have a similar product made of yellow plastic, which also includes an integral air filter to prevent the ingress of dirt that could block the restrictor hole, or damage the internal surfaces of the air rams. It is also possible to restrict the air flow by using wheel collets over the tubing, and squashing it with the grub screws, but this soon damages the tube, and it is difficult to obtain the same restriction on two tubes - for instance when trying to match the operation of a pair of retracts, wheelbrakes or speed brakes.

Mechanical Retracts

The majority of mechanical retract units require a special 'retract' servo to operate them, which are normally expensive, and often quite large and heavy to provide sufficient power. They operate a little more slowly than standard servos, and most do not have adjustable travel or end-points, the servo always completing it's full travel of between 160° & 175°. This means that the linkage geometry must be adjusted mechanically, which can be difficult in the limited space available in many jet models - especially in thin wing sections.

There are very few commercially available mechanical retracts that are suited to the weights and sizes of normal jet models, perhaps the most common being the BVM units manufactured pre-1995. However many custom, or own-design, retract systems for special projects often use mechanically operated gear although increasingly these are being converted to pneumatic power by the addition of individual air rams.

Generally the wire linkages are difficult to fabricate accurately, even harder to maintain reliably, and prone to stalling the servos at the slightest mis-alignment, after a hard landing for example, which can drain the nicad quickly and result in the inevitable demise of the model.

For these reasons the use of mechanical types is in rapid decline, and there are now few suitable commercial items available, except for some smaller units designed for lightweight airframes.

Electric Retracts

Electrically operated retracts are quite rare, but since 1994 there has been a little resurgence of interest, partly due to the much improved nicads and recent developments in small electric motors and electronic controllers. Most are very powerful, which is useful for operating heavy scale undercarriage systems and wheels, and they are most commonly installed in large scale models, such as the multi-engined airliners that have been constructed in Holland and Germany during the last couple of years. It is preferable for electric retracts to have a separate nicad from the flight battery, in case of stalled retracts and, although electronic interference is seldom a problem, stringent range checks should always be carried out before flight.

The most popular electric retracts are these from Giezendanner Technik in Switzerland. They are very powerful & reliable, and are only a little more costly than equivalent pneumatic types.

In Europe the most common type are those from Giezendanner-Technik, in Switzerland, which were updated in about 1995 and offer very reliable operation at a reasonable cost. These units are very powerful and operate at a nice scale-like speed, pre-set at 5 seconds, and typical of Swiss engineering they are beautifully made from high quality composites and aluminium alloys. Several different sizes are available for model weights from 5 - 20 kg. Each retract unit is completely independent, and has it's own internal motor, clutch and travel limiting system which allows retraction angles of between 80° & 100°. A standard 4.8v nicad supplies the necessary power, and they come with an electronic switch and controller which is plugged directly into the receiver, needing no separate servo. The weight of a complete system is comparable to many pneumatic retracts, typically a complete tricycle set for 7 kg model weighing about 280 grams, and dimensions of each unit are also similar.

WIRE LEGS & OLEO STRUTS

There are two choices of undercarriage leg; either plain wire legs or oleo struts. Most standard retract sets include wire legs of 5/32" (± 4 mm) or 3/16" (± 4.5 mm) diameter, usually with a one or two turn coil spring near the top to allow some deflection in the event of a hard landing without damaging the retract unit or mounting system. Wire legs are quite sufficient for most sport jets and models up to about 6.5 kg in weight, although I recommend using the larger 4.5 mm diameter wire, but they do accentuate the models tendency to bounce on landing - especially on hard surfaces. However they are inexpensive, easy to replace, and can be straightened several times without weakening the wire unduly. The quality of the wire varies considerably between manufacturers, some being much stiffer than others, and a few are plated to prevent corrosion. The bottom ends of the legs are either bent through 90° to form axles for he wheels, or separate metal axles can be bolted or soldered onto them. If using the bolt-on axles remember to file a 'flat' spot on the axles at the bolt loca-tion, to prevent varia-tions in wheel align-ment. However it is preferable to solder the axles onto the wire legs, giving accurate leg length and wheel alignment, and I recom-mend that low-tempera-ture silver solder is used, for example the excellent 'Stay-Brite'(available from BVM dealers).

Oleo struts incur a small weight penalty, but reduce unwanted bounc-ing tendencies and

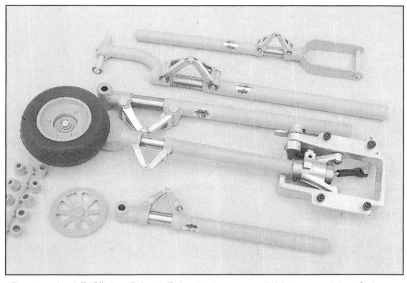

The standard 3/8" dia. Robart Robostruts are available in a variety of shapes & lengths, and now come with 'E' clips & machined grooves on the axles for wheel retention. There are also 7/16" dia. Robostruts, these being more suitable for jets over 7 kg weight. Also shown is a Robart wheel on the Trim Aircraft twist & turn nosegear in retracted position. These wheels are very commonly used on jets, but require the foam inserts for models over about 6kgs, & preferably the plastic bushes (seen left of photo) replaced with brass types.

improve ground-handling characteristics, as well as looking far more realistic. They are far stronger than wire legs, but once they have been bent in an accident they need to be replaced. There are 2 com-mon methods of attaching them to the retract units. The simplest is by using a short length of wire or a machined steel pin as a connector, retained in each part with grub screws, which provides a sacrificial link that can easily be replaced if bent. The alternative method is to fit the oleo struts directly into suit-ably sized holes in the retract pivot blocks, and several manufacturers offer this on their larger retract units. The holes are normally 3/8" diameter, to accept the majority of common oleos, and some retracts include adapter sleeves or bushes for other sizes or wire legs. This direct connection method gives far more rigid mounting, but the oleos are more eas-ily bent in a bad accident.

Three typical oleo legs, from PMP for the Gripen & Jim Fox Models for the BAe Hawk, all use wire stubs for connection to retract unit. Economically priced & quite sufficient for most applications.

There is a huge range of generic oleo struts available from model accessory companies, retract manufacturers, and specialist jet product manufacturers. They are two main types; those with 'drag-link' mechanisms at the base of the leg, simulating many full-size oleos, and the simpler and less costly sort which uses a bolt or pin that slides in a slot machined in the outer tube to limit the travel and maintain alignment. Most commercial oleos only contain single or twin springs of various compression rates, and these are quite adequate for most instances. However there are superior units available which also include a 'damping' mechanism, either util-ising air or oil to further reduce the bouncing effect, and these provide even better characteris-tics.

One of the most popular ranges of generic oleo struts are those from Robart, whose huge range of plain sprung units includes many different styles, lengths and configurations, and these are commonly used on jets up to about 9kg weight. However the torque-link mechanism at the base of their smaller oleos wears quite quickly, especially when used on models at the heavier end of this range, which gives variable wheel alignment and causes poor steering. Adjustment of the drag-link can alleviate this temporarily, but a more permanent cure is to bush both the pivot pins with short lengths of brass tube to prevent the deformation of the stamped metal parts.

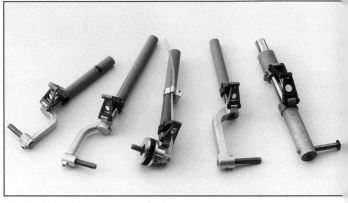

BVM's 'Durostrut' range of air damped & sprung oleos are extremely well engineered & strong, giving excellent ground handling & low 'bounce' - even when used on grass strips or rough runways. Struts are available for their whole range of models, as well as generic types which fit standard 3/8" dia. retract pockets. The torque link mechanism is particularly strong, cast from beryllium copper, and then machined, ensuring that wheel alignment remains constant.

Several of the established kit manufacturers also have specific oleos for their scale jets, closely representing the style of the full-size aircraft oleos, most especially the noselegs that are often so conspicuous. The installation of these, together with a little dressing-up of the legs and perhaps the addition of dummy landing lights etc, transforms the realism of scale models.

WHEELS

The majority of contemporary jets have higher takeoff and landing speeds than conventional models, and frequently increased weights and narrower undercarriage tracks, which cause higher loads and stresses on the wheels and tyres. For these reasons careful selection and installation of the wheels is required.

Most sport and scale jets up to about 7 kg are fitted with standard plastic model wheels and these are usually adequate, however the axle holes in the plastic hubs wear surprisingly quickly, especially if flown from hard surfaces, again resulting in varying wheel alignment. This can be overcome by using a type that has replaceable axle bushes, such as the wide range from Robart which are lightweight and very popular. The bushes supplied with these are plastic, but several companies (eg: Philip Avonds, Trim Aircraft, Jim Fox Models) stock replacement brass bushes which extend the useful life of the wheels considerably and also give smoother wheel rotation. There are also foam rubber inserts available for the range of Robart wheels, which prevent the tyres squashing flat under the load of heavier jets.

Three of the range of over 50 beautiful exact scale jet wheels from Glennis Aircraft, mostly machined from 6061 T-6 aluminium, and available for most of the best quality scale jets. Many of the world's top jet pilots use these in contests. Disc brakes are also available for the main wheels in many cases.

Larger jets, and scale types, benefit from the fitting of wheels with metal hubs and bushes and harder rubber tyres - although these are heavier and more expensive than the plastic ypes, and often require more powerful retract units to operate them reliably. Lots of jet companies (JMP, BVM, Yellow Aircraft, CJM, Avonds, Glennis etc.) make suitable wheels for their own kits, both sport and scale, as well as generic types that can be fitted to most other models as well, and some of these now have the option of brakes. If fitting wheels with metal hubs, don't forget to occasionally lubricate the axles with a very small amount of grease; almost any type will do - Robart S03 is quite commonly used and is also useful for many other model applications.

Wheel retention

The method of using collets and grub screws to retain wheels on the axles is not recommended for any jets due to the higher loads, especially on hard surfaced runways, normally resulting in the wheels coming off at the most inopportune moment! All jet wheels should be retained by either small washers soldered onto the axles on both sides of the wheel, or by similarly positive systems such as E-clips or circlips. Many of the bolt-on and solder-on axles incorporate the latter method, as well as the better oleos, with the circlips fitting into machined grooves or slots in the ends of the axles.

When soldering metal washers onto axles either side of plastic wheels, use a piece of thin cardboard or lithoplate as a spacer to ensure free wheel rotation and also act as a heat shield to protect the plastic hubs. Use a powerful (75 watt min.) soldering iron, and complete the joint as quickly as possible. Be very careful to clean the joints properly if using an acid flux, otherwise metal wheels or bushes will quickly rust onto the axles !

Wheel alignment

The alignment of the main wheels in relation to the centreline of the fuselage is extremely important to ensure good ground-handling characteristics. In all cases the wheels should be carefully adjusted to point directly ahead, or preferably with a very slight toe-in angle, which helps to prevent unwanted turns on take-off and landing rolls. If there is a little 'slop' in the wheel alignment, be sure that the wheels cannot twist outwards of the directly ahead position; too much toe-in being preferable to any degree of toe-out. Poor ground handling or steering characteristics of most models can usually be attributed to incorrect wheel alignment, and this should be the first thing to check if you are experiencing difficulties.

The degree of castor (forward or backward rake between the axle and the pivot point of the retract unit) of noselegs also has a pronounced effect on the steering effectiveness, and you should be careful to follow the kit manufacturers advice on this aspect.

WHEEL BRAKES

Since the early 90's brakes have become an increasingly popular option for both scale and sport jets, not only increasing the realism and 'fun' elements, but also improving safety factors. On turbine models they are especially useful as the high idle thrust often makes it difficult to hold the model stationary, & the use of brakes whilst the motor spools up to take-off power considerably shortens the ground roll.

The vast majority of wheel brakes are air operated, having many of the same advantages of pneumatic retracts, often utilising the same air storage tank as brakes consume very little air volume per operation. Most commercial & home-made systems use either a ring of tubing or a large 'O' ring inside the wheel hub which is expanded by the air pressure to provide sufficient friction to stop the wheel turning, but the brakes from Glennis Aircraft & Westbury Products use miniature disc brake systems. Operation of all types is by a simple spring-loaded air valve, either controlled by a dedicated servo connected to a separate receiver channel, or by combining the brake operation with another function. In the latter case the application of full down elevator is often used, the air valve or microswitch usually being actuated by a wire pushrod from the elevator linkage or servo arm, (see right).

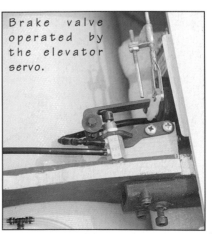

Brake valve operated by the elevator servo.

To ensure equal braking on each main wheel, so that no turning moment is induced, it is important that exactly the same amount of air is supplied to each brake assembly, and therefore the lengths of tubing between the 'tee' piece and each hub should be identical. It can be advantageous to insert a single in-line restrictor is into the supply tube to each brake, which reduces the tendency for the brakes to lock on suddenly. As with the installation of pneumatic retracts, it is wise to fit a 'quick-disconnect' into each brake tube close to the leg or oleo, to facilitate the removal of the retract for maintenance or repair.

Currently I'm not aware of any suitable commercially produced mechanical or electrical brake systems, but Fiorenze Hobbies markets an interesting set of hydraulically operated brakes that can be fitted to some wheel types on 5/32" diameter axles. The system uses a master cylinder filled with water, actuated by a standard servo, pressurising the water which, in turn, expands a ring of tubing inside a brake drum attached to each wheel hub. Only a small amount of water is contained in the system, which is quite lightweight, and they are easy to install.

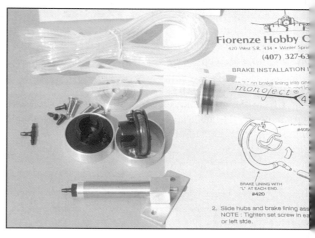

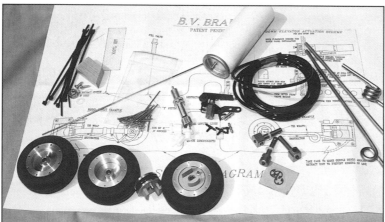

(Above) Bob Fiorenze Hobbies makes a unique set of hydraulically operated brakes, which are very compact and can be fitted to quite small wheels.

(Above) BVM sport-jet wheels, wire legs and brake system is suited to most jet kits and fits many standard retracts. A full range is also made for their scale jets.

Wheel & brake system from Jet Model Products for their large T-33.

Simple brakes from Modellbau Klühr, which fits inside larger sized (3.5"+) Robart wheels.

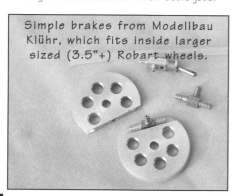

The use of wheel brakes increases tyre wear, especially with many of the wheels originally designed for conventional models as the rubber compound is quite soft. However it is not necessary for brakes to be so powerful that they lock the wheels solid - in fact this can be a distinct disadvantage as if they are applied inadvertently when the model is not rolling straight it may tip over and damage the airframe. If using the same air storage tank as for the retracts, usually at around 6.5 bar (100 psi) pressure, this can cause the wheels to lock, but there are several variable and dual-rate brake valves available to rectify this, as well as a few that are designed to give fully proportional braking. Alternatively fit a separate smaller air tank and fill it to a lower pressure, to give just enough power to hold the model stationary at about 75% throttle before take-off, and to slow the model quickly without skidding. This option of a separate system has other advantages also; if a fault develops in the brake system you won't lose the air pressure needed to operate the retracts, and the weight penalty is only the few grams of the air tank.

Pneumatic Operating Valves

Apart from the commonly used 'shuttle' valves, such as the excellent Robart #167 and many similar types, and the 'toggle' valves used with Spring-Air units, there are a number of air control valves available which provide additional features. Generally these offer extra outlet nipples for the controlling of gear door systems, and some also incorporate miniature needle valves to allow the operation speed to be controlled - acting like an adjustable restrictor.

The most well-known are from Ultra Precision, whose wide range includes several units for combining retract operation with both sequencing and non-sequencing doors, proportional brake control, & a special valve for speed control of single-line systems like the widely used 'Spring-Airs'. They also make a neat 'low pressure safety system', which is an electronic unit that fits between the receiver & retract servo that automatically extends the retracts if the air pressure drops below 3.2 bar (50 psi), or any level set by the user.

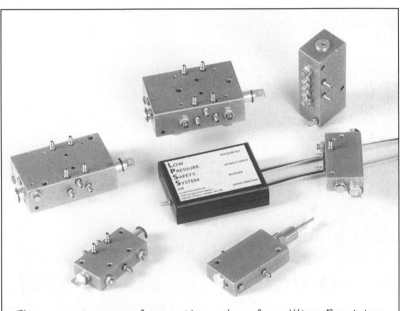

The current range of operating valves from Ultra Precision.

When installing any shuttle valves be careful that the servo doesn't push the shuttle off-centre in the valve guide as it operates, otherwise the 'O' ring seals will wear or be squashed, resulting in air leaks.

INSTALLATION

The installation of retracts in jets follows similar methods to that of conventional models, although often the wings are of a thinner section requiring more accurate work and slimmer retract units. Most are simply fixed to plywood plates (usually 6mm thick) in the wings and fuselage, either with self-tapping screws, or small bolts and captive nuts. The latter method, although stronger and making regular maintenance and removal easier, also has the disadvantage that in a very hard landing the gear can also rip out the plywood mounting plate or bulkhead as well - so you must make your choice of fixing system !

As in several other instances the range of kits from Bob Violett Models uses a different method. All retracts are screwed to sacrificial plates or arms, manufactured of carbon-reinforced nylon, which are in turn screwed of bulkheads or spars. In the case of a hard landing these pieces (called 'flex-arms' and 'flex-plates') are designed to break and cause minimal consequential damage to the airframe, retracts and undercarriage legs. The replacement of these parts, a simple 10 minute job which can be carried out on the airfield, is usually all that is necessary to make the model flyable again. This is an admirable system (which I have had occasion to use several times!), and so far no other manufacturer has introduced anything similar. Its only disadvantage is the cost of the replacement flex-arms and plates, but at just a few $ each most pilots regard this as a small price to get back in the air again quickly.

Seen above is a typical main gear installation in a BVM F-80, showing the retract, flexplate, air operating cylinder, and microswitch below the foam pad that closes the inner gear doors.

Gear Doors

Gear doors seem to cause more problems than almost anything else, however they are an advantage on scale and speed models, increasing performance when properly closed and enhancing the realism and looks of a scale jet. They are also useful for increasing the drag during landing, particularly those doors that are perpendicular to the flight direction, and can be surprisingly effective. Most need regular maintenance and adjustment, and are the first thing to get damaged in any "less-than-perfect" landing, but with proper installation they can be extremely reliable.

Generally the use of individual servos to operate gear doors is not recommended, not only being expensive and heavy - but also costly in terms of replacing servo gear sets almost every time a door is damaged. The best method of operating doors is either to use mechanical linkages (wire or spring) between the door and undercarriage leg, or separate miniature pneumatic rams to each door, and often a combination of both is used on complex multiple door systems. Simple mechanical linkages are generally easy to devise and install, although they sometimes need tweaking between flights to ensure proper door closure, and a couple of common methods are shown in the figures nearby. Some commercial oleos incorporate attachment points for door linkages, and both CJM and BVM offer separate attachment brackets that will fit a variety of oleos. Of course it is easy to make your own door linkage attachment points on wire legs - just solder on a short length of brass tube to accept the wire link.

For more complex installations, with both 'sequencing' (doors open for undercarriage to extend, and then close) and 'non-sequencing' doors (doors stay open when undercarriage is down), for instance on a scale model, then a pneumatic system using individual air rams is the most reliable method. The miniature air rams used for door actuation are available from many companies (eg: Ultra Precision, PMP, BVM, JMP, Avonds, CJM and Braeckman), and most offer a range of stroke lengths between 25 - 50 mm. Almost all use twin air lines, and incorporate attachment points on the ram body and the actuating arm for easy connection to the airframe and doors. They are usually of about 8 or 9 mm diameter, lightweight and powerful, and will last indefinitely with almost no maintenance. Several of the Ultra

Precision valves mentioned above are specially designed to provide the correct sequencing of multiple air rams for both types of gear doors, or you can easily make your own system using standard 4-way shuttle valves.

COMBINED RETRACT & GEAR DOOR SYSTEM..

A very simple and reliable operating method developed by myself and Ralf Ploenes for my F-15 used at the '95 Jet World Masters, and now used by many modellers on their scale jets, uses a single servo to operate the pneumatic retracts and both sequencing and non-sequencing doors. It was designed around a pair of the standard Robart blue #167 (or #157VR) valves, but most similar 4-way shuttle valves will suffice. You can use this system with any type of pneumatic retracts, either single or twin air line types, but if you use single airline units (eg: Spring-Airs) then the gear 'down' nipple on the retract operating valve must be blocked off. The gear doors are operated individually by small air rams, as mentioned above, and a single air supply is used for the whole system, a pair of standard sized retract air tanks tee-ed together normally giving sufficient capacity. Each operation of the undercarriage and 6 door rams uses about 15 psi, allowing at least 3 complete cycles of the gear and doors on each flight, using an initial tank pressure of around 110 psi (7 bar).

The servo and valves are fitted on a small plywood plate, which is installed anywhere convenient in the model after the system has been finally adjusted. A little experimenting is necessary to find the exact

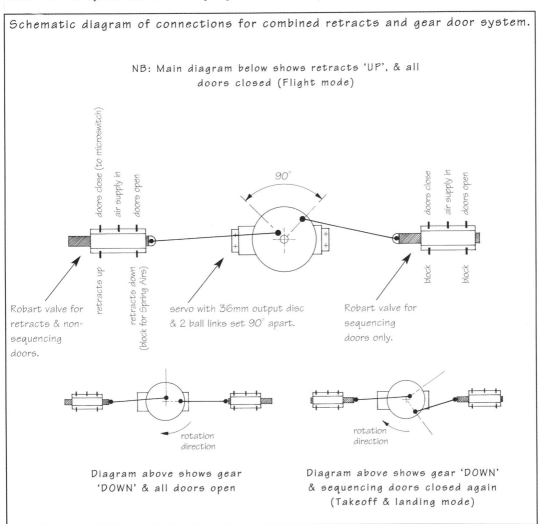

Schematic diagram of connections for combined retracts and gear door system.

NB: Main diagram below shows retracts 'UP', & all doors closed (Flight mode)

90°

doors close (to microswitch)
air supply in
doors open

doors close
air supply in
doors open

retracts up
retracts down
(block for Spring Airs)

block
block

Robart valve for retracts & non-sequencing doors.

servo with 36mm output disc & 2 ball links set 90° apart.

Robart valve for sequencing doors only.

rotation direction

rotation direction

Diagram above shows gear 'DOWN' & all doors open

Diagram above shows gear 'DOWN' & sequencing doors closed again (Takeoff & landing mode) locations of the two ball-links on the large servo output disc, but remember that they must be at 90° to each other, and that the shuttle in the valve that controls the 'sequencing' doors must move twice as far as the one that controls the retracts and 'non-sequencing' doors, therefore its ball link must be further out from the centre of the output disc. The non-sequencing doors are shut by using a 'normally closed' type of air micro-switch (BVM #5753 or equivalent), which is actuated by the last gear leg to go up, completing the air circuit and allowing the air rams to close the doors.

The servo used doesn't need to be powerful (even a mini will do) but it must be capable of about 140° rotation, and most standard servos can be made to do this by setting the end points to the maximum values in your transmitter. If you have a servo-slow facility in your transmitter this can be used to control the servo speed, otherwise I recommend an add-on electronic unit is utilised to allow this - about 4 to 5 seconds between servo end-points works well. It is very wise to use different coloured air tubing for each

'up' and 'down' line, otherwise the plumbing can get confusing! To make sure that there is enough time delay between the doors opening and the gear going down, and also to slow down the whole operation and make it look more realistic, you may need to add some in-line restrictors in the 'down' tubes to the main retract units, and also the 'up' tubes from the sequencing gear door rams. Make sure that these restrictors are positioned in each pair of tubes at an equal distance from the air rams or retract units, to give similar operation speeds. This system is particularly simple to construct and easy to maintain, and has recently been adopted by a couple of the larger jet manufacturers for use on all their scale kits.

Door Hinging

The hinges for gear doors need to be strong enough to take the loads imposed by the operating system, as well as any shocks and moments imposed on them by the undercarriage itself during landings. The most commonly used hinges are the 'offset' type, their geometry increasing the gap between the door and the airframe as they open, allowing narrow hinge gaps to be maintained. Excellent offset hinges are manufactured by BVM and Usher Enterprises, and these are available from many good jet equipment dealers. In some

Absolutely astonishing hand crafted main undercarriage by Einar Johnsson, from Sweden, for his very large own-design 1/8th scale Saab Viggen. He made the whole assembly, including; retract units, sprung oleos, trunions, links, wheels, gear doors, brakes and tyres. Still, they have long winter nights in Scandinavia!

cases you can use normal nylon model hinges, the type with metal pivot pins are recommended, but the gluing faces need to be well abraded with 80 grit sandpaper or a coarse sanding tool before gluing in position. Hinges can be glued in place with a quick-setting epoxy (30 minute is ideal), preferably with a little milled-fibre mixed into it to increase the strength of the bond and stiffen the epoxy to prevent it running into the pivots.

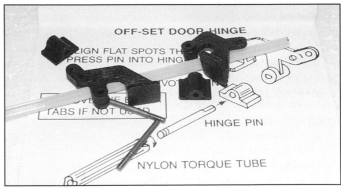

OFF-SET DOOR HINGE

LIGN FLAT SPOTS TH
PRESS PIN INTO HING

TABS IF NOT US

HINGE PIN

NYLON TORQUE TUBE

The best way to hinge gear doors is by using a proprietary 'Offset' door hinge, such as the BVM type shown above, or similar items from Usher Enterprises Inc. To ensure the narrowest possible gap around the door, and the maximum opening angle, it is important to fit the part that is fixed to the main airframe (the smaller part) right on the very edge of the cutting line for the door.

Doors can be quickly cut out of fibreglass mouldings using a cutting disc (eg: Dremel or Permagrit) on a miniature high-speed drill, although it's easy to slip and damage the door or adjacent airframe, or finish with a wide hinge gap after straightening the cuts with a sanding block. For these reasons I prefer to use an X-Acto saw blade, which cuts fibreglass well enough (if a little slowly), but it is safer and makes perfectly straight and narrow hingelines. Drilling a very small hole in each corner of the door location to give a starting point for the saw blade is a great help.

To obtain really smooth door operation it is imperative to locate the hinges accurately - not only must they be at right angles to the edge of the door, but also multiple hinges on the same side of the doors must be in line with each other. The BVM hinges mentioned above can be connected together with the tubing provided to ensure parallel installation, and you can effect the same result with some others by using a length of inner snake on the pivot pins of adjacent hinges. The trick to getting really good operation, however, is to glue the hinges in place before finally cutting the doors free from the airframe. Mark the exact door location and the hinge positions and cut through at all the corners and the hinge locations, leaving just enough uncut material to retain the door in place. Then glue the hinges in position and, after it has completely cured, cut through the last parts to release the door, and finally clean up the door edges with a sanding block. Once you are happy with the door operation the hinges can be further secured with a single very small self-tapping screw through the airframe into each hinge body, if you wish, this also making it easy to relocate them in exactly the same position if they need repair in the future. You'll find that this method guarantees perfectly operating door hinges and the narrowest possible hingelines.

Offset door hinges shown glued in place, and finally retained with a single small 'polyply' self-tapping screw through the fuselage into the nylon hinges. In this Spectre the nosegear oleo closes the door by actuating a motion transfer arm (BVM part) which pulls the door closed behind it. Extremely simple method, but very effective.

Maintenance

If properly installed most pneumatic undercarriage systems require little maintenance - until damaged during an 'arrival'! Some manufacturers advise on the maintenance required for their units, but generally you should not apply any oil or grease to the retracts as it only attracts dust and grit which speeds up wear and causes binding. The best way to look after retract units & oleos is to keep them free of grit; cleaning with a blast of compressed air, or methylated spirits & soft bristled brush, are recommended.

After a considerable period of use (say 50 flights) a single drop of pure silicone oil on the piston actuating rod of all air rams will eventually find it's way to the 'O' ring seals and lubricate them. The same silicone oil also benefits the 'O' ring seals in shuttle valves, & the nylon bushes in most retracts, when they become dry or stiff. Only apply a very little high melting-point grease or light machine oil to wheel axles if brakes are fitted - otherwise you will find that your brakes don't work! Gear door hinges need checking for security regularly, and a small blob of Robart S03 grease, or similar, on the pivot pins keeps them free. You will soon know if any of the air lines need replacing, because of leaks, but if pneumatic brakes are fitted check the air lines where the undercarriage leg pivots for kinks and splits occasionally. Often air leaks are caused by grit in the air filling valves, and you should try & position these in the model where they can't get dirty, and remember to keep the air filler nozzle clean as well.

Electric retracts require almost no maintenance, the moving parts being totally enclosed, but if a separate nicad is used to power them remember to fully cycle it occasionally as it rarely gets completely discharged. Mechanical systems generally need a little more attention than pneumatic types, with regular cleaning and occasional greasing of pivots and bushes ensuring reliable operation and long life.

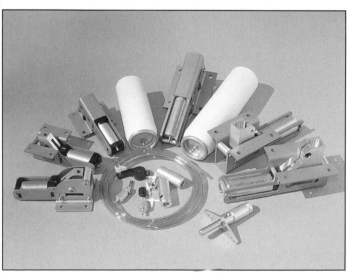

9 - Accessories

There are two sorts of accessories; those that enhance the visual appearance of a model, and those that improve the operating functions or safety of it, some sorts contributing to both aspects. All of these add some weight and complexity, and often newcomers to the jet scene load so many extras onto their models that they are barely able to fly, and more time is spent adjusting these than maintaining the main functions of the model - I know, because I've also been guilty of this !

Some of the items here can be added after the first few flights when you are used to the individual flying characteristics of the model, but others need to be either installed, or provision made for them, during the original construction. It is impossible to list every optional extra here, otherwise it would fill the whole book, so I've concentrated on the more common ones and just given a brief overview of their function, and where to obtain the commercially available parts. The addresses of companies mentioned will be found in Appendix 1 at the back of the book wherever possible, though some items may also be available from good model shops.

RELEASABLE STORES & ORDNANCE

Many of the scale jet manufacturers also make optional drop tanks, bombs, missiles etc. for their kits, and although these are purely aesthetic they do add a great deal of extra realism. The larger ordnance gives a little extra drag and weight to the model, but this is not normally sufficient to affect the performance unduly. It is relatively easy to make most ordnance releasable during flight, thereby injecting a little extra fun to your flight schedule, as well as enhancing the realism and points gained during competitions.

The most commonly used commercial release mechanism used is the 'Vortac'. This consists of a small grey plastic mini-pylon with an internal spring-loaded sliding plate, which has two slots in it that engage with a pair of plastic teeth fitted to each item of ordnance. They can be operated by a mini or micro servo, either using a wire linkage or a pull string if the servo is remotely located - especially useful when fitting stores onto wings or pylons that are not thick enough to enclose a servo. The Vortac mechanism is strong enough to support weights of around 250 grams, but large items need 'sway braces' or rubber pads to prevent them wobbling around during flight. These can easily be made from short lengths of threaded rod or small cap-head bolts, with rubber washers or 'O' rings cyanoed onto the ends to protect the ordnance. A similar, but much simpler and lower quality, release mechanism is made by SLEC in the UK and this comes complete with bright red plastic 2-part bombs that can be filled with talcum powder for extra effect !

There are also plenty of ways to make your own release mechanisms, the system used on BVM F-80 Shooting Stars for the tip-tan release being just one example. This uses a length of thin piano wire from the servo bay in the inboard part of the wing, passed through a plastic snake guide tube to the wingtip, which then locates in a metal eyelet in the top of each tip-tank. A small slot is cut into the balsa tip block and lined with plywood, with a pair of holes to positively

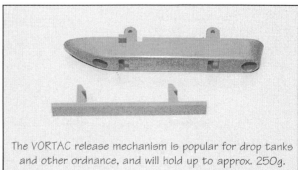

The VORTAC release mechanism is popular for drop tanks and other ordnance, and will hold up to approx. 250g.

locate the piano wire. Short pieces of silicone tube glued into blind holes in the top of each tank provide enough 'spring' to release the tanks properly every time the system is operated, and a small locator pin at the front and back of the wingtip positions the tank laterally, parallel to the fuselage centreline.

Of course it is not necessary to make all the stores releasable during flight, just the addition of external weapons on a model of a military aircraft adds considerably to the realism. A large range of missiles, bombs, tanks, guided weapons and other accessories is made from lightweight ABS by Eagle Miniatures (USA) in several suitable scales, FTE manufactures several different styles and scales of bombs, and it is not difficult to make your own - either using thin ABS with a vacuum-forming machine (now quite inexpensive), or even moulded from epoxy and glass-cloth over a wooden or foam plug.

Do make sure that each item is properly fitted onto the model before each flight, and that they release reliably every time, as trying to control a model which has an asymmetric load is fraught with danger at landing speeds, normally producing a pronounced yaw. Remember that for authenticity tanks should 'tumble' in the air, and bombs or other heavy ordnance should 'fly'. A central Centre of Gravity for tanks, and a few grams of lead in the nose of bombs helps to give this effect. Wing and fuselage pylons are usually constructed from lightweight balsa sheet with litely formers, and can be made removable by screwing them to hardwood plugs fixed into the structure of the model, or that can be permanently

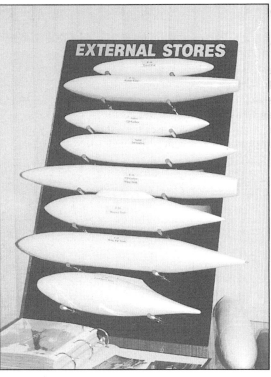

Most of the reputable current jet kit manufacturers have a range of external stores for their scale jet kits. The wingtip tanks, centreline tanks and stores pods are part of the range from BVM. All are moulded in very lightweight fibreglass.

Tom Robertson shows off the underside of his fully loaded F-16 Fighting Falcon. Most of these drop tanks are releasable during flight, and the model flies quite well with all in place, although the extra drag is especially noticeable in crosswinds & during landing approaches.
Underside view also shows the specially manufactured scale undercarriage gear on this BVM kit to advantage.

glued into position. Make sure that both ordnance and pylons accurately line up with the centreline of the fuselage to prevent trim problems during flight.

Note: In many countries the firing of any propelled type of ordnance from a model, for instance missiles propelled by miniature rockets (eg: Estes types), is strictly forbidden - and can be dangerous.

ADJUSTABLE TAILCONES

The ability to vary the diameter of the jet nozzle at the outlet of the exhaust duct during flight gives enhanced realism, and also allows adjustment of exhaust velocity and volume to suit the flight profile. In the fully open position, almost parallel with the rear section of the exhaust duct, these give increased static thrust but reduced exhaust velocity - which is useful for take-off and in a 'go-around' situation after an aborted landing, as well as for vertical climbs. Conversely, reducing the size of the nozzle in the correct proportion increases the exhaust velocity allowing higher model airspeeds, and this has been used to good effect on some dedicated 'speed' models.

A great example of the Bob Fiorenze adjustable exhaust nozzle, fitted to a Yellow Aircraft F-16 Fighting Falcon. After final installation it was sprayed & weathered to enhance the realism.
The owner wasn't certain if it gave any performance increase on his jet - but it looks very impressive !

There are two adjustable exhaust nozzles available at the moment, one from Bob Fiorenze Hobbies and the other from Pauls Jet Products (both in the USA), both requiring the existing jet nozzle to be cut off the model and replaced with the new part. The Fiorenze nozzle is aimed mostly at scale jet models, the turkey feathers being beautifully made from very thin aluminium sheet, and it can be made to fit many current ducted-fan kits with exhaust duct outlets of 87 - 105mm diameter. Operation is by a standard servo and a nyrod snake, the tailcone assembly weighs only about 70 grams, and it comes pre-assembled with full instructions. The 'Variable Exhaust Nozzle' from PJP was originally designed for installation on BVM sport jets, but can be also fitted to some other types with diameters of approx. 105 mm. It is fabricated from precision moulded carbon and kevlar strips which are interleaved to form an airtight nozzle, and controlled by drawstrings and a snake in a similar manner to the Fiorenze item. It comes in kit form and needs several hours of careful building, but it is creditably light at around 40 grams.

As the latest ducted-fan units reach towards the higher limits of efficiency possible, then in-flight adjustable nozzles may well provide a method of extracting just a little more performance, but for most modellers they are only a method of enhancing the appearance of their jets.

ISOLATION MOUNTS

Since the early 90's isolation, or anti-vibration, mounting systems have become the most popular and effective way of reducing the transmission of vibration from the motor and fan unit to the airframe, also helping to reduce resonance and noise levels. They work by preventing direct rigid contact between the fan unit and the main fuselage structure that supports them, normally consisting of rubber or silicone isolating material around the fixing bolts and under the mounting flanges on the fan unit, effectively 'soft-mounting' it. High-frequency vibration is the major killer of electronic equipment, also affecting the structural integrity of the airframe and all of it's associated parts, and therefore it is highly recommended that isolation mounts are installed in every ducted-fan model. All fragile electronic items in the airframe, such as the receiver, should still have their own foam packing to give extra protection - but the installation of high quality isolation mounts goes a long way towards prolonging the life of servo potentiometers and switch contacts, and therefore your model.

All of the commercially produced isolation mounts raise tractor fan units a little, to lift it clear of the support bearers and prevent direct contact, therefore it is usually necessary to install these during initial construction as otherwise the fan shroud won't line up with the inlet and exhaust ducts. Of course some vibration is still transmitted to the airframe via the ducting, which is usually tightly attached to the fan unit and airframe to prevent air leakage, but the reduction produced by isolation mounts is definitely well worth having.

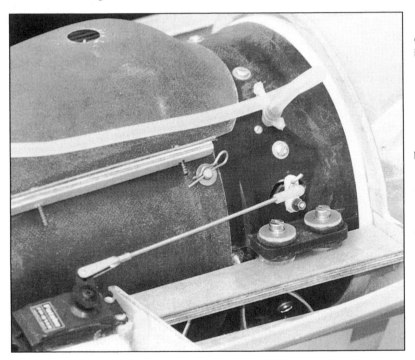

Most manufacturers of current D/F units produce isolation mounts for their fan, but there are also several after market types. The system shown fitted in a Gripen model on the left is from PMP, simple to fit to a Ramtec or Dynamax, and is commonly used in Europe. Weston UK make another type of mount, that raises the fan less and is also effective, but it is more bulky and heavier (see advert).. Notice also the clever throttle transfer linkage through the side of the shroud on this fan unit.

A couple of the manufacturers of contemporary tractor type ducted-fan units (Viojett & Ramtec) offer isolation mounts for their units, either included with the unit or as an optional extra, and these are also available separately for use with other fans. There are also several good after-market systems specifically designed for this purpose, my favourite being the mounts from Performance Model Products which are particularly effective and only raise the level of the fan unit by 3.5 mm.

It is also quite simple to make your own anti-vibration mounts for either tractor or pusher fan units. Enlarge the holes in the mounting flanges or brackets of the fan unit to accept the fixing bolts with a sleeve of thick-walled silicone fuel tubing around each, allowing a loose clearance fit. Then bolt the fan unit to the support bearers (or bulkhead in the case of a pusher type fan) with a large steel or fibreglass washer and then a rubber washer under the head of each bolt, and another rubber washer and finally a steel washer under the nut on the other side of the support bearer. The silicone tube sleeve should be a couple of millimetres longer then the thickness of the mounting bracket, so that when it is compressed by the bolts it will expand to grip the sides of the holes, and just keep the fan mounting brackets clear of the support bearers or bulkhead. Note that if you tighten the bolts up too much the fan unit will become rigidly mounted, negating the effect of the isolation mounts. Another, even simpler, method is to fit the fan unit to the support structure using 'rubber-nuts', more commonly used in the building industry for fixing to plasterboard material, although these aren't as effective. Don't forget to add a pad of silicone or rubber to the base of the tuned-pipe hanger bracket, which not only helps to isolate the vibration, but also protects the bracket from heat.

Having tried many anti-vibration mounting systems it is difficult to determine which has the greatest effect - but it is extremely noticeable that models with these fitted don't give your fingertips the same 'buzz' when you touch them!

HUSH-KITS

These are acoustic panels fitted inside jet models that absorb some of the noise produced by the ducted-fan unit, motor and the high speed airflow, reducing the overall sound levels emitted during operation. Commonly called 'hush-kits' (actually the name given to this product by BVM), they usually consist of acoustic foam panels wrapped around the outside surfaces of the inlet ducts, with the outer surface sealed by either lightweight fibreglass or ABS panels. The wall of the inlet duct has thousands of very small holes drilled in it to allow the noise to enter the acoustic foam, where it is then absorbed. This system adds a little weight to a model, but is very effective in reducing the noise levels - in some cases by as much as 4 dBA at 7 metres (depending on the surface area of the acoustic panels), and it is definitely a worthwhile addition.

Construction is easy, though drilling the holes is time-consuming, but it must be completed during the initial construction of the model as inlet ducts are normally glued permanently in place. First plan the areas of inlet duct that have sufficient space around them to fit a hush kit of about 13 mm thickness without fouling the fuselage sides or control linkages. Make paper templates to match these shapes and draw around them on the outside of the inlet ducts. Next the 0.5 mm diameter holes are drilled in the inlet duct walls, using a pattern guide to ensure correct and even spacing(approx. 2 apart) and then acoustic foam of approx. 12 mm thickness is glued over the outside of the ducts to completely cover the areas of holes. The outer surface of the foam pads are then covered with very thin fibreglass or ABS sheet to prevent the noise escaping. Lastly the exposed edges of the foam are sealed with a mixture of 24 hr epoxy and a large percentage of microballoons to give a very stiff consistency - almost like icing a cake! Some final sanding and sealing of the panels with a fuelproof primer completes the job.

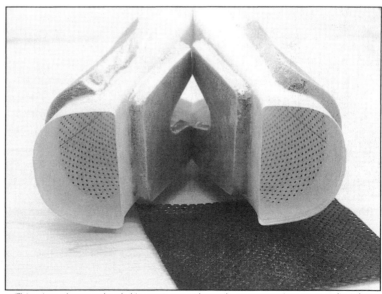

This view shows a hush kit part way through construction on a split inlet duct for a Maverick. Notice the punched fabric template supplied in the BVM hush kit to ease drilling of the thousands of holes, which need to be accurately spaced. Finally the acoustic foam panels are clad in thin sheet and the edges sealed with a mixture of epoxy & microballoons.

Other plain panels of acoustic foam may also be used inside ducted-fan models to reduce resonance and noise levels, often stuck to the inside surface of hatches and large flat areas of fibreglass that can otherwise vibrate like a drum. However care is needed that these exposed foam panels do not become fuel-soaked over time, not only increasing the weight of the model, but also gradually affecting the Centre of Gravity location - possibly so slowly that it isn't noticed until it's too late !

Several of the larger jet kit manufacturers (BVM, Avonds, Trim Aircraft etc.) offer tailor-made 'hush-kits' for their models as well as generic hush-kit packs, and a few jet accessory companies (eg: Braeckman Modellbau & Jim Fox Models) also stock the special foam for those who wish to make their own acoustic reduction panels. Some foam types are self-adhesive, the glue used being relatively fuel-proof in most cases, and thicknesses of between 6 - 18 mm are commonly available. Experiments with other types of lightweight foam have not produced such a noticeable noise reduction as when the special acoustic type is used.

SMOKE SYSTEMS

The addition of an on-board smoke system in a jet, whether sport or scale, enhances the 'fun factor' and is a great option for displays. Many full-size jets use smoke systems for aerobatic routines at airshows and these are normally remotely mounted smoke generator pods, often on the wing tips instead of missiles, and electronically ignited by the pilot as required.

Miniature smoke generator capsules are available from theatre prop companies in a wide variety of colours and these are ignited electronically - normally requiring about 3 volts, easily obtained from a couple of dry cell batteries and a microswitch in the model. However they are quite small, approx. 30 mm diameter and 75 mm long, usually have a burn time of less than 1 minute and the smoke is not really dense enough to give sufficient visual impact at high speeds. They also constitute a fire hazard to both the airframe and the ground, and are therefore not recommended.

On ducted-fan models the usual method of producing smoke during flight is to use a separate tank of smoke liquid, and inject it into the hot exhaust as it leaves the motor, where it burns and exits the tuned pipe as dense white cloud. Petroleum dyes may also be added to the smoke mixture, to give various colours, but these stain everything that they come into contact with, and so should be used with great care. The best system I have seen is that of Canadian jet modeller Martin Lefevbre, employed to excellent effect in his OS91 powered model of an Aermacchi MB339, as used by the famous Italian aerobatic display team 'Frecce Tricolori'. It consists of a separate tank to hold the smoke liquid, which is a 50/50% mix of diesel fuel and automatic transmission oil (ATF). A capacity of 300 ml (10 fl.oz) provides 4 - 5 minutes of smoke, but all of the tubing and the tank stoppers must be of the type used for gasoline motors (rubber or neoprene), as silicone is rapidly destroyed by the smoke mixture. The smoke mix goes through an in-line filter to an electric fuel pump, again of the type used for gasoline, and many companies advertise these in modelling magazines. From the pump it passes through a needle valve, of the type that just squashes the tube, to allow fine tuning of the flow, and finally a one-way valve before entering the vapouriser coil. This consists of half a dozen turns of 3 mm diameter annealed brass or copper tube wrapped tightly around the tuned pipe, immediately behind the motor, and is used to

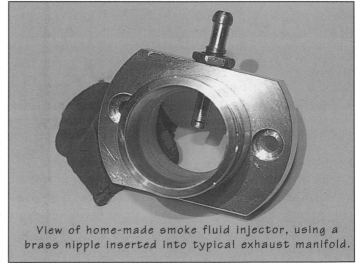

View of home-made smoke fluid injector, using a brass nipple inserted into typical exhaust manifold.

pre-heat the mixture before it enters the exhaust manifold through an injector nipple. The vapouriser coils are soldered together, using a low-temperature silver solder such as 'Stay-Brite', and wrapped in reflective aluminium foil to help retain the heat.

The injector tube in the exhaust manifold is made from a standard brass threaded nipple, of the type commonly used in the caps of fuel containers. Before fitting it the bottom end is blocked with silver solder, and then a very small slot is cut in the side of the tube, just above the end so that it is close to the centre of the manifold, using a sharp razor saw. Drill and tap the manifold to suit, and fit the injector nipple with the slot facing towards the tuned pipe, not towards the motor.

To set up the system start the motor and let it warm up for a minute or so, with the mixture set as normal. Then at full throttle, switch on the pump (using a separate channel, switch & nicad) and open the smoke mixture valve slowly until a dense trail of smoke is produced, without the motor speed reducing more than 200 or 300 rpm. After a little practice, and some experimenting with the exact ratio of diesel to ATF, you will achieve reliable dense smoke with almost no rpm drop at all. Only operate the smoke system when at least 70% throttle is selected, otherwise the motor may stop or run roughly. If your motor has a removable exhaust manifold then no permanent modifications to the model are necessary, and the system is simple, reliable - and produces a very impressive result!

LIGHTS

Navigation, position and landing lights can all be simulated quite easily, and these may be either working or non-working. Almost without exception every full-size jet aircraft has some sort of lighting, usually in a conspicuous position, and the omission of these will be noticed immediately by the judges in any scale contest.

Many aircraft types have landing lights on the noseleg oleos which are very prominent, usually consisting of one or more conical reflectors in a circular housing, which are quite easily machined from aluminium by a friend with a small lathe. Very small high-intensity bulbs that operate on low voltage (3 - 4.8 volts) can be obtained from small torches (such as mini-Maglites®), or from specialist suppliers such as Ross Mansell in the UK. The bulbs are retained in the reflectors by a blob of clear silicone, connected with fine wires to a small on-board battery pack, and controlled by a microswitch operated by a cam on the retract servo output disc, automatically switching them on when 'gear down' is selected. Generally the heat produced by the high-intensity lamps is sufficient to melt clear plastic lenses placed in front of the bulbs, so the lights have to remain open at the front.

Various electronic lighting units are also available commercially, usually pre-connected to a series of red, green and white high-intensity l.e.d's, and these can also be installed behind plastic lenses as they don't get very hot. The only company that I know of that makes scale light units for jet models is Glennis Aircraft, whose products are manufactured from lightweight resin mouldings and which are available for a number of scale models, notably the BVM scale jet range.

Non-working position lights, such as the red and green ones on wingtips etc., can be easily represented by cutting and sanding the correct shape from small pieces of coloured nylon toothbrush handle, and then repolishing the external surface with a car paint restorer compound, such as 'T-Cut'. These are glued in place as required, sometimes with a small piece of silver foil behind them to increase the reflectiveness, and they look very realistic indeed.

Glennis Aircraft make several scale light units from moulded resin, this one for the F-80 or T-33 Shooting Stars.

Note: If you install any operating light system in your model, ensure that there is no interference caused to your R/C system by completing a proper range check before flying.

ON-BOARD GLOW DRIVERS.

The glowplugs currently used in ducted-fan models are specially designed to suit the characteristics of these motors, giving reliable transition and low idling speeds on properly adjusted motors. Therefore there is generally no need for a separate glowplug driver system and these are very rarely seen. Very occasionally, however, on a multi-engined models, or contest models specifically set up for use in a very restricted airspace, an on-board glow-driver system can be an advantage. These either utilise a microswitch controlled by a cam on the throttle servo, or a commercial electronic unit, to connect a small 1.2 volt nicad to the glow plug at low throttle settings to prevent inadvertent engine cutting.

BRAKING PARACHUTES

Many current high-performance military jets (Phantom, Mirage 2000 series, Tornado etc.) and a few older types, make use of drogue 'chutes to enhance their wheel brakes and shorten landing rolls. The addition of a 'chute to a scale jet model enhances not only the appearance, but can also be useful in the case of an emergency landing - but do ensure that it absolutely cannot be deployed accidentally during flight, and be careful if using them in a crosswind as it can be difficult to steer the model. There aren't many proprietary drag 'chute systems for models that I know of (BVM has a drag 'chute system for their F4, and CJM make a 'chute for their F-100/F-105 kits), and therefore the operating system is normally own-design. However there are some parachutes which can be utilised from toys and R/C parachutists, and it's not difficult to make your own from thin rip-stop nylon fabric, especially if you know someone who's handy with a sewing machine. Do make sure that both the material and cords are strong enough to take the sudden loads imposed when released behind a 10 kg jet doing 100 kph down the strip !

Most 'chutes are stored in a small tubular or conical fairing above or below the jet nozzle at the tail of the aircraft, and a simple hinged door to this fairing operated by a micro servo suffices. It is usually necessary to put some sort of spring loaded circular plate inside the fairing to eject the 'chute, and careful folding and packing is necessary every time it is reloaded to make sure that it opens fully.

Vern Montgomery's large twin-engined F4 Phantom, shown in flight earlier in the book, has an operating drogue 'chute system, which he deploys as soon as the model has touched down. It is quite effective, as well as looking spectacular.

BATTERY MONITORS & BACKERS

Probably one of the most commonly installed accessories is an on-board battery state indicator, so that you can check the level of charge of your flight nicads before every flight - and these have certainly saved many models. Even the highest quality nicad packs can die suddenly, or have one cell fail, which spells disaster for the model and could cause a dangerous crash. Many commercial units are available, some more complex and costly than others, and most display the nicad charge remaining by a series of coloured l.e.d's - usually ranging from red, through orange/yellow to green to indicate 'no fly' and 'fly' situations. My advice is to fit the type that checks the level of your nicad charge 'under load', which is normally accomplished by rapidly moving both sticks on the transmitter around the extremes of travel and watching the display or l.e.d's to assess the charge state. Of course fitting one of these units is of no use if you don't actually check it before each flight, so make sure that it is installed in a readily visible location, such as under the canopy or engine starting hatch.

Personally I think that fitting a battery level monitor of some sort is just plain common sense, and one more way to ensure the safety of your model - hence all my jets have these little units installed. However on-board monitors are no substitute for regularly cycling and checking the capacity of your flight nicads using a decent charger/cycler unit, and high-quality nicads, which will warn you of any problem with your nicad pack before you arrive at the flying site. There are also a number of electronic 'Battery-Backer' modules that allow the installation of a second, normally smaller capacity, nicad in the model - and if the level of charge in the main nicad drops below a certain pre-set level these units automatically switch over to the other nicad pack. Although I've never used these myself, I have seen them used successfully, especially in models with a large number of high-power servos.

ON-BOARD TACHOMETERS

One of the most recently introduced electronic aids is the on-board tachometer, which gives you a visual display of the real-time engine rpm (useful before take-off), and some of these also memorise and store the maximum rpm achieved during the last engine run, and display it when the engine is stopped. Most of these units have a pair minute electronic or optical sensors that are easily installed in the back of the spinner plate to read the rpm's, sending the data to a small electronic module located under the cockpit - or in any position where it is easy to read the display. This system has many advantages over the common 'hand-held' tachometer, especially in ducted fans where it is often difficult to use a normal tacho as the spinner is hidden deep inside the model.

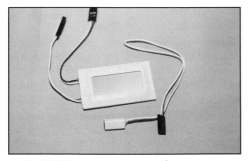

The PMP Tachometer monitors engine rpm during each run, records the highest rpm reached, & displays it when the engine is stopped. Useful for setting up motors. It also has an integral nicad level monitor.

On-board tacho's can be helpful in optimising tuned-pipe lengths and types, fuels and mixture settings, and also for synchronising motors in multi-engined models. Interestingly the use of these in the last couple of years has, finally, proved that the rpm of the majority of ducted-fan motors does not rise dramatically in flight - even during power dives. Several companies manufacture these units, but my only experience is of the 'Performance Monitor' from PMP, which has a large digital readout and has proved reliable and accurate, and which is also combined with an on-board battery monitor.it is commonly fitted below the cockpit canopy or under another hatch that is normally removed for engine starting, also allowing an rpm check before every flight - which could warn of any impending engine problems.

OPENING COCKPITS

This is one of the ultimate options on a scale jet, but requires a high level of building skill to ensure that it works correctly & realistically - and most importantly that the canopy cannot open accidentally during flight. Whether the canopy is hinged at the back or side, or sliding, it should take at least 5 seconds to open to look realistic. If operated by a servo this requires a 'servo-slow' facility, and if using a pneumatic ram then restrictors need to be inserted into the air tubes. The difficult part is to fabricate a positive mechanical lock to keep the canopy tightly closed during flight. If the canopy is operated by a powerful servo the operating linkage should be adjusted so that, in the closed position, it is positioned at an 'over centre' position with the linkage directly in line with, but on the opposite side of, the servo output shaft. Another method, used by Jerry Caudle in an F-16, used a long-stroke miniature air ram to operate the canopy, combined with an air micro-switch set into the cockpit side rail that actuated a second small pneumatic ram that operated a locking bolt at the front of the cockpit when the canopy touched it in the fully closed position.

Opening cockpits, operated from the transmitter, are at the pinnacle of scale jet model building. Here is one of the few examples seen recently, on david Ribbe's F-16 at the 1995 Jet World Masters.

PNEUMATIC SYSTEMS

These are covered in Chapter 8,but pneumatic systems are becoming popular for operating all kinds of accessories & special functions, such as speedbrakes, undercarriages & doors, spoilers, speed brakes etc,. There are many advantages; the miniature air rams generally used are lighter, smaller, less expensive, generally more reliable & more powerful than individual servos, and easy to install. A huge variety of shapes, sizes and throws are available from manufacturers such as Ultra-Precision, JMP, BVM, PMP etc, and these can be combined with many of the various different operating valves that are marketed by several companies (eg: Robart, Rhom-Air, Spring Air, Ultra-Precision). In particular the operation of accessories that could result in high current drain due to operating loads, or items that could stall a servo, such as gear doors, are better operated pneumatically.

10 - Turbines

At the time of writing the growth in numbers of turbine powered models is increasing at a colossal rate, and it is probably the fastest expanding area in jet modelling. However the current cost of commercially manufactured gas-turbine motors is about 5 or 6 times that of a complete ducted-fan system, which is the main limiting factor in the expansion of this power source. This is likely to remain the case for the conceivable future, although if a large manufacturer starts true mass production of a turbine motor it may reduce the cost differential a little, and bring the possibility of owning these superb pieces of engineering within the reach of a larger proportion of jet modellers.

The ratio of turbines to modellers in Europe is far greater than anywhere else at present, often over 10% of models at European jet meetings being propelled in this manner, and in particular the USA has been slow to join the jet-set initially, mostly due to this countries 'sue happy' society and therefore complex regulations and insurance requirements. Australia and Asia have also embraced the turbine scene rapidly, and gas-turbines are now becoming extremely popular all over the world - especially at model shows where they are usually the biggest attraction.

In 1997 there is little doubt that the French JPX turbines are the most popular and numerous, mostly because they were first to be commercially available, but also due to their proven reliability and performance during the last 5 years. Nevertheless several other makes of turbine, most especially the Dutch AMT Pegasus, are now becoming a more common sight world-wide. All of the 5 present commercially produced units (described below) have proved sufficient integrity and reliability to be approved for use in North America by the AMA, which is quite a demanding test procedure. In the next couple of years you can expect to see a larger share of the market taken by the motors from Turbomin, GWM, AMT and Sophia Precision, and there is little doubt that other companies will also manufacture similar turbines shortly, especially as more suitable airframe kits become available.

One thing is certain - the sound and performance of a real turbine in a jet model represents the very pinnacle of R/C modelling, offering the ultimate realism for scale models, and there are a growing number of modellers who are prepared to pay the price to achieve this.

Thrust units
Commonly modellers talk about the thrust produced by turbine motors in either kilograms (kg) or pounds (lb), but this is actually incorrect as both of these are units of mass rather than force. Strictly speaking thrust is measured in Newtons (N), which approximate to a static thrust of 10 times kg, or 5 times lb (10 N = approx. 1 kg = approx. 2.2 lb). However I have mostly used more common terminology of kg here, as it can be more easily imagined by modellers.

Gas-Turbine or Turbo-Jet ?
There is some confusion about the correct term for the miniature turbine motors used in our models; Are they gas-turbines or turbo-jets? Well, although it is really of little importance, they are all gas-turbines, as they use a turbine to produce thrust and the working medium is air, albeit in a gaseous form. Note that the word 'gas' in the type of motor refers to the working medium, not the fuel type used. It is generally accepted that a gas-turbine becomes a turbo-jet when the useable energy in the exhaust gases from the turbine are concentrated using a convergent nozzle to harness some additional thrust, and this is the case in all the miniature turbines used in our models. However, in this book I have tended to use the word 'turbine' to save any confusion.

HISTORY

Way back in 1983 English modeller Gerry Jackman and his team made modelling history by being the first to design, build and successfully fly a miniature turbine in a radio-controlled jet model. This event took place on March 20th at RAF Greenham Common in southern England, witnessed by an astonished crowd, and was the catalyst for a whole new era of jet models. The specially designed model, named the 'Barjay', was of the pod fuselage and twin tailboom type (of similar style to a D.H. Vampire), which needed no exhaust ducting and obviated most of the problems of hot exhaust gases burning the stabilisers, and this airframe configuration has also been used more recently by many operators of Schreckling and other home-build type turbines. The turbine was a single shaft motor, with a home-made axial flow turbine wheel, annular combustion chamber and centrifugal compressor and was fuelled by propane. At 340 mm in length and 110 mm diameter it weighed about 1.8 kg (4 lb) and produced about 3.5 kg of thrust. In the following years many individuals and companies tried to emulate Gerry's achievement, even to the stage of advertising ready-to-fly turbines for sale in several model magazines but, to the best of my knowledge, none of these were produced

In 1983 this group of English modellers and engineers made history by being the first to build and fly a gas turbine powered radio-controlled model aircraft.

Seen in this photograph on the actual day of the event, with the Barjay, are the team that made it happen. (left to right) Barry Belcher, Ray Carter, Gerry Jackman, Chris White & David Sitch.

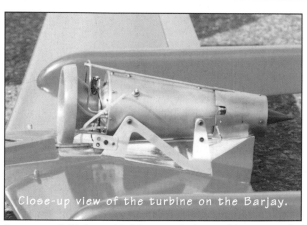

Close-up view of the turbine on the Barjay.

commercially, and very few of them were actually flown. Kavan in Germany, and both Seegers and Continental RPV in the USA all flew prototype miniature gas-turbine motors at least once (thrusts varying from 5 kg for the Seegers motor to approx. 22 kg for both others) during the late 1980's, but at the time there was insufficient interest for the investment required to undertake further development and commercial production.

Eventually in 1990, at the famous model show 'La Ferte Alais' in France, Michel Serrier thrilled the modelling scene by making several flights with his own-design turbine, named the 'Viscos', in a semi-scale Dassault Mirage model. An engineer by trade, and an enthusiastic modeller, Serrier had actually completed the design and working prototype in 1986, but it took four years to build the final motor. The turbine was similar to the Schreckling designs, using a centrifugal compressor wheel, a home-built axial flow turbine wheel, and was fuelled with liquid propane, producing about 40 Newtons (4 kg) thrust. The model turbine revolution started right there and then, with JPX, a high-tech company with aviation engineering skills and CNC equipment (they also produce pistons and other parts for Ferrari and Williams Renault Formula 1 racing cars) purchasing the rights to the motor immediately. Further development and testing continued rapidly and the production motors were released for sale in early 1992.

Roughly on a parallel time base a noted German modeller and engineer, Kurt Schreckling, was also working on a model-sized turbine design, and the first flights were made with his FD2 prototype installed in an own-design model called the 'Elkete' in Germany on 10th September 1989 - almost a full year before Serriers public demonstration of the 'Viscos'. The motor also used an axial flow turbine wheel design, but in this case it was fuelled by diesel with 10% unleaded petrol added to aid combustion, and produced only 2.1 kg of static thrust. However Schreckling's motor was strictly a home-build design and not originally intended for series manufacture, although it is now available in a much developed form in the guise of the Golden West Models FD3/67.

The complete story of Herr Schrecklings achievements, and the many developments of his design over the last few years are detailed in several books (available in both English and German languages), which are highly recommended reading for any budding jet pilot. Another young German engineer, Thomas Kamps, has also written a book in conjunction with Kurt, detailing his 'Microturbine' of similar design and this also contains a lot of interesting and useful information. More recently Schreckling has developed a new motor in collaboration with Spanish engineer, Jesús Artés, called the KJ66. This motor, although based on Schrecklings original design, features many new parts and a completely revised combustion chamber and produces more than 7 kg of static thrust from a motor which weighs only 900 grams - a tremendous feat! The major parts for home construction of this motor, together with building instructions and detailed drawings, are available from either Schreckling or Artés (see Appendix I). Since 1990 Schrecklings design has been the basis for most of the

Jacques Buchoux (left) and Michel Serrier, the designer of the original Viscos in 1990, which led to the JPX turbine we know today. An astonishing amount of development has been achieved in the last 7 years, and the turbine motors from the reputable companies are now reliable, powerful & safe.

Kurt Schreckling with his own design FD2 installed on the 'Elkete' model, after having made the first successful flights in September, 1989. A very clever engineer, who is continuing to achieve great improvements in turbine design today.

home-build turbines, as well as several commercially manufactured motors produced in the USA, UK, Germany and Scandinavia, and he is one of the most innovative and talented people in this field.

Anyway it was the derivative of Serriers 'Viscos' that went in to series production first, emerging as the famous JPX Turborec T-240. This started the rush to find suitable airframes, the most popular and successful choice being the Sagittario sport model produced by Zanin in Italy, originally designed for pulse-jet propulsion. Although the turbine was essentially hung on the underside of the fuselage, just behind the wing, the simple access and good cooling air flow gave instant success & many of these converted Sagittarios have been flown all around the world, making quite good turbine-trainers.

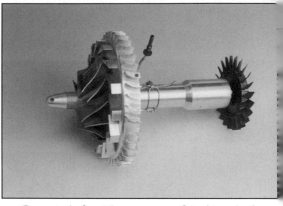

The mainshaft, with compressor & turbine wheels attached, of the latest Schreckling/Artes KJ66 motor, expected to be produced commercially soon. Astonishing performance from this very lightweight kerosene-fuelled axial flow turbine, which can be home-built using commercially produced main parts.

The reliability and performance of the JPX turbine also convinced several experienced European modellers to work on designs for improved airframes, and perhaps the best of these (and the first to go into production) was the 'StarJet', designed by German father and son team Harald and Harald Pigisch. This was a further development of the Sagittario, with an almost fully cowled-in turbine, but still no exhaust ducting - the jet nozzle exhausting directly to atmosphere. However with a more aerodynamic fuselage shape and better wing and tailplane design, this model was a vast improvement over the converted Sagittarios.

Further flying experience gained with the StarJet, and other similar types, demonstrated the necessity of efficient high-drag devices to allow landings at a higher idle rpm, which made 'go-arounds' possible without too much turbine-lag, and the addition of large flaps and crow-braking systems improved the 'flyability' of the model even further. At this stage the design and license to manufacture the StarJet were purchased by Eric Rantet of Aviation Design, in France, and since then it has become a legendary sport model, having won many performance awards world-wide, consistently achieving straight-and-level speeds of over 350 kph (220 mph).

The next step was to develop ducting systems that allowed a turbine to be fully enclosed inside a model, without overheating or thrust loss problems. Several ducted-fan companies, and a handful of individual modellers, worked on this problem for a couple of years before real success - and in 1995 we started to see some completely internal, and fully ducted, turbine installations which proved feasible and reliable. Currently there are about a dozen manufacturers that produce dedicated turbine versions of some of their original ducted-fan kits, as well as a new models specifically designed for turbine propulsion. In addition a few of these companies produce universal 'turbine conversion kits' consisting of full-flow ducting systems that can be used in other suitable airframes.

BASIC THEORY

The most common misconception is that turbine engines propel the aircraft by the force of the exhaust gases pushing against the air behind the jet nozzle. Actually the majority of the thrust is produced by the airplane's reaction to the ejected gases, as described by Isaac Newton's 3rd law of motion, which basically states that: "For every force acting on a body, there is an equal and opposite reaction". In the case of a gas-turbine the 'body' is the mass of air passing through the motor, which is accelerated. The 'reaction' to this acceleration is what provides the majority of the thrust attained, and not the exhausting of high velocity air out of the jet nozzle at the back of the motor, which only contributes a relatively small amount.

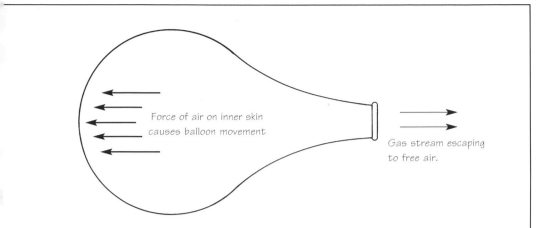

Force of air on inner skin
causes balloon movement

Gas stream escaping
to free air.

The 'reaction' is what provides the majority of the thrust attained, and *not* the exhausting of high velocity air out of the jet nozzle at the back of the motor.

Perhaps the simplest way to explain this is to imagine what is probably the most basic form of 'jet reaction'. Take a party balloon and inflate it to bursting point, and then let go - it accelerates out of our hands in the opposite direction to that of the stream of escaping air. The thrust making the balloon accelerate is not that caused by the jet of air escaping, it is mostly caused by the force exerted on the inner surface of the balloon opposite to the outlet.

The working cycle of a gas-turbine motor is similar in principle to that of a normal piston engine, ie: air is used as the working fluid (gas) which is induced into the engine, compressed to the required pressure, then fuel is added and ignited which heats and expands the air, and finally it is exhausted to the atmosphere. However in a turbine the process is continuous, rather than in cycles, and hence far more powerful than a reciprocating piston engine.

In the miniature turbine engines used for our models the actual process happens like this: Air is ingested by the spinning compressor wheel (impeller) at the front of the motor, and accelerated. The accelerated air is forced past stator blades into a diffuser of divergent channels, which convert the increased velocity

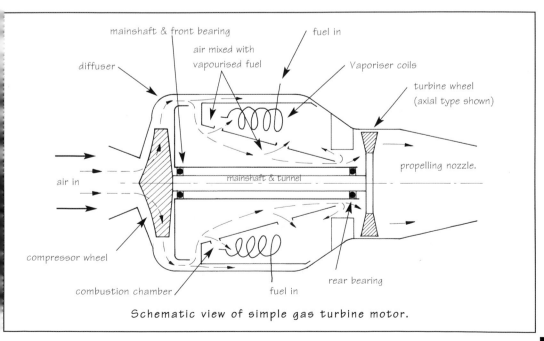

mainshaft & front bearing

air mixed with
vapourised fuel

fuel in

diffuser

Vaporiser coils

turbine wheel
(axial type shown)

air in

mainshaft & tunnel

propelling nozzle.

compressor wheel

combustion chamber

fuel in

rear bearing

Schematic view of simple gas turbine motor.

into increased pressure. It then passes into the combustion chamber where it is mixed with the fuel and ignited, causing a rapid expansion of the air and it's subsequent rearwards acceleration. Before escaping to the atmosphere through the jet nozzle at the back of the motor this hot, high velocity gas flow is directed through a turbine wheel (another impeller), causing it to rotate at high revolutions. As the turbine wheel is connected to the compressor wheel on a single shaft it, in turn, spins the compressor ingesting more air.... and so the cycle is repeated again & again.

All present model turbines are of the single shaft type, with the turbine wheel on the back of the shaft, and the single

Main internal parts of a typical model gas turbine, in this case the axial flow AMT Pegasus. (left > right) Compressor, diffuser stage with shaft tunnel, precision ground mainshaft, and turbine wheel. Also shown are the front & rear bearings which are of the ceramic hybrid type in most model turbines.

centrifugal compressor at the front (inlet) end. The single compressor system, of necessity due to the small size of the motors, limits the pressure ratio to a certain extent, and most model turbines have a pressure ratio of between 2 or 3 to 1. This means that they compress the air sucked into the turbine by 2 or 3 times it's natural atmospheric pressure (of 1 bar) to 2 or 3 bars pressure. Full-size turbines have much higher pressure ratios (often in the region of 25:1) because they use multi-stage axial compressors, and this results in their increased efficiency and performance.

Axial or Radial Turbines

There are two distinct types of model turbine design, separated by the type of turbine wheel used, either the 'Axial' or 'Radial Inflow', and the diagram below should make the major differences clear. Axial turbine wheels are simpler to design and manufacture than radial inflow types, but there are lots of commercially available radial wheels (for vehicle turbochargers) of a suitable size, which is the main reason why many manufacturers incorporate these to reduce design and production costs. Axial turbines have some advantages over radial types, perhaps the most conspicuous being that they have substantially

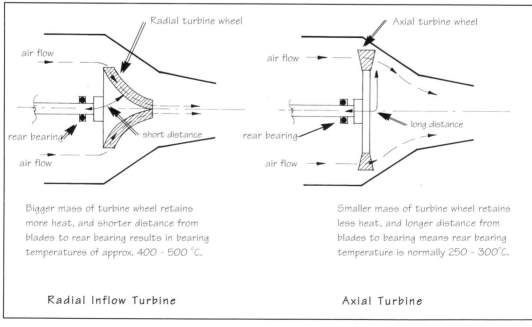

Bigger mass of turbine wheel retains more heat, and shorter distance from blades to rear bearing results in bearing temperatures of approx. 400 - 500 °C.

Smaller mass of turbine wheel retains less heat, and longer distance from blades to bearing means rear bearing temperature is normally 250 - 300°C.

Radial Inflow Turbine

Axial Turbine

less mass, usually around 60% for the same diameter. This means that there is less inertia, and therefore faster acceleration and deceleration times. Also due to this lower mass they don't retain as much heat as the radial type which means that less heat is transferred to the rear bearing, especially just after shut-down, which consequently increases bearing life or allows a less complex material to be used. However at the relatively low temperatures and pressure ratios in our miniature turbines there is very little notice-able performance or maintenance difference between radial and axial turbines, except for the acceleration & de-celleration times.

FUEL SYSTEMS

The majority of 'model-sized' turbines are liquid fuelled by kerosene, paraffin, Jet-A1 or similar, just as per full-size turbines. Many of them use gas from a small canister of liquid propane to pre-heat the com-bustion chamber for the initial start-up as it is easier to ignite than kerosene, which then allows the combustion chamber to quickly reach sufficient temperature to burn the kerosene fuel. When the turbine has reached self-sustaining temperature and idle rpm, the fuel supply is switched over from the external gas supply to the liquid fuel in the internal tanks. A couple of the commercial manufacturers (Turbomin and JPX) have recently succeeded in enabling their motors to start directly on liquid fuel, using high pressure pumps and microscopically small fuel nozzles in the combustion chamber to vaporise it effi-ciently so that it will ignite, and these are currently going through final development stages. You can

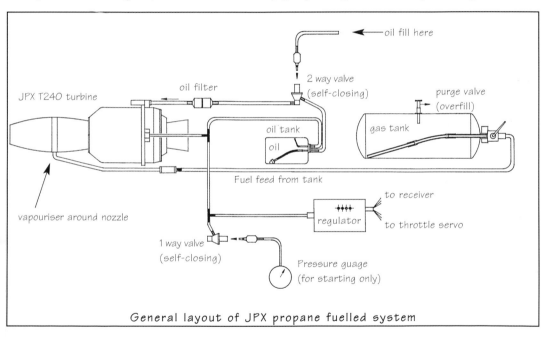

General layout of JPX propane fuelled system

expect that more of the liquid fuelled turbines will follow this arrangement in the near future, reducing the amount of ground-support equipment required.

The most notable exception to the liquid fuelled turbines are the current range of JPX motors which are all started and run on propane gas, which is contained in a specially manufactured stainless steel tank in the aircraft. The tank is filled with propane in a liquid state from a larger bottle, such as those used for fork-lifts and domestic gas heaters, and this gives enough pressure in the tank to provide a constant sup-ply of fuel to the motor, by which time it has vaporised, and enters the combustion chamber as a gas. The pressurised tank system is extremely reliable, clean and safe, but has a slight drawback in that the single tanks are quite large which can limit their location in some models - often meaning that they are some distance away from the Centre of Gravity location, giving trim changes during flight as fuel is consumed. However the latest motor from JPX, expected in mid-1997, runs on kerosene which precludes this inconvenience.

Conversely liquid-fuelled turbines use an electronic pump to supply fuel to the motor - the combined weight of the plastic fuel tanks, pump and its nicad pack usually being a little more than the weight of a metal propane tank of capacity for equivalent flight duration (typically 1.5 - 2 litres for 7 minutes). These fuel pumps need to be specially designed for this application, and these have sometimes proved to be a weak link in the overall propulsion system of some turbines. They must be capable of providing reliable and continuous high pressure, with linear flow control between idle and full power, and yet be lightweight and operate from the limited capacity of an on-board nicad. Most of the major turbine manufacturers have been using their own pumps, but I understand that a couple of them are now using the new fuel pump from Rhom-Air because of its fine performance. This high precision unit was especially developed for liquid fuel turbines, operates of 6 volts, meets all the necessary criteria, and is very efficient due to the computer generated port design and teflon lip seals. It should also be very suitable for use with most of the home-built turbine designs.

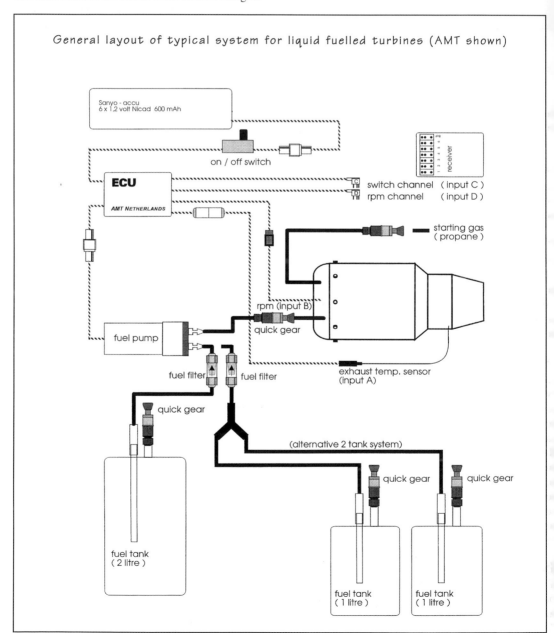

General layout of typical system for liquid fuelled turbines (AMT shown)

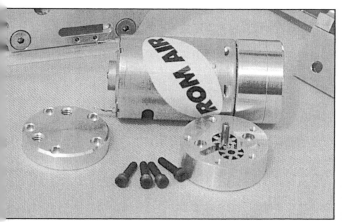

The fuel pump from Rhom Air, designed for liquid fuelled turbines, is a high precision unit of light weight & high performance. It features graphite impregnated teflon lip seals, diamond lapped gears, & computer generated design for high efficiency.

An advantage of liquid fuelled motors is that they can use multiple fuel tanks which can make installation simpler, especially in scale models, often allowing location closer to the Centre of Gravity. Some turbine manufacturers recommend the use of flexible plastic plasma bags (used in hospitals) as fuel tanks which permit them to be fitted into complex shaped areas, such as in wing roots or between inlet ducts. The plastic fuel tanks normally used in ducted-fan models are resistant against kerosene, paraffin and Jet A1 type fuels, and most of these can be used. However, depending on which fuel is being used, the tank stoppers and all of the fuel supply tubing must be made of the correct material so that it is not degraded or dissolved by the fuel, and this is usually supplied by the turbine manufacturer. The normal silicone fuel tubing used for i.c. motors is not suitable for either kerosene or propane fuelled motors.

For both propane & liquid fuelled motors it is extremely important that the fuel is clean, & free from grit and other particles, & therefore it should be filtered before filling the tanks. If using tanks for liquid fuel which have no air return/vent line, such as plasma bags, then it is also imperative to exclude all air bubbles from the fuel system, which is easily done during filling.

The actual location of the fuel tanks is relatively unimportant for reliable operation, and both propane and liquid fuelled types are capable of handling fuel supply tube lengths of about 600 mm with ease. However the level of the oil tanks in both types of motor, and the fuel tanks in the case of liquid fuelled motors only, relative to the turbine centreline level should be taken into consideration to prevent siphoning into the motor when it is not running, as both are a cause of 'wet starts'. If the tanks are higher than the motor and this becomes a problem, then a manually controlled valve can be installed in the feed tubes.

Propane v liquid fuels

The debate over whether propane or liquid fuelled miniature gas-turbines are better or safer is one which will probably never end. Personally I think that there is little difference; propane is more flammable and needs a little more care when transporting it in a vehicle, and in the pit area when a no-smoking policy must be adopted. Kerosene, and most similar liquid fuels, are slightly more difficult to ignite accidentally and easier to transport, but any leaks make the airframe smelly - especially in a vehicle on a hot day! During flight there is no difference, but in the event of a crash the propane is contained in a strong pressure vessel which is less likely to be punctured, although if it is the gas burns quickly in a fairly brief burst of flame. On the other hand the plastic tanks used for liquid fuels are more likely to be ruptured, and the kerosene will burn - with less intensity, but for longer, if it comes into contact with hot turbine parts etc. Therefore both fuel types have their advantages and disadvantages, and it should be left up to the modellers personal choice which type of fuel, and therefore motor, to use - rather than by official regulations.

INSTALLATION

The installation of turbine motors requires several extra criteria to be taken into consideration, compared to ducted-fan propulsion. The most obvious of these is the higher temperatures produced by the motor, which can affect the integrity of the model, as well as being a possible source of ignition and fire. Also bear in mind the much increased velocities of the inlet and exhaust air in the ducting, as well as the considerably higher flight speeds achievable, which require additional structural integrity of the airframe and its flight controls. It is not simply a matter of taking out your ducted-fan system and dropping in a turbine - a procedure that could be dangerous if carried out by an inexperienced modeller. Nevertheless it is possible to adapt many of the existing ducted-fan airframes for turbine propulsion and there have been some very successful conversions during the first few years of turbine modelling.

Ducting

The most demanding part of the progress in the last couple of years has been the design of the ductwork for fully enclosed turbine installations, using a continuous duct from the inlet, around the turbine, and to the exhaust outlet at the rear of the model. This system gives the highest efficiency and thrust. However, not all turbine models need fully ducted systems, many proving quite powerful enough with separate inlet and exhaust ducts, and the motor simply mounted in between them. For instance the range of turbine kits from Aviation Design follows this principle, it's owner Eric Rantet believing that simplicity and easier access for maintenance is more important than extracting the last few percent of performance. The Golden West Models FD3/67 turbines are also commonly used without being fully ducted, sometimes without any inlet duct at all, and generally turbine performance is not reduced a great deal by turbulent air ingested into the compressor.

The suction in front of a turbine is higher than any ducted-fan unit, especially in the case of fully ducted installations, and therefore the inlet ducts must be more rigid so that they cannot collapse. Inlet ducts, if thin fibreglass, are normally strengthened by adding hoops of carbon-fibre or heavyweight glasscloth tape. Current sizes of model turbines require far less air inlet area than 5" diameter fan units, typically only about one third of the area, and therefore in most cases the inlets can be quite small, rather than slightly enlarged as in many scale D/F models. As rule of thumb the total cross-sectional inlet area should be at least twice that of the turbine's compressor intake, but always follow the manufacturers guidelines.

BVM has a generic gas turbine conversion package, suited to the JPX range, for retrofitting to other kits, which is similar to that provided for their own F-80 & T-33. It is complete with their 'Bypass' ducting, motor mounts, exhaust duct with heat shield, & very comprehensive instruction manual.

Then consideration needs to be given to the motor itself. Not only does it require sufficient air to supply the compressor without it stalling, but some air must also be passed around the turbine to cool it, and the exhaust ducting. For the simpler systems, not using a fully ducted installation, there is normally enough excess air from the inlets to be sucked past the motor and into the exhaust duct for cooling. In the case of fully ducted systems this is an exacting science, the amount of air required depending on the particular turbine type, and most of the major manufacturers have employed aeronautical engineers to design efficient 'bypass' systems. All of these bleed a proportion of the inlet air around the turbine, the ductwork expanding in a bulbous shape to allow this, and then reducing in size again behind the jet nozzle. Several of these companies not only manufacture complete ductwork systems for their own range of kits, but also 'generic' full ducting systems for installation into other jet models. Of the ones that I am aware of the systems from Bob Violett Models (BVM 'Bypass' duct), Westbury Products ('Free-Flow' duct) and Philip Avonds Scale Jets ('Full Flow' duct), have all proved to work extremely well and are recommended for converting a ducted-fan airframe to turbine power.

Access to the turbine in fully ducted installations is slightly less easy than in the simpler systems, but all of the three types mentioned above use a horizontally split bulbous duct around the motor. This allows the top half to be removed quickly for maintenance and examination - a bit similar to the engine

Philip Avonds Scale jets have developed special bifurcated jet nozzles (below) that fits directly to JPX turbines, for use in twin outlet models, such as their own F-15 Eagle (seen right) and Rafale.

After over a year of flight testing it is now fully proven, and does not invalidate the JPX warranty. Notice the short stainless steel tailpipes set into the rear of the F-15 to protect the fuselage from heat behind the jet nozzle outlets.

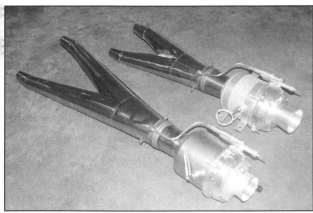

cover cap in a tractor type ducted-fan model.

The exhaust duct is the most technically challenging part of the system, particularly in a fully ducted installation. It must withstand not only the heat produced by the turbine, (approx. 350°C behind the jet nozzle), but also the high velocity and pressure of the exhaust flow, and protect the surrounding airframe and flight controls from the heat. These ducts are usually formed from .010 inch (0.2 - 0.25 mm) stainless steel sheet, or occasionally .004" titanium sheet for lightness, spot welded into a tubular shape, and sometimes use additional heat shield insulation on the outside of the duct made from ceramic felt or similar material. It is very important that the exhaust duct is centred on the turbine's jet nozzle, and held rigidly in position. Failing this there will be temperature differentials in the duct, and also caused in the turbine itself which could damage it, as well as resulting in substantial thrust loss.

The actual design of the exhaust duct is complex, and much trial and error is usually required to ensure that no loss of thrust occurs - and with clever design it is actually possible to enhance the thrust levels in some instances. The diameter of each end of the exhaust duct is dependant on several things; most importantly the particular turbine used and the total length of the duct, but also governed at the outlet by the diameter of the fuselage itself. The design formula used for the exact determination of the most effi-

A view of the BVM ducting system, fully assembled, showing the heat shielding around the exhaust duct and the quick-remove cap cap that allows very fast access to the turbine.

cient duct dimensions are fairly complex, and sometimes closely guarded secrets, but most of the commercial turbine manufacturers should be able to advise you on the requirements for their motors, and in many cases guidelines dimensions are included in owners manuals.

The most recent innovation is the bifurcated exhaust ducting, developed by Philip Avonds, which allows a single turbine to exhaust through twin outlet nozzles. It was designed specifically to suit his F15 and Rafale models, taking more than a year of work to ensure that no overheating of the turbine or ducting occurred. The final design is extremely effective, with no loss of thrust, and has been fully approved by the JPX factory who confirm that the use of these ducts from Philip Avonds will not affect their normal Warranty. No doubt other turbine manufacturers will follow this ground-breaking development in the near future.

Turbine Mounting

Turbine motors get hot during operation, and therefore need to be mounted in the model using a heat-resistant system. This normally consists of a pair of steel rings that fit tightly around the outer casing of the motor, at the front and back, which are then bolted to a pair of horizontal bearers or brackets in the fuselage, one on either side of the motor. Ensure that heat transferred from the motor through the mounting system cannot soften fibreglass, or burn wooden parts, of the airframe. The GWM turbine, and some other Schreckling based derivatives, can also be mounted directly into a suitable aperture cut in a vertical bulkhead, using the attachment studs on the front casing.

Most turbines are mounted in the model using a pair of split hoops that clamp around the main motor casing. These are then bolted to metal bearers installed in the airframe, which project through the side of the ducting around the motor.
Shown is the new AMT Olympus turbine which has 17 kg thrust.

Pay attention to the ease of access for starting and operation; allowing for fuel filling, compressed air connectors for starting, external gas supply for ignition if necessary, pressure gauge, ignition system connections, and any external testing and calibration equipment. Where the turbine is installed in close proximity to the airframe, and not enclosed in a fully ducted system, it is may also be necessary to protect the fuselage from the heat. Self-adhesive reflective aluminium foil is commonly used for this, and is sufficient in most cases.

OPERATION

To start all turbines it is only necessary to rotate the compressor wheel, and hence the turbine wheel, at a high enough RPM to compress the fuel/air mixture, and with a hot enough combustion chamber for the fuel to vaporise and ignite. Four of the commercially produced motors use a stream of compressed air (from a Scuba tank) directed onto the compressor blades to attain the minimum required rpm for starting. The exception is the GWM FD3/67 motor, and most of the smaller kit motors and home-builds, which use a modified 12 volt hair-dryer to give enough air flow over the compressor wheel.

Once the minimum rpm is achieved then fuel, either gas or liquid, is fed into the combustion chamber and ignited. Ignition is normally by either a piezo electronic spark generator (as used in many cigarette ighters), or a normal model engine glow-plug which has had its platinum wire element pulled out of the body of the plug a little to ensure good ignition. The fuel/air mixture ignites and expands rearwards through the blades of the turbine wheel, turning it and therefore the compressor wheel - which in turn sucks in more air to mix with the fuel to continue the cycle.

Lubrication

Internal lubrication is required both to lubricate and cool the bearings that the main shaft runs in during operation, and also to protect the internal parts of the motor from corrosion when it is not being used.

There are 2 methods used to provide this. The most common is the 'Total Loss' system, consisting of a small separate oil tank in the model, which normally feeds oil into the motor using the pressure differentials in the turbine to supply a little positive pressure to the tank - just like in a ducted-fan fuel system. In most cases the oil is supplied through a separate small tube either directly onto the bearings, or into the tunnel that houses the shaft and bearings. Any excess oil is burned during the combustion process, and a few manufacturers recommend that after use a small amount of oil is injected into the motor to prevent corrosion during storage.

The second method is to mix a small percentage of oil with the fuel itself, usually about 5% by volume. A small amount of this fuel/oil mixture is supplied through a separate tube directly to the bearings, and the oil in remainder of the fuel mixture vaporises in the combustion chamber, and leaves sufficient residue after shut-down to protect the internal parts until the next start-up sequence. This method may offer a very slight advantage in that it prevents damage in the case of forgetting to refill the oil tank between flights, and also generally requires no additional lubrication to protect the internal parts from corrosion during storage.

The oil that must be used is specified by the turbine manufacturer, normally a type designed especially for gas-turbines, for example Aeroshell 500 or Exxon 2380. It is fair to say most turbine damage and failures are caused by insufficient lubrication, and a careful eye should be kept on the oil system, and the amount consumed during each flight, for any indication of leaks or blockages.

Wet-starts

One of the things to avoid when starting a turbine is the 'wet-start'. This is caused by excess fuel or oil being in the combustion chamber when ignition is achieved - and it causes a spectacular, but short-lived, flame from the jet nozzle. It can, of course, be dangerous, but need never happen if manufacturers instructions are followed every time. In most cases the prevention of this only requires blasting a short burst of compressed air through the turbine before starting, and ensuring that no fuel or oil can siphon into the motor from the tanks when the model is stationary after filling.

In the case of a wet-start, the fuel supply should be shut off immediately, and the compressed air left on for a few seconds to clear any remaining fuel or oil, and cool the turbine. Of course wet-starts can over-heat the exhaust duct and damage the surrounding airframe, and these must be thoroughly checked for structural integrity before any attempt is made to restart the motor or fly the model. Happily this phenomenon is now a rare occurrence, but still one which should be guarded against - especially in ensuring that no persons are positioned directly behind the jet efflux during starting procedures, and ensuring that a fire extinguisher and operator are close by.

ECU's

All of commercially produced model turbines (except JPX T240, T250 and T260P motors), and most kits and home-builds, use an electronic control unit (ECU) to prevent over-speeding of the motor, and this is usually contained in a small box about the size of a standard receiver. The ECU normally works by restricting the amount of fuel supplied to the motor to pre-set levels, based on the data which is constantly monitored by RPM and EGT (Exhaust Gas Temperature) sensors on the turbine. However most of the latest ECU's are much more complex than this, including additional software that provides 'assisted' or fully automated start-up and shutdown procedures, as well as restricting the speed at which the throttle can be opened or closed. This is necessary to prevent too much, or too little, fuel in the turbine during throttling up or down, which could cause compressor stalling or surging, and therefore overheating. The JPX motors mentioned above use a mechanical gas pressure valve combined with a throttle speed regulator to govern the motor.

There are also some add-on electronic units available which give additional safety features and enhance the capabilities of the standard turbine control systems, and the vast majority of these are designed for the propane fuelled JPX motors which use a mechanical regulator rather than an ECU. Mini-Hobby in Florida manufacture the 'Jet Guard' unit, marketed by Bob Violett Models, which includes a programmable throttle servo controller, a fire detection loop and 'Airframe over-temperature sensor' which can be installed by the motor and adjacent to the rear of the exhaust duct, and an 'engine failure sensor' which immediately closes the fuel valve if the engine should stop during flight to prevent a fire. Philip Avonds Scale Jets market three units; an 'Electronic Emergency Shut-off Device' (EESD) which closes the gas valve if the pressure drops below a pre-set level, an 'Electronic Immediate Shutdown' (EIS) which is installed in conjunction with the EESD to fully close the throttle servo automatically, and an Electronic Idle Regulator (EIR). Jet-

This is the Philip Avonds EESD unit.

Tech, from Switzerland, manufacture a 'Druckshalter' device which is similar to the Philip Avonds EIR, and which automatically detects the pressure at idle and constantly adjusts the throttle servo to set the minimum safe rpm.

Some turbine manufacturers also offer small external plug-in modules which display vital engine data on l.e.d screens during start-up and these are becoming more common. To my knowledge only AMT and GWM offer these at the moment, but there are several more being developed.

Note: Just using a simple 'servo-slow' unit to control the throttling speed of any turbine is NOT a safe method, and operators should never be tempted to use this rather than the manufacturers calibrated ECU, or other pre-set regulator system.

AMT's 'Engine Data Terminal' which is plugged into the ECU during start-up, & displays the following data in real-time mode: Current EGT & RPM, posn.of throttle channel, ECU status, and error codes. it will also show the software version of both the ECU and EDT, as well as the current status of the nicads.

COMMERCIAL TURBINES

Since the early 90's there have been many companies that have promised the release of miniature gas-turbines, many of these pledging extremely low prices - but few have actually materialised! At the time of publication there are really only five companies that manufacture turbines on a proper commercial basis, these being JPX, AMT, Turbomin, Sophia Precision & Golden-West Models. All these companies have detailed brochures on their motors, explaining the specific properties and functions, and giving more information than it is possible to include here. Each turbine supplied normally includes everything needed to install and operate the motor; usually comprising a pre-run and tested turbine, fuel and oil tanks, ECU, RPM & EGT sensors, comprehensive owners manual, all necessary tubing and connectors, mounting brackets, and sometimes the Nicad packs for the ECU and pumps. Below is a list of the main technical data of these motors, and a brief overview of each turbine.

Turbine	Date released	Fuel	Pressure ratio	Max. thrust	Max. rpm	Unit weight	Length x Diameter
JPX T-240	1992	propane	2.15:1	45 N	122,000	1.7 kg	295 x 116mm
JPX T-250P	1995	propane	2.15:1	55N	120,000	1.6 kg	295 x 116mm
JPX T-260P	1996	propane	2.15:1	60 N	120,000	1.8 kg	290 x 116mm
JPX T-260HP/K	1997	liquid	2.15:1	60+ N	120,000	1.2 kg	290 x 116mm
AMT Pegasus Mk.3	1995	liquid	3:1	100 N	105,000	2.1 kg	270 x 120mm
AMT Olympus	1997	liquid	4:1	170 N	105,000	2.4 kg	270 x 130mm
Turbomin T-60	1997	liquid	2.1:1	75 N	100,000	2.4 kg	365 x 136mm
Turbomin T-100	1996	liquid	2.4:1	100 N	105,000	3.0 kg	415 x 148mm
Sophia Precision J-450	1996	liquid	2.3:1	60 N	125,000	1.7 kg	335 x 120mm
Golden West FD3/67	1996	liquid	1.5:1	40 N	90,000	0.9 kg	220 x 110mm

JPX PROPULSEURS (FRANCE)

All JPX turbines utilise a single stage centrifugal compressor and a radial inflow turbine, these being modified from a standard vehicle turbocharger part in the T240 and T250 motors, but specially designed and cast parts for both the T260 units. The external dimensions of all versions are very similar, making it easy to upgrade the performance in any model by swapping motors. The T240, T250 and T260P turbines are fuelled by propane, and therefore no separate external gas supply is required for starting. The propane is stored in the model in specially manufactured stainless steel fuel tanks, of which several different sizes (1.25 - 4 litres) and shapes are available to give flight times of between 7 - 10 minutes. The propane fuelled motors do not need an ECU, instead they use a mechanical regulator valve to supply propane to the motor at a constant pressure, and JPX's own servo-slow system to control the acceleration and deceleration times. A 'total loss' lubrication system is used in these 3 motors, with a separate oil tank, the special turbine oil lubricating both the front and rear ceramic bearings, and the waste being exhausted to atmosphere. Starting of all JPX motors is achieved using compressed air from a 'Scuba' tank, and ignition is by their own piezo electronic spark generator to a sparkplug in the combustion chamber.

The latest JPX T-260HP/K, released in June 1997, is started using a small external canister of propane/butane gas, like several other commercial turbines, and is then switched over to run on liquid fuels (kerosene, Jet A1 etc.) which can be contained in single or multiple plastic fuel tanks. The turbine uses a specially developed electronic pump to supply fuel at the correct pressure and volume, and it is regulated by an Electronic Control Unit, which also has an optional fully automatic starting system. Lubrication is achieved by a small percentage of turbine oil mixed in with the liquid fuel, directed to the bearings, which also vaporises in the combustion chamber and protects the motor during storage.

JPX have also been working on a larger kerosene fuelled 90+ N thrust motor, designated the T-280K, for several years but it is unknown when this will become available. There is an extensive world-wide dealer network, and the majority of the current turbine kits are suitable this range of motors. The JPX turbines are simple to use, and have proved extremely reliable - with many thousands of successful flights since 1992 all over the globe.

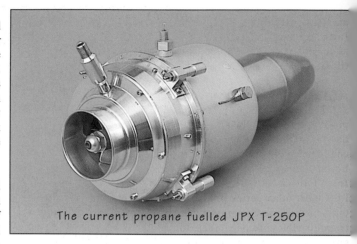
The current propane fuelled JPX T-250P

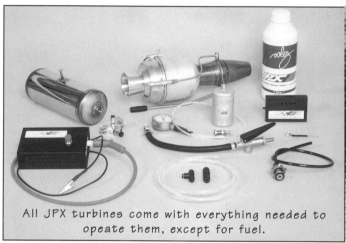
All JPX turbines come with everything needed to opeate them, except for fuel.

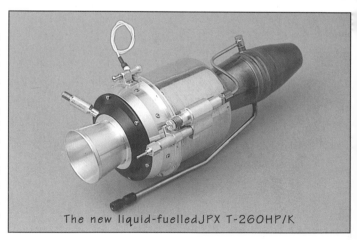
The new liquid-fuelledJPX T-260HP/K

AMT NETHERLANDS (HOLLAND)

Advanced Micro Turbines were the second company to offer a commercially manufactured gas-turbine motor that was specifically designed and manufactured for model aircraft. The mainstay of their program is the Pegasus Mk.3 (100 N) which has been available since 1995, and they also released a larger motor in early 1997 for experienced customers and special applications, named the Olympus, with a rating of 170 N (approx. 36 lb). Both motors have centrifugal compressors, annular combustion chambers and axial flow turbine wheels - the latter giving extremely fast acceleration and deceleration times.

AMT turbines are started using a small external canister of propane which is shut off once the motor reaches minimum rpm and temperature, and then run on liquid fuel (kerosene, Paraffin, Jet A1 or even White Spirit). Like most other series produced turbines they use compressed air, from a scuba tank or similar, to spin the motor for starting. Ignition is by a normal model glowplug, installed in the primary zone of the combustion chamber. No separate oil tank is needed as lubrication is handled by the fuel, which is pre-mixed

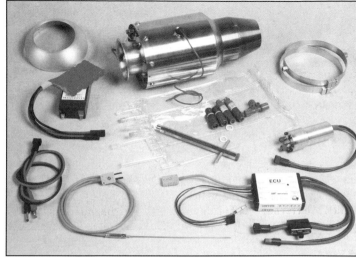

Both the AMT Pegasus & Olympus motors come as a complete package, with everything required for installation & operation of the motor, and an extremely detailed instruction manual, which includes guidelines for designing & making exhaust ducting, and its installation.

with a 5% of Aeroshell 500 turbine oil. Notably the AMT turbines run at a higher pressure ratio than others, due to the very efficient diffuser stage. Fuel is delivered by a specially designed electric pump, which is powered by the same Nicad pack as the Electronic Control Unit. The ECU is a particularly good module, based on a microprocessor chip and using surface-mount technology. It not only regulates the motor and calibrates the idle constantly, using data received from the EGT and RPM sensors in the motor, but also offers fully automated start-up, shut-down and emergency stop programs to facilitate safe turbine operation.

Various optional equipment has been developed, including a 'telemetry' software option to allow real-time visual display of data (incl. RPM, EGT, throttle posn., ECU status & error codes) on a PC computer screen. An inexpensive 'Engine Data Terminal' is also available which provides the same data on a small LCD display. There are an increasing number of dealers and service agents throughout the world, and the Pegasus is becoming very popular.

A view of the AMT Pegasus Mk.3 turbine, with main outer case removed, showing the compressor and diffucser stage, and the combustion chamber. The small wire at the front is the cable for the rpm sensor, which is installed in the inlet bellmouth during manufacture.

Here you can see the precision CNC engineering required to manufacture these micro turbines.

Mike's JET BOOK

TURBOMIN (SWEDEN/USA)

Turbomin produce two motors, the T100A rated at 100 N, and the smaller T60A, with 75 Newtons thrust. Both motors are of similar design, consisting of a centrifugal compressor, annular reversed flow combustion chamber and radial inflow turbine wheel. The reverse flow combustor allows a very short mainshaft to be used, reducing both the loads on it and the temperature at the rear bearing. The fuel used is kerosene (or Jet A, Jet A-1, diesel) and Turbomin motors both start and run directly on the liquid fuel, no external gas supply being necessary, however for starting the fuel is supplied to the motor at a higher pressure than normal to ensure efficient vaporisation. A specially developed high pressure fuel pump feeds fuel from the plastic or plasma bag tanks to the motor, and this is powered by a Nicad battery.

Starting uses a compressed air supply, from a scuba tank or similar, and ignition is by a piezo spark plug in the combustion chamber. A separate tank is used for the total loss lubrication system, utilising the pressure differential between the compressor and bearing housing to pressurise the tank via a small bleed nipple. The ECU monitors compressor pressure, P2, EGT and RPM and regulates the voltage to the fuel pump based on this data, also controlling the acceleration and deceleration rates. The motors come complete with an external Start-Box unit, which automates start-up procedure, and also includes displays for monitoring EGT and pressure data.

Although these motors have only become readily available quite recently, they are based on a training motor manufactured by Turbomin since the 1980's for use in universities and similar educational institutions, and the company has a great deal of experience and expertise in this field.

The Turbomin T60 (left) and T100 motors, which both are started & run on liquid fuel (kerosene, Jet A1 etc), but use a separate oil tank and total-loss lubrication system. Fully revised turbines are expected in 1998.

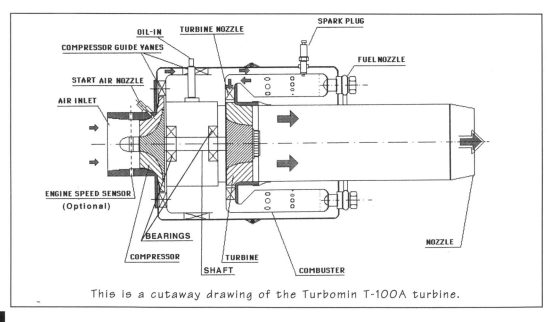

This is a cutaway drawing of the Turbomin T-100A turbine.

GOLDEN WEST MODELS (USA)

The FD3/67 LS is a licensed derivative of the original Schreckling FD3 design, now further developed and manufactured in the USA by Golden West Models LLC. It is by far the smallest and lightest of the commercial motors available, at only 900 grams, but still gives plenty of thrust for 5 - 6.5 kg models, and is most commonly used in conversions of existing ducted-fan kits. It uses a radial compressor, axial turbine wheel, and an annular combustion chamber and vaporiser coil. It is not necessary to use compressed air for starting, a simple 12 volt blower or modified hair-dryer being sufficient. A small external canister of propane, or propane/butane mix, is used for the starting sequence only, and the turbine then runs on liquid fuel consisting of Kerosene with 15% gasoline to improve combustion. Ignition is by normal model glowplug, with the coil pulled out of the body a little, and lubrication is by an 'oil mist' (total loss) system using a separate small tank which is lightly pressurised from a nipple on the motor.

As in all of the other turbines mentioned here, the ECU for the FD3/67 monitors both EGT and RPM, thereby regulating the fuel flow to the motor, as well as limiting the speed at which the throttle can be opened and closed. It features a simple system of multiple coloured l.e.d's to give visual display of the turbine status, and offers assisted start-up and shut-down sequences. An optional RS232 interface allows downloading of data to a personal computer, and the optional GSU (Ground Support Unit) is a hand held terminal that provides the operator with a visual readout of turbine's status, using 5 l.e.d's and a three line LCD display.

With it's very lightweight design, and simple installation, this motor is becoming quite popular for conversion of the smaller ducted-fan airframes.

A GWM FD3/67 turbine installed in a much modified JHH Cougar kit, which flies extremely well. You can see the single fuel tank, fuel pump (left), ECU & propane to kerosene changeover valve, & oil tank (back/right). They have also been flown in several 1/10th scale Yellow Aircraft F/A-18 Hornets, and a pair fitted in a Philip Avonds F-15, which give it a very convincing flight performance.

The GWM turbine comes complete with all items needed to install & run it, even including the hairdryer, together with a very comprehensive instruction manual and video.

SOPHIA PRECISION (JAPAN & USA)

The J-450 was originally a development of the JPX design, modified to run on liquid fuel which was stored in a metal fuel tank, pressurised by a small CO2 cartridge. The turbine has a single stage centrifugal compressor and a radial inflow turbine and starts and runs directly on liquid fuel (white gasoline), no separate external gas supply being required.

In 1996 a complete redesign of the fuel system took place and all production motors now use an electric pump to supply the fuel, and therefore normal plastic fuel tanks, or plasma bags. The 'total loss' lubrication system is taken care of with a separate tank, using a separate electric pump to supply the required amount of oil, and this also primes the ceramic bearings before each start-up. Compressed air from a Scuba tank is used for starting and ignition is by a modified model glowplug, located in the combustion chamber. The ECU supplied not only regulates the motor using data from it's RPM and EGT sensors, but also offers semi-automated start-up and shut-down sequences. It also has facilities for storing data from the last 30 minutes of running for retrieval through it's RS232 interface, and an external Status Display Board featuring 3 l.e.d's for engine status. A GSU (Ground Support Unit) is available as an optional extra, this small unit being plugged into a socket in the model, and giving readouts of various data (RPM, EGT, pump voltages etc.) on a two line LCD display in real-time mode.

Although the J-450 is one of the most recently introduced turbines, there are already several national dealers and service agents, and the motor is just starting to be seen at a few jet events - especially in Europe and the Far East.

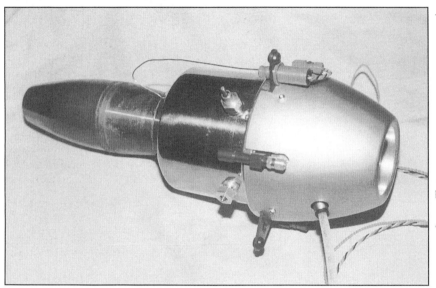

The Sophia Precision J-450 turbine was based on the original JPX T-240 design, but has undergone many changes & much development since 1995. It uses separate electric pumps for both the fuel & oil supplies, & a new ECU was released in 1997, which is designed to improve starting sequences & provide better engine control.

Note: In addition to the companies above, all of whose motors are now well proven, Thunder-Tiger (Taiwan) have shown prototypes of their P-15 turbine for future release, and Sim-Jet (Denmark) have produced a handful of motors (one competed in the '95 Jet World Masters), although little is know about their current.

Home-Builds and Kits

As well as the commercially produced turbines above there are a few smaller companies and individuals who produce kits or semi-kits of the main parts, and in a few cases complete motors, in very limited quantities. The vast majority of these are further developments of the original Schreckling design, and many are flown successfully - albeit on an occasional basis. However, in almost all cases they are a bit more difficult to operate, require greater understanding of turbine operation, and are somewhat less reliable than the commercial motors. This is not to say that you should dismiss them, just that they are more for modellers interested in turbine motors themselves - rather than jet pilots who wish to fly a model powered by a turbine, and are hence beyond the scope of this book. Advertisements from many of these companies can be found in current issues of many modelling magazines, in particular 'R/C Jet International', and several are also listed in the Appendix at the back of this book.

Those of you that are interested in building your own turbines would be well advised to read the books of Thomas Kamps and Kurt Schreckling, available in German and English languages, and also to contact the GTBA (Gas Turbine Builders Association), which is a mine of useful information and has members all over the world. Another book worth obtaining is 'The Jet Engine', published by Rolls Royce (ISBN

0 902121 049), which contains a comprehensive explanation of the principles of jet propulsion, associated systems, maintenance and operating procedures as well as many examples of full size motors, and is regarded as a 'bible' to turbine developers.

AIRFRAME KITS

In 1997 there are not many jet kits available that have been properly designed, or upgraded, to suit turbine propulsion - although this situation is changing rapidly! Several of the more established jet manufacturers are currently making the essential alterations to some of their existing ducted-fan kits, as well as designing completely new airframes, and many smaller companies are also working on similar kits for turbine power. The modifications to existing D/F kits to make them suitable are often quite substantial, as mentioned above, and are normally based around a particular turbine, or thrust range of motor. Certainly for your first G/T powered model it would be good advice to build an airframe that has been specifically designed for this propul-

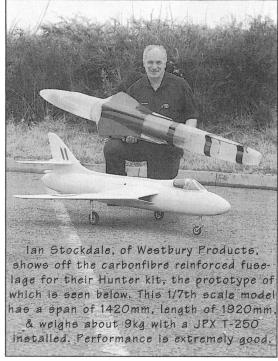

Ian Stockdale, of Westbury Products, shows off the carbonfibre reinforced fuselage for their Hunter kit, the prototype of which is seen below. This 1/7th scale model has a span of 1420mm, length of 1920mm, & weighs about 9kg with a JPX T-250 installed. Performance is extremely good.

sion mode by an established manufacturer, before embarking on your own conversion of an existing D/F airframe, Below is a brief summary of the kits that I am aware of which are available now, and those that are expected shortly.

AVIATION DESIGN

The 1:9 scale Rafale, Exocet and StarJet were designed for a single JPX motor, the 1:6.8 scale Rafale for twin JPX motors (or similar), and the large Mirage 2000 for a single AMT Pegasus motor, or equivalent.

Rafale C - 1:9 scale jet. 1.70m length, 1.21m span, 6.0kg.
Rafale C - 1:6.8 scale jet. Fully composite, twin engine. 2.25m length, 1.6 m span, 1kg.
'Exocet' - sport jet. 1.80m length, 1.60m span, 6.6kg.
'StarJet' - sport jet. 1.70m length, 1.62m span, 6. kg.
Mirage 2000 - 1:6.8 scale jet. Fully composite. 2.1 m length, 1.34m span, 8.5 - 11kg.

BOB VIOLETT MODELS

All the BVM kits below are designed for JPX turbine installation. The Mig.15 is expected to be released in late '97.

'Bandit' - sport jet. Fully composite. 1.83m length, 1.62m span, 8.5kg.
T-33 - 1:6.5 scale jet. 1.75m length, 2.035m span, 9.5kg.
F-80 Shooting Star - 1:6.5 scale jet. 1.625m length, 1.83m span, 9kg.
Mig. 15 - 1:6 scale jet. 1.73m length, 1.73m span, approx. 8kg.

PHILIP AVONDS SCALE JETS

All the kits below were designed for the JPX range of turbines, but should also accept Sophia J450 or similar types.

Rafale A - 1:9 scale jet. 1.78m length, 1.26m span, 6.7kg.
F-15 Eagle - 1:9 scale jet. 2.16m length, 1.4 m span, 7.8kg.
F-104 Starfighter - 1:7 scale jet. 2.39m length, 1.1m span, 6.9kg.

FIBER CLASSICS
The F86 is suitable for Sophia J450 turbines, and larger motors such as Turbomin & AMT. The Turbine-Trainer is a delta configuration model, and will fly on motors with thrusts from 40 - 100 N.

F-86 Sabre - 1:6 scale jet. Fully composite. 1.85m length, 1.92m span, 10kg.
Turbine-Trainer - sport jet. 1.50m length, 1.65m span, approx. 4 - 7kg.

AIR CHAMP MODELS
These kits were designed to suit the 10 kg thrust turbines, such as the Turbomin TN100 and AMT Pegasus.

F-15D - 1:8.5 scale jet. 2.29m length, 1.60m span, 10 - 11kg.
A-4 Skyhawk - 1:6 scale jet. 2.032m length, 1.40m span, 10kg.

JET MODEL PRODUCTS
T-33 Shooting Star - 1:6 scale jet. Fully composite. 1.95m length, 2.16m span, 12 - 13kg.

This conversion was designed for the AMT Pegasus turbine.

FAN-JETS/PETER NYE
Mig.15 - 1:5 scale jet. 2.025m length, 2.025m span, 10kg.
DH Venom - 1:6 scale jet. 1.68m length, 2.13m span, 7.5kg.

The Mig. 15 has been designed around the AMT Pegasus unit, but is also suited to others with 7 - 10 kg thrust, and the Venom is designed for 5.5 - 7 kgturbines.

TOP GUN AIRCRAFT
F-16C Falcon - 1:6 scale jet. 2.50m length, 1.65m span, 12 - 14kg.

This kit was designed to suit 7 - 12kg thrust turbines, such as the Turbomin T60, T100 and AMT Pegasus.

TRIM AIRCRAFT
F-86 Sabre - 1:7.2 scale jet. 1.61m length, 1.59m span, 6 - 8kg

A conversion kit will be released at the end of 1997, for turbines with a thrust range of 5 - 8kg.

JET-TECH/FRANZ WALTI
Rafale BO1 - 1:6.65 scale jet. Fully composite, twin turbine. 2.30m length, 1.64m span, 15kg.

Designed for two JPX motors, or similar.

WESTBURY PRODUCTS
Both the kits below are designed to suit the JPX range of turbines.

Hawker Hunter - 1:7 scale jet, 1.92m length, 1.42m span, 8.5 - 10kg,
DH 108 Swallow - 1:6 scale jet. 1.40m length, 2.44m span, 7.5 - 10kg.

BYRON ORIGINALS
Hope to release turbine-modified versions of the kits listed below towards the end of 1997. All have been designed around the 10kg thrust turbines, such as the Turbomin TN100 and AMT Pegasus.

F-20 Tigershark - 1:6 scale jet. 2.285m long, 1.425m span, 7.5 - 9kg.
T-33 - 1:6 scale jet. 1.83m length, 2.085m span, 9 - 11kg.

YELLOW AIRCRAFT
Expect to release the turbine retrofit conversions for the following D/F kits during 1997. All are suited to the GWM FD3/67, and ducting kits may also be available for the Turbomin T60 and Sophia J-450 in future.

F/A-18 Hornet - 1:10 scale jet. 1.715m length, 1.20m span, 5.5 - 7kg
F-16C Falcon - 1: 9 scale jet. 1.70m length, 1.12m span, 6 - 7kg.
F4E Phantom - 1:10 scale jet. 1.73m length, 1.115m span, 6 - 7kg.

REGULATIONS & SAFETY

Thankfully there aren't many extra official restrictions on flying gas-turbine powered models, in Europe at least, although there are quite strict laws in North America. Nevertheless a turbine, just like any other mechanical device, can be dangerous if misused or operated by inexperienced persons, and there are some general guidelines and tips that apply to all operation of miniature turbojets - whether being run on a test-bench, or in a model at the airfield.

1) Never operate a turbine on your own - always have a second person nearby with a CO2 fire extinguisher, who is competent in using it and knows what to do in case of a fire.

2) Be careful that there is no debris in front of the turbine inlet that could be ingested.

3) Don't fill fuel tanks if there is any risk of a fire, due to hot motor parts or persons smoking nearby.

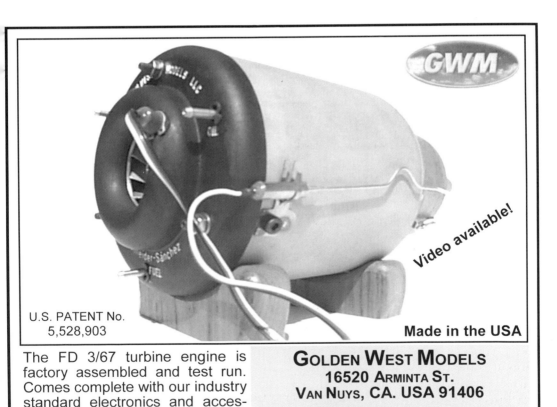

4) Carefully check the whole fuel and lubrication system for leaks before every flying session.

5) Before starting a turbine ensure that there are no persons directly behind the turbine, or at the sides in line with the rotation axis - except for the necessary assistants. At most established jet events there is a separate start-up and preparation area for turbine models and, if available, these should always be used for fuelling and starting procedures.

It goes without saying that pilots should be fully competent at flying very fast models, or similar ducted-fan types, before attempting to fly turbine powered models. At the moment only North America has regulations to control the competence of turbine pilots, and I feel it would be a retrograde step to impose general restrictions in Europe, or anywhere else. Pilots should also be aware of the turbine delay during throttling up and own procedures, and you can actually practice this by using a servo-slow on the throttle in a ducted fan model - set at about 5 seconds from idle to full power.

Most of the reputable manufacturers, or their authorised agents, offer new customers an introductory session to learn how to operate turbines correctly and safely and I highly recommend that you complete this - and ask for it if they don't offer it !

....and finally, a very famous jet pilot perfectly described the transition from ducted-fans to gas turbines thus: *"It's not difficult - but it is different"*.

11 - Operation

Most of today's jet models are no more difficult to operate than any other high performance R/C aircraft, unlike many of them a few years ago. The arrival of fixed length tuned pipes, efficient tractor fan units and engines specifically designed for this purpose, as well as advances in airframe technology and design, has finally killed off the belief that there is some kind of magic to the operation of jet models. However jets are a little more complex than an average propeller powered sport model, requiring extra concentration and a more methodical approach to ensure safe and reliable operation.

Likewise most of the current jet kits are relatively easy to fly, the ones mentioned as suitable for beginners in the 'Airframes' chapter are not much more difficult than good a .60 sized low-wing pattern model. The major differences are the slower acceleration, particularly at take-off, the complete lack of torque effect produced by ducted-fans or turbines, and the lack of any propeller braking effect when the throttle is closed. The absence of any wash from a propeller also makes the stabiliser control surfaces rather ineffective at slow speeds, making good nosegear steering imperative during take-off and landings.

Once in the air contemporary jets need smooth controlling to prevent undue speed loss, and it is quite common to set reduced throw rates on elevators and ailerons for use during normal flight. Exponential servo throws on the elevators and ailerons can also make many models much easier to fly around the neutral control throw positions, 25% exponential being an average setting to begin with.

With the generally higher wing loadings, the use of flaps and other similar high lift and drag devices are a big advantage on jets, and proper use of these makes landings and takeoffs much slower and easier. If you are new to retractable undercarriages you will immediately notice how much drag they give when they are extended, and in emergency 'dead engine' situations they should not be lowered until necessary.

Models with large wing areas, or delta planforms, like this very popular Rafale from the Philip Avonds kit, are a good choice for newcomers. They also make flying from grass strips much easier. The Rafale also has the option of working canards which permit astonishing manoeuvres to be performed once you are completely at home flying it - for instance inverted flat spins, which are one of Philip Avonds favourite display tricks !

Aviation Design also makes a similar sized Rafale.

The Law & Insurance
All countries have some sort of statutory laws governing the flying of model aircraft, and it is absolutely vital to have adequate insurance before flying a jet. In most countries membership of the national modelling federation or association automatically includes third party insurance in your own country, and often some others, but if you plan to fly abroad you should check that your association has a reciprocal agreement with the country that you are intending to visit. The USA, in particular, has different laws for model flying, and in most cases it is necessary to become a member of the AMA if you wish to fly your jet in the 'States.

You should also bear in mind that some countries have restrictions on the maximum height above ground level that you can fly a model, this usually depending on the weight or size of it, and therefore the amount of damage it could cause to a full-size aircraft if they should collide.

Transporting Models
Of course no-one would be so silly as to build a model that wouldn't fit in their car when completed, would they ? However this point is worth checking before construction begins, and certainly in Europe, where the cars tend to be smaller than in the USA, for instance, models with removable wings are almost a necessity.

Transporting large models in vehicles can still be a tricky operation, and often more damage is done to the airframes getting them to the airfield than during actual flying! A good method is to connect the grab-handles inside the roofs of most cars together with elastic straps, protected with foam water-pipe

Beginners are well advised to choose a model with especially good access to the engine and R/C bays, for example this JMP Starfire, which makes installation and removal of the fan unit and other equipment much easier while you are learning about operating a jet model.

This view shows the Dynamax fan, OS91 motor, tuned pipe retained by a spring, in-flight remote needle valve & servo, hopper & main saddle tanks & plumbing — all very easily accessed by just removing one large moulded fibreglass hatch which takes a couple of seconds.

insulation, and carry the model upside down on these, against the roof lining of the car. However don't forget to drain the fuel tanks completely before using this method.

It is simple and cheap to make sleeves for wings and other delicate parts from sheets of bubble-wrap, taped together, or there are several companies that make custom shaped fuselage and wing bags to protect your pride and joy.

Flying Abroad

In the last few years a lot of jet modellers have travelled abroad by air with their models to fly in other countries, especially to visit some of the big events in the USA, and this is not as difficult as it first seems. There are a few simple guidelines for doing this.

1) Contact the airline that you wish to fly with at least 3 weeks before departure, and explain that you want to take a model aircraft with you on holiday. As long as you don't exceed the normal baggage allowance, (usually 2 x 32 kg per person for intercontinental travel) most airlines are quite helpful, and won't charge you any extra. However they normally won't accept model crates over 2.2 metres length. You will usually have to check-in one or two hours early, and may have to deliver the model crate to a separate cargo bay instead of the passenger check-in area.

2) Construct a crate to carry your model, making it very light but strong. Care is needed to keep the weight of the model and box under 32 kg. A frame work of 18 mm square softwood, clad in 4 mm plywood is quite sufficient. Although it must be securely fixed, make sure that you can open the lid at the airport in case customs wish to inspect the model. Ensure that you disconnect the nicads, and completely empty the fuel tanks before packing the model. You cannot take fuel with you, and will have to arrange for a supply at your destination. Very clearly mark the box with 'Top' and 'Fragile' markings.

3) Put your transmitter, well protected, inside your luggage suitcase, but make sure you disconnect the internal battery. Occasionally I have carried my as hand luggage, but some airlines don't like this. If in any doubt ask their advice before going to the airport.

4) When entering some countries the Customs dept. may ask you to prove that the model is a personal possession and is not being imported. If it's not a new jet, then there should be no problem as they will be able to see that it's had some use - but if it looks immaculate then take some proof of ownership.

Personally I have transported several of my models all over the world in this manner, including Australia, Japan, Thailand, the Americas and Italy etc., mostly travelling with Virgin Atlantic Airlines, and so far I have incurred no costs or damage whatsoever.

You will also need to check what R/C frequencies are used in the destination country, as these vary throughout the world, and you will need the correct transmitter modules and receivers before you are allowed to fly.

Field Support Equipment

The equipment and spare parts needed at the flying field should be fairly obvious to anyone who has built a jet kit, but for beginners to ducted-fan operation this simple checklist may be helpful.

ELECTRIC STARTER - A powerful type is often needed with the .90 size engines, the Sullivan Dynatron being very popular, and it can also run at 24 volts although this is rarely necessary. Make sure your 12 volt battery is in good condition, and fully charged. My advice is to buy the best starter you can afford, it will last for years.

STARTER PROBE OR BELT - Make sure that the drive end is in good condition and fits the cap head socket bolt or nut properly, and don't forget to lubricate the end with a very small amount of grease every 5 or 6 starts. Occasionally the free-wheeling sleeve on the outside of the shaft should also be lubricated with thin machine oil.

GLOWPLUG DRIVER - Personally I prefer the self-contained glowdrivers, such as the type from McDaniel or similar, and these are quite sufficient for a days jet flying before they require charging. However if you use a very cold plug, such as a Rossi R8 or OPS300 they draw a lot of current, sometimes as much as 5 amps, and in this case a power panel running off a 12 volt battery may be better. Don't forget to take a glowplug spanner.

AIR PUMP - For pneumatic retracts. The type with an integral pressure gauge is worthwhile, and I have relied one of the Spring Air units for many years with no problems. The use of miniature electric compressors, easily obtainable at camping shops etc., is on the increase - but it's just something else to carry around, or fail at the worst moment.

TOOLS - take all the hand tools, hex keys, pliers and screwdrivers you used during building of the model. Don't rely on other modellers having the correct tools for your jet. Once you have had a few flights and the model is reliable, then you will be able to leave the majority of them at home.

FUEL - A standard .90 capacity motor uses about 500 ml (17 fl. oz) in a typical flight, so a gallon of fuel is usually enough for a good days flying. Don't forget to filter it properly before you fill the model, and make sure that there is sufficient quantity of high quality oil in it - unless you wish to waste money on engine repairs.

FUEL PUMP - For reliability many jet pilots use a simple mechanical hand pump, as most of the electric types seem to leak after a short while. However they do make it much quicker and easier to fill and empty the large fuel tanks that are common in jets.

SPARES - For a typical ducted fan model that is well maintained, the most commonly required items are tuned pipe 'O' rings or seals, glow plugs, and undercarriage spares. If you are using wire legs in your retracts it is quite a good idea to have a spare set in your flight box, already bent to shape and cut to length, as it's not easy to straighten wire legs on the airfield in case of an 'arrival' !

CHARGER AND NICAD CHECKER - Field chargers, that will top up your receiver nicads from the 12 volt electric starter battery, are very handy, especially the fast types, but ensure that your nicads are designed to accept fast-charging. If you don't have an on-board Nicad checker, then use a remote type before every flight.

CLEANING MATERIALS - Although the majority of the exhaust residue gets blown out of the back of the exhaust duct, a considerable amount always manages to dribble underneath the back of the fuselage. It's a good idea to look after your investment by giving it a quick wipe over after a days flying; common household window cleaning fluid and paper towels are excellent for removing grease and fuel from jet models.

This APU, from Mini Hobby, is a clever self-contained field box that holds everything you need for operating a jet, and has proved quite popular in the USA. It is very compact, contains its own rechargeable 12 volt battery which powers the starter output, a glow plug analyser and driver, electric fuel pump, and an integral electric air pump. A very neat bit of kit.

Starting

• Fill the fuel tanks. Open the main needle valve by the amount recommended in the motors instructions (normally about 3 - 4 full turns). Check that the glowplug is glowing bright orange, not white.

• Prime the motor. If tuned-pipe pressure is being used then open the throttle fully, block the end of the tuned pipe and turn the motor over with the probe and electric starter for 3 or 4 seconds. If this fails, then remove the glowplug and dribble a few drops of fuel into the motor. For models using impeller or puffer pressure the easiest method is to have a brass tube connector in the pressure line close to the top of the fan unit where it is easily accessible. Disconnect the tube to the tanks, open the throttle fully, and blow into the tube to apply some positive pressure to the fuel.

• Close the throttle to a slow idle setting, insert the starter probe (or connect the drive belt), and spin it with the electric starter for about 5 seconds without the glowplug supply connected. If the motor spins easily then it is probably primed sufficiently, and not either dry or flooded. If it is still dry then re-prime. If it is flooded then the excess fuel must be removed before attempting to start (remove the glowplug, pinch off the fuel supply and spin the motor over with a rag over the plug hole).

• Check that there are no loose objects, starter or glowdriver wires, rags or clothing that can be sucked into the inlets.

• Connect the glowplug supply, check that the throttle is set at a very low idle (about 1.5 mm of the hole in the carburettor barrel visible).

• Push the electric starter onto the probe, and spin the engine. If it doesn't start, or at least fire, after 10 seconds then stop. Don't keep spinning the motor, as you will heat up the end of the starter probe driver and damage it. Remove the glowplug and check to see if it is damp, indicating a roughly correct fuel supply, very wet (flooded), or dry (not enough, or no fuel). Correct flooding as described above, and close the needle valve some more. If the plug is dry check the fuel supply for pinched tubes, and if no other restriction is found then open needle valve by 1 turn and try to start again

• Once the motor is running reliably, let it warm up for 30 seconds or so at a fast idle, before opening the throttle further. Replace the engine cover cap if you have removed it during starting. Then set the correct mixture for flight, ensuring that it is a little rich to ensure adequate motor cooling. It is advisable to get some assistance from an experienced jet pilot with mixture settings until you are conversant with it.

This BAe Hawk from Jim Fox Models has a 1350mm wingspan, and has introduced many newcomers to jets - although not quite as easy to land as some of the delta types, unless you install flaps. This particularly well built and finished example has a forerunner of the GWM turbine installed. & proved to be very exciting to fly.

This view of the engine bay of the Franz Walti's huge 1:6.8 scale Dassault Rafale shows the twin JPX gas turbines which gave amazing performance during the 1995 Jet World Masters. It has a wingspan of 1.60m, length of 2.25m, and weighs around 13kg. Although not available as a kit from his company, Jet Tech in Switzerland, a very similar model is now manufactured by Aviation Design in France.

Safety

With the modern, powerful and fast ducted fan and turbine models safety cannot be overemphasised! The same guidelines apply as for conventional models, but due to the higher speeds the separation distances that must be allowed between flying models and spectators or other pilots should be at least 50% greater. Never, ever, fly above the spectators or pits areas, even at high altitude.

Ducted fans and turbines have a surprisingly high suction effect in front of the inlets, and you should therefore be most careful that there are no loose objects or clothing that can be sucked into the impeller blades. When running a ducted-fan model on the ground, don't point the exhaust at other people or their models.

Final Tips

It is a very good idea to make the first flights with any new, or first, jet model while it is still in primer. This allows any necessary alterations or minor repairs to be made without damaging the final paint finish. The addition of some high-visibility orange fluorescent labels on the wingtips and vertical stabiliser help enormously when trying to see a grey or white model in the air.

Don't be too proud to let a pilot with plenty of jet experience, preferably with a similar aircraft type, make the first flight with your new model. If anything should go wrong, they will have a far better chance than you of getting it on the ground with as little damage as possible!

Marinus van der Wal, from Holland, with his 3050mm long 1/16th scale A-310 Airbus, powered by a pair of Ramtec fans driven by OS91 motors. The model is a good and reliable performer.

This impressive 1/15th scale A340 Airbus, built and flown by Frenchman Henri Wild, has a 4.1m span, weighs 45kg, took 4000 hours to design and build, & is powered by four JPX T250 turbines. Over 20 public display flights to date, including several off grass strips.

Not for beginners! (D. Boddington photo)

Appendix

MANUFACTURERS & SUPPLIERS.

AEROLOFT DESIGNS
7919 E. Mawson Drive,
Mesa. Arizona - 85207. USA.
Tel: 001 480 380 4799

AIR MAGIC MFG
3200 Dutton Ave, Suite 116.
santa Rosa. CA 95407
USA. Tel: 001 707 542 5721

AMT - NETHERLANDS
Postbus 128, Heistraat 89
NL-5701 HJ Helmond
Netherlands
Tel: 0031 492 545801
Fax: 0031 492 550379

ARTUS, Jesús
C/Venus 10
08012 Barcelona. Spain.
Fax: 0034 379 50719

AVIATION DESIGN
2 Rue de la plaine Jonville
F-77310 Ponthierry. France
Tel/Fax: 0033 1 6065 7881

BERTELLA, G
Via Matteotti 248,
Gardone V.T.25063
Brescia. Italy

BOB VIOLETT MODELS INC.
170 SR. 419, Winter Springs,
FL-32708. USA
Tel: 001 407 327 6333
Fax: 001 407 327 5020

BOLLY PRODUCTS
Unit 8-9, 100 Hewittson Rd
Elizabeth West - 5113
S.Australia.
Fax: 00618 255 9666

BOSAK, Pavel
33901 Klatovy 111, Zahradni 731
Czech Republic.
Tel/Fax 0042 186 22042

BRAECKMAN MODELLBAU
Breitbenden Str.22
D - 52080 Aachen
Germany.
Tel: 0049 241 554719
Fax: 0049 241 552079

BOB DIVELY MODEL PRODUCTS
38131 Airport Pkwy.
206, Willoughby
OH-44094. USA
Fax: 001 216 953 9311

CENTURY JET MODELS INC.
11216 Bluegrass Parkway
Louisville. KY-40229
USA.
Tel: 001 502 266 9234

CHART HOBBIES
Station Rd. East Preston
West Sussex. BN16 3AG
England.
Tel: 0044 1903 773170

CS MODELS
9522 Biggs Way
Windsor. CA-95492
USA. Tel/Fax: 001 707 837 9920

DELUXE MATERIALS
Thornton House, Soke Rd.
Silchester. Reading.
Berks. RG7 2NS
England. Fax: 0044 1734 701579

DGA DESIGNS
16 Main St. Phelps.
NY-14532. USA
Tel 001 315 548 3779

DL AÉROMODELES
4500 Kimber, Suite 8
St.Hubert. QC.
Canada. J3Y 8K5

FANTAIL RPV'S
Bakerside. Morelieigh.
Totnes. Devon.TQ9 7JH.
England.

FIBER CLASSICS
Andreas Geitz
PO. Box 1247.
D-65371 Oestrich-Winkel
Germany. Tel: 0049 6723 8797
Fax: 0049 672 87971

FIORENZE HOBBIES
Bob Fiorenze Hobbies.
PO Box 953042.
Lake Mary. FL-32795.
USA. Tel/Fax: 001 407 330 1448

FLITETECH MODELS
1441 N.Mayfair Road,
Milwaukee. WI-53226
USA
Tel: 001 414 257 1923
Fax: 001 414 771 2092

FTE
15300 Estancia Lane
West Palm Beach. Florida-33414
USA. Tel: 001 561 795 6600
Fax: 001 561 795 6677

FRANKEL, Mark
1525, Lafayette road
Gladwyne. PA 19035. USA

FUCHS MINERALOELWERKE GmbH
Juulicher Strasse 82
D-52249 Eschweiler
Germany. Fax: 0049 2403 77284

GENESIS MINIATURE TURBINES.
11 Audley Avenue, Torquay.
Devon. TQ2 7BP. England.

GIEZENDANNER-TECHNIK.
Ifangstr. 5. CH-8335 Hittnau.
Switzerland. Tel: 0041 1950 4264
Fax: 0041 1950 4797

GLEICHAUF MODELLBAUTECHNIK
Zeppelinstrasse 14
D-78166 Donaueschingen
Germany. Tel: 0049 771 5047

GLENNIS AIRCRAFT
5528 Arboga Road.
Linda. CA - 95901
USA. Tel/Fax: 001 916 742 3957

GER-LLY SCALE PRODUCTS
5523 So. Ward way
Littleton. CO-80127
USA. Tel/Fax: 001 303 932 1403

GOLDEN WEST MODELS
16520 Arminta Street.
Van Nuys. CA - 91406.
USA. Tel: 001 818 781 7364
Fax: 001 818 781 4112

GRAUPNER GMBH
Henriettenstrasse 94-96
D-73230 Kircheim/Teck
Germany. Fax: 0049 7021 722200

HÄWE Modelltechnik
Schützenstrasse 39
D-50126 Bergheim
Germany. Tel: 0049 2271 42426

JE PE FIBERATELIER
Jean-Paul Schlösser
Engelsweg 3b
NL 5705 AB Helmond
Holland. Tel/Fax: 0031 492 554196

JOSH HAREL MODELS.
286 Hawthorne Ave,
Derby. CT-06418.
USA. Tel: 001 203 732 0532

J.D.MODEL PRODUCTS
PO.Box 386. Pacifica.
CA-94044. USA
Fax: 001 415 359 5833

JET HANGAR HOBBIES INC.
10595 Bloomfield Street
Los Alamitos. CA-90720
USA. Tel: 001 310 493 0260
Fax: 001 310 467 0261

JET MODEL PRODUCTS
211 N.Mullen Rd
Belton. MO-64012
USA. Tel: 001 816 331 0356
Fax: 001 816 331 3930

JOHNSSON, Einar
O.A.vägen 6. 178 38 EKERÖ
Sweden

K & B MFG., INC
2100 College Drive. PO. Box 3000
Lake Havasu City
AZ 86405. USA
Fax: 001 602 453 3559

KRESS JETS, INC.
800 Ulster landing Rd.
Saugerties. NY-12477. USA.
Tel: 001 914 336 8149

LESHER MODEL AVIATION
330 Rexmont Rd.
Lebanon, PA 17042-8845
USA. Tel: 001 717 272 2616

MAKIN MODELS
PO Box 328. Manhattan
IL 60442-0328. USA
Fax: 001 815 485 5211

MANSELL, Ross
93 Whitemoor Rd,
Kenilworth. Warks.
CV8 2BN. England
Tel: 0044 1926 511274

MARSDEN, Peter
1 Solent View Cottages
West Common, Langley
Nr. Southampton.
Hants. SO4 1XJ. England.

McCOY MODEL GLOWPLUGS INC
2117 N. 2nd Avenue
Upland.CA-91784
USA. Fax: 001 909 946 6823

MEY'S HI-TECH HOBBY
96 Taunton Hill Rd,
Newtown. Conecticut
CT - 06470. USA
Fax: 001 203 744 0626

MGA Enterprises
P.O.Box 5631
Fresno. CA-93755
USA. Tel: 001 209 224 4170

MICRO-MOLD
see Chart Hobbies

MIKES MODELS
3-5 Brockwell Road, Kingstanding,
Birmingham. B44 9PE.
England.
Tel: 0044 121 360 4521
Fax: 0044 121 360 7350

MODEL SPECIALITIES Inc.
1220 Sylvan Rd
West Chester
PA 19382. USA.
Tel: 001 215 692 4139
Fax: 001 215 692 9427

MODELLBAU KLÜHR.
Hausen 15.
D-5208 Eitorf/Seig
Germany
Fax: 0049 2243 3943

MULTIPLEX GmbH
Neuer Weg 15
D-7532 Niefern/Oschelbronn 1
Germany. Tel: 0049 7233 7313
Fax: 0049 7233 7399

NYE, Peter
Barn Cottage, Christophers
Withycoombe.Minehead
Devon. TA24 6PZ. England.

OPS
Via Matteotti 128 - 20041
Agrate Brianza (MI)
Italy. Fax: 0039 39 653842

P & J PRECISION ENGINEERING
27, The Knole. Istead Rise
North Fleet. KENT.
DA13 9DJ. England.

PAULS JET PRODUCTS
13430 Sundance Ave.
Whitier. CA-90605. USA

PERFORMANCE MODEL PRODUCTS
17 Beacon Ave, Dunstable
Bedfordshire. LU6 2AD
England.
Tel/Fax: 0044 1582 661562

PERMAGRIT TOOLS.
The White House
Pointon. Sleaford
LINCS. NG34 0LX.
England. Tel: 0044 1529 240668
Fax: 0044 1529 241026

PHILIP AVONDS SCALE JETS
Doornhofstraat 6
B-8670 Koksijde. Belgium
Tel: 0032 58 514451
Fax: 0032 58 517253

PRO-MARK INC.
751 Airport Road, Metropolis.
IL - 62960. USA
Tel: 001 618 524 2440
Fax: 001 618 524 3617

R/C JET INTERNATIONAL
see: Traplet Publications Ltd.

ROBART MFG.
PO Box 1247.
St.Charles.IL-60174.
USA. Fax: 001 630 584 3712

ROSSI MOTORS AND ELECTRONICS.
Via Caporalino 5
I-25060 Cellatica (Bs)
Italy. Tel:0039 30 252172
Fax: 0039 30 2522282

SCALE MODEL RESEARCH
3114 Yukon Ave
Costa Mesa
CA-92626. USA
Tel: 0101 714 979 8058
Fax: 0101 714 979 7279

SCALE MODEL SERVICES
17 Rothwell Drive
Solihull.W.Midlands
B91 1HG. England
Fax: 0044 121 744 4766

SCHLEICHER JETS
Frankfurter Str.46
D-63584 Gründau-Rothenbergen
Germany. Tel: 0049 6051 15708
Fax: 0049 6051 15704

SCHLÖSSER: see: Je Pe Fiberatelier

SCHMALENBACH, Peter
8755 Alzenau
Cranach Str. 19a
West Germany
Fax: 0049 6023 2693

SCHRECKLING, Kurt
Edelrather Weg 153
D-51375 Leverkusen
Germany.

SIM-JET
TAKS a/s, Villingerødvej 71
DK-3230 Graested,
Denmark

S.M. SERVICES
18 Orchard Way. Cranfield. Beds.
MK43 0HU. England
Tel/Fax: 0044 1234 751095

SOLARFILM LTD
Ackhurst Rd
Chorley. Lancs.
PR7 1NH. England
Fax: 0044 1257 276203

SPEEDMASTER
550 Primrose
Odessa, Texas.
TX-79765. USA

SPRING-AIR PRODUCTS
PO Box 37-3218
Satellite Beach
FL-32937. USA
Tel: 001 407 728 9002
Fax: 001 407 728 2881

TAGS GRAPHICS
2787 Stage Center Drive.
Bartlett. Memphis.
TN - 38134. USA
Fax: 001 901 386 7676

TECHNO-WELD LTD
4/5a Aston Works
Back Lane. Aston
OX18 2BX. England
Tel: 0044 1993 851028
Fax: 0044 1993 851036

TELSTAR VIDEO PRODUCTIONS INC.
483 S.E. Monterey Rd
Stuart, Florida-34997
USA.Tel: 001 561 286 2535
Fax: 001 561 220 4849

THORJET
Glaston Garage, Main St. Glaston.
Oakham. Rutland.
LEICS. LE15 9BP
England. Tel: 0044 1572 823394

TRAPLET PUBLICATIONS LTD
Severn Drive, Upton-on-Severn
Worcs. WR8 0JL.
England. Tel: 0044 1684 595300
Fax: 0044 1684 594586

TOP GUN AIRCRAFT
410 W.Jefferson St.
Ottawa. IL-61350
USA. Tel: 001 815 433 6132
Fax: 001 815 433 5596

TRIM AIRCRAFT
14 Collins Rd, Melton. Vic - 3337
S.Australia.
Tel: 00613 9743 7161
Fax: 00 613 9743 0435

Turbomin AB.
Författarvägen 19
S-161 40 Bromma
Sweden. Fax: 0046 8704 1898

UNITRACTS INTERNATIONAL.
87-89 Farleigh Road,
Warlingham. Surrey.
CR6 9EJ. England
Tel: 0044 1883 627240
Fax: 0044 1883 622003

USHER ENTERPRISES INC
1017 SE Frontage Rd
Box 511, North Plains
OR-97133. USA
Fax: 001 503 647 1015

VORTAC MFG. CO
PO Box 469. Oak Lawn
IL-60453. USA.

VÖSTER MODELLBAU
Münchinger Str.3.
D-71254 Ditzingen.
Germany.
Fax: 0049 7156 951666

WALTI, FRANZ/JET-TECH
Bleichhubelweg 10
CH - 4852 Rothrist
Switzerland
Fax:0041 062 794 3785

WESTON UK Ltd.
84-88 London Rd
Teynham. Sittingbourne.
Kent. ME9 9QH. England
Tel: 0044 1795 521030
Fax: 0044 1795 522020

YELLOW AIRCRAFT.
203 Massachusetts Ave,
Lexington. MA- 02173.
USA. Tel: 001 781 6749898

ZANIN
Via Bertuol 32
I - 31020 Frescada (TV)
Italy.

ZONE 5 AIRCRAFT
P.O. Box 402441
Hesperia, CA 92340-2441
USA. Fax: 001 760 956 1693

GTBA
Hollybank. Main Road
Swardeston. Norwich
NR14 8AD. England.
(www.gtba.cnuce.cnr.it.)

IJMC - INTERNATIONAL JET MODEL
COMMITTEE.
Stauffenbergstr. 42
D-5308 Rheinbach
Germany. Fax: 0049 2226 7097

JET DANMARK
Torshøjvænget 106 Kolt
DK- 8631 Hasselager
Dänemark

JMA/JET MODELLERS ASSOCIATION
23, Springfield Avenue
Bridgewater
SOM. TA6 7JA
England.

JPO/JET PILOTS ORGANISATION
3088 Bragg Blvd, NW.
Orangeburg.
S.C - 29115.
USA.

GTCTA
Grupo de Trabajo de Constructores
De Tourborreactores Para
Aeromodelismo.
Guillermo Day Contreras
C - Allemendro, 7, 2 - 1
Torrellano. 03320 Alicante
Spain. Fax: +34 6568 0277

Jet SIGS, Associations & National Federations.

AMA
Academy of Model Aeronautics
5151 East Memorial Drive
Muncie. IN 47302-9252
USA. Tel: 001 317 287 1256
Fax: 001 317 289 4248

FAI/CIAM
93 Boulevard du Montparnasse
F-75006 Paris
France

IMPERIAL - METRIC CONVERSION FACTORS (APPROX.)

Length
1 inch	= 25.4 millimetres (mm)
1 mm	= 0.0394 inches (ins or ")
1 foot	= 0.305 metres (m)
1 yard	= 0.91 metres (m)
1 metre	= 1.094 yards (yds)
1 mile	= 1.609 kilometre (km)
1 km	= 0.621 miles.

Volume (capacity)
1 ml	= 0.034 fluid ounces (fl.oz)
1 fl.ounce (UK)	= 29.6 millilitre (ml)
1 cu. in	= 16.387 cubic centimetres (cc)
1 cc	= 0.061 cubic inches (cu. in)
1 litre	= 0.264 US gallons (galls)
1 litre	= 0.22 UK gallons (galls)
1 US gallon	= 3.8 litres (l)
1 UK gallon	= 4.546 litres (l)

Velocities
1 mph	= 1.61 kph
1 kph	= 0.621 mph.

Mass
1 gram	= 0.035 ounces (oz)
1 ounce	= 28.35 grams (g)
1 pound (Lb)	= 0.45 kilogram (kg)
1 kg	= 2.20 pounds (Lb)

Power
1 Horsepower (hp)	= 0.745 kilowatts (kw)
1 Kilowatt	= 1.3 horsepower (hp)

Torque
kg/cm x 13.86	= ounce/inches
oz/inch x 0.072	= Kg/cm

Temperature
Degrees Fahrenheit	= (°C x 1.8) +32
Degrees Celsius	= (°F - 32) x 0.56.

Pressure
2.0 bar	= 29 psi (lb/in^2)
100 psi (lb/in^2)	= 6.8 bar

Force
1 lbf	= 4.45 N
1 kgf	= 9.81 N

ABBREVIATIONS ETC.

The following abbreviations are generally used throughout this book:

D/F - Ducted-Fan
G/T - Gas-Turbine
rpm - revolutions per minute
JFM - Jim Fox Models
JHH - Jet Hangar Hobbies
JMP - Jet Model Products
PMP - Performance Model Products
BVM - Bob Violett Models
RPM - Ralf Ploenes Models
Byron - Byron Originals
PASJ - Philip Avonds Scale Jets
IJMC - International Jet Model Committee
i.c - internal combustion

BIBLIOGRAPHY

Books on Jet Modelling:

DUCTED-FAN RC AIRCRAFT.   Dick Sarpolus (1981)
Published by Kalmbach Books, USA. ISBN 0 89024 038 8. English language.

R/C DUCTED FANS.   Frank Fanelli (1987)
Published by Motorbooks Int'l, USA. ISBN 0 87938 279 1. English language.

DUCTED FANS FOR MODEL JETS.   D.James (1989)
Published by Argus Books, GB. ISBN 0 85242 977 0. English language.

IMPELLER.   Heinrich Voss (1989)
Published by Neckar-Verlag, Germany. ISBN 3 7883 0618 1. German language.

ENGINES FOR DUCTED-FANS.   David James (1990)
Published by Argus Books, GB. ISBN 1 85486 017 8. English language.

STRAHLTURBINE.   Kurt Schreckling (1992)
Published by VTH, Germany. ISBN 3 88180 120 0. German language.

GAS TURBINE ENGINES.   Kurt Schreckling (1994)
Published by Traplet Publications,GB. ISBN 0 9510589 1 6. English language.

MODELLSTRAHLTRIEBWERKE.   Thomas Kamps (1995)
Published by VTH, Germany. ISBN 3 88180 071 9. German language.

MODEL JET ENGINES.   Thomas Kamps (1995)
Published by Traplet Publications, GB. ISBN 0 9510589 9 1. English language.

IMPELLER.   Heinrich Voss (1996)
Published by Neckar-Verlag, Germany. ISBN 3 7883 1618 7. German language.

IMPELLER FÜR ELEKTROFLUGMODELLE.   Hans Wekkeli (1995)
Published by VTH, Germany. ISBN 3 88180 076 X. German language.

ELEKTRO-IMPELLER.   Ludwig Retzbach (1997)
Published by Neckar-Verlag, Germany. ISBN unknown. German language.

NEWSLETTERS:

The following jet associations, companies, or modelling groups publish regular newsletters about jet modelling.

Bob Violett Models (The INLET)

Jet Modellers Association (FANFLASH)

Jet Pilots Organisation (CONTRAILS)

Gas Turbine Builders Association (NEWSLETTER)